MW00849435

THE ALIITES

CLASS | NEW
2 | STUDIES
0 | IN
0 | RELIGION

EDITED BY Kathryn Lofton AND
John Lardas Modern

Books in the series:

Hunted: Predation and Pentecostalism in Guatemala
by Kevin Lewis O'Neill

Faking Liberties: Religious Freedom in American-Occupied Japan
by Jolyon Baraka Thomas

Credulity: A Cultural History of US Mesmerism
by Emily Ogden

Consuming Religion
by Kathryn Lofton

Death Be Not Proud: The Art of Holy Attention
by David Marno

THE ALIITES

Race and Law in
the Religions of Noble Drew Ali

SPENCER DEW

The University of Chicago Press
Chicago and London

The University of Chicago Press, Chicago 60637
The University of Chicago Press, Ltd., London
© 2019 by The University of Chicago
All rights reserved. No part of this book may be used or reproduced in any manner whatsoever without written permission, except in the case of brief quotations in critical articles and reviews. For more information, contact the University of Chicago Press, 1427 E. 60th St., Chicago, IL 60637.
Published 2019
Printed in the United States of America

28 27 26 25 24 23 22 21 20 19   1 2 3 4 5

ISBN-13: 978-0-226-64796-8 (cloth)
ISBN-13: 978-0-226-64801-9 (paper)
ISBN-13: 978-0-226-64815-6 (e-book)
DOI: https://doi.org/10.7208/chicago/9780226648156.001.0001

Library of Congress Cataloging-in-Publication Data

Names: Dew, Spencer, author.
Title: The Aliites : race and law in the religions of Noble Drew Ali / Spencer Dew.
Other titles: Class 200, new studies in religion.
Description: Chicago : The University of Chicago Press, 2019. |
Series: Class 200, new studies in religion
Identifiers: LCCN 2019005338 | ISBN 9780226647968 (cloth : alk. paper) | ISBN 9780226648019 (pbk. : alk. paper) | ISBN 9780226648156 (e-book)
Subjects: LCSH: Ali, Drew, 1886–1929. | African Americans—United States—Religion. | Moorish Science Temple of America. | Religion and law—United States.
Classification: LCC BP232 .D49 2019 | DDC 297.8/7—dc23
LC record available at https://lccn.loc.gov/2019005338
♾ This paper meets the requirements of ANSI/NISO Z39.48-1992 (Permanence of Paper).

CONTENTS

PREFACE

Dialing in to Contemporary American Religion

EVERY SUNDAY, AT 8:00 P.M. EASTERN, 5:00 p.m. in California, the members of the Empire Washitaw gather over a conference call. The call of October 1, 2017, starts the way all Sunday calls begin, with an "acknowledgment of the ancestors" giving thanks to "the Greatest Spirit" for placing callers within the Washitaw community, the world's oldest sovereign nation. Descendants of those mound-builders who first settled the New World, themselves refugees from the land of Mu, a continent that disappeared in catastrophe, contemporary Washitaw have reconstructed their glorious past through arduous historical research. The resulting historical narrative is central to the prayer recited each week at the start of the call. This prayer expresses gratitude to a lineage of empresses, from she who sent her people forth from Mu before its destruction to a legendary nineteenth-century woman who lived through what Washitaw call "the Turbulent Years," when, they believe, the Supreme Court decided in favor of their claims to legal ownership of the land of the Louisiana Purchase. The prayer gives honor, as well, to the modern figure who founded the Washitaw movement, whose research allows the community to continue its struggle for legal recognition and return of its land, and whose son now leads this community and convenes this call. The text of the prayer also lays out a map of Washitaw settlements, past and present, describing a trajectory of ancient mounds built from China to South America, up through the Yucatán Valley, and on to Mississippi and the most important of ancient sites for the Washitaw, Poverty Point, in what is today Louisiana. Other sites are mentioned, generally those in proximity to specific Washitaw on the call, individuals scattered across the country—in California, in Baltimore, in New Jersey, in North Carolina, locations associated with some of the "over 150,000 mounds and pyramids throughout the earth" acknowledged in this prayer. Such mounds stand not only as "sacred" sites, but also as evidence of ownership. This Sunday-night "nation-building" or "state of the empire" call unites the Washitaw for the purposes of "getting the land back," of having their legal claims recognized such that they might by able to establish a reservation, remaining within America but with a degree of self-determination and autonomy, living as "a nation within a nation," running their own businesses, able to raise and educate their children in peace. The only way to regain their ancestral land, the Washitaw repeatedly insist, is through the U.S. legal system, by appeal to historical legal precedent as well as to what Washitaw understand to be true law, that transcendent and eternal force, synonymous with justice and with the Creator, the Most High. The Washitaw express a fervent faith in a better future through law, and they imagine and engage law in order to transform society, themselves, and their own community. Such work— the theory and practice of law within the Washitaw and related religious movements—is the subject of this book.

This community has been participating in such calls for eighteen years, and, since 2011, most Sundays I've called in as well. From the call I have learned specifics of Washitaw thought—one of the three connected religious traditions discussed in this book—but I have also learned about the *form* of contemporary American religion, its mercurial and fissiparous nature, its reflexive rebellion against authority paired with a desire, even a *need*, to court and coopt such authority. Empowered by belief in their own agency in the world, their own ability to interpret and innovate, the callers on this line represent an extreme of the Protestant legacy, all of them radically subjective individual thinkers, able to use varied technologies to publicize their thoughts: self-publishing books, running their own conference calls, posting videos, or creating websites. Simultaneously, however, these callers are devoted to community, coupling their engagement in schism and disagreement with claims of unbroken lineage and tradition. The ceaseless creativity of thought displayed on this call, finally, exists and is explicitly framed in relation to external power—the potentially destructive power of the state, of the legal system and its law enforcement agents, the power of the media to (mis-)represent Washitaw claims, but also the other side of the power of the state, the power to reward and accommodate, to grant and acknowledge rights and claims. The religion central to each Sunday-night call is a matter of identity—ancestral culture, community—but also always a matter of negotiating racial categories. Such identity is understood always as legally consequential—implying inheritance, for instance, but also opening up an array of opportunities and responsibilities under and in relation to law. Each Sunday-night call reminds participants and listeners that existence is inextricable from the power of the state—the power that racializes, that excludes, but also the power that can recognize, that can include, that can be transformed by its own citizens.

Conference calls are the Empire Washitaw's primary mode of fellowship, communal worship, and exchange of ideas. Such calls are preferable to communicating via the internet because not everyone in the community has reliable internet access or the necessary skills. The Empire Washitaw website is rarely updated and occasionally inoperable. After the prayer, each Sunday's call features a few minutes devoted to the business of announcing the other weekly calls, giving out the telephone numbers and access codes. The Monday-night call is devoted to the community's letter-writing campaign, a campaign of outreach to elected officials, trying to persuade them to honor the Supreme Court decision mentioned in the opening prayer. While explicitly focused on helping Washitaw members write letters and start petitions, the host of this call makes a point of saying that all are welcome to just "stop by and say hello, talk about Washitaw, it's open." This week a new Tuesday-night call was announced, for the purposes of planning the community's annual "family reunion" in celebration of its most important holiday, to be held this June in Louisiana. But few can afford the expense of travel, and such events are sparsely attended. Every Wednesday the community members call in for a public reading of their scripture—a book compiled by their founding empress, primarily a collection of legal and historical documents related to the Louisiana Purchase, with the purpose of proving that the Washitaw are the true owners of that land. On Thursday nights there's a call devoted to genealogy. For a donation, you can receive a chart that traces the bloodline of the royal family, back to the thrones of France and Spain. The man who prepares such charts claims to have come to this knowledge miraculously, after fainting one afternoon and regaining consciousness speaking a language he did not know. For another donation, he can work out your personal genealogy, based only on your last name. There used to be a Friday-night call, focused on religion, but its theology was judged too exclusive by the community and the call's host pulled away from active participation. For a brief while, too, a group of Washitaw women who felt excluded from the Sunday-night call set up their own weekly call, and a second group of women who felt excluded from that call set up their own, alternative women's call. The Washitaw are a "matriarch society," as the men who run the call frequently note.

After each of the male leaders has spoken in regard to his own weekly call, the call's convener, called the Dauphin, talks vaguely about conversations he has had throughout the week with people who are interested in Washitaw. He spends most of his time "answering phones for Washitaw" and is quick to give out his home number for anyone who wants to speak privately.[1] Tonight he's worried about a copy of the Washitaw scripture—he calls it "Mama's book," since his mother compiled it—that he mailed to Pontiac, Michigan, and that was returned. This time, he assures the line, he has a tracking number, and he hopes he got the address right. The Dauphin reminds callers that this open Sunday-night call is a chance to ask questions and to propose concrete plans for the betterment of the Washitaw nation. Speaking of his own plans, he says, "There's lot of things that are going on that we would like to speak on, but we can't."

"We'll let you know when the news comes out before the other news media gets it. We will be straightforward and let you know," he says, but he has nothing more to offer at this time, so he opens the call to the community. "Anybody have anything to say?" he asks, before remembering that the Washitaw is "a matriarch society" and so "the sisters are always first" to speak. Tonight, the sisters are silent, so the call is open to anyone who has questions about the Washitaw movement.

The first caller to raise a question wants what many callers want: identification papers, proof of nationality. He wants to change his status, he says, from "African American" to "indigenous." He wants to know the procedure, how this can be done. He is given a version of the answer every caller with that question has received—at least since I started listening to these weekly public calls in the fall of 2011. He's told no paperwork is being issued at this time, that the community has to make sure that the status change is legal, that it's recognized. It needs to be recognized by all governments, and by the United Nations and the FBI. It must be legitimate, not the sort of fraudulent paperwork being produced and sold by certain criminals. This is a community of law, and only through obedience to the law—as citizens and through the work of citizenship—can their salvation be achieved.

The next caller claims to have paid for genealogical paperwork that he never received. The rest of the hour devolves into a debate, with some (including the likely guilty party) casting blame on an unpopular female leader, recently excommunicated. But the handful of members who are speaking tonight are split on this accusation, and that former leader, alerted by another community member, calls in after many months of absence to defend herself. Legal accusations and interpretations are mobilized, threats of lawsuits, defenses predicated on having been in jail at the time of the events in question. Several leaders express confusion over who controls access to the community's PayPal account, and several build on each other's arguments to raise suspicion about the validity of connecting last names to ancestry, citing slavery and maroonage, the unreliability of certain Native American rolls, and a general sense that the dark-skinned predecessors of those on tonight's call might have been forced or might have opted to change their names.

Finally, on the notion of racism and racists who want nothing more than for such communities to be divided, the call's leader is able to find common ground, and he ends the hour on a conciliatory note, which, as usual, he frames as pragmatic. Unity is necessary for survival. "We have to learn how to agree to disagree," he says. "And we have to learn how to respect each other." He thanks everyone for their participation, insisting that "these are the kind of phone calls we need," the sort that "give us our faults" and "don't just say that we're doing good. We're not doing good," he insists, because we're not arguing before legal and political bodies, "we're not before the United Nations or getting the attention of Congress, we're not on the world scene complaining about our situation." Exercising its rights, speaking the true law before representatives of the state and other legal bodies: that is what the community must do, the only way their circumstances will improve. He ends the call by requesting that everyone call again next Sunday and leaves his community with his standard farewell: "Have a good week on purpose."

The October 1 call, like most weeks' calls, is messy, alternating between discord and commitment to unity, earnestness and hypocrisy, individual ego and communal purpose, the pomp of prayer and folksy chatting, the palaver of imagined empire and bickering over reputation. Most of the hour involved a fight over "one hundred or one hundred and twenty-five dollars." The man who paid for proof of his indigenous origin couldn't remember the exact amount. He also kept saying that he wasn't that upset about the money. He didn't want it back. He just wanted proof of his legal status and his rights.

In the years of research leading to this book, I have heard callers weep with gratitude at learning of their true ancestry, heard callers scream with rage against the racist violence of the state. I have heard callers testify to miraculous experiences, offer personal memories of the movement's founder, and debate the present leadership and course of the movement. I have heard callers share their desires and fears, their frustration and sadness, their theories of chemtrails, their UFO sightings, and their recipes for healthy food. I have heard callers plug their new album or their brand of skin-care products, describe ideas for alternative power sources and commemorative coins honoring Washitaw history. Individual figures have risen to prominence and been driven away, have departed after expressing bitterness or have been blocked from the call, banned. Tribal councils and royal councils have likewise been created and swept away, sometimes by election, sometimes by appointment. Weekly calls have been initiated and have ceased. I've been present as the community held moments of silence in the wake of tragedies like the massacre at the Pulse nightclub in Orlando or the murder of police officers in Dallas, as members collected funds to help pay electrical bills or supply diapers and baby food to other Washitaw experiencing misfortune, as they checked in with each other after a storm or discussed their worries in the wake of the most recent nationally publicized instance of police killing, the most recent acquittal, the most recent protest, the most recent election.

The call is open to the public. It is recorded, both out of a sense of commitment to creating an accurate historical record and as a self-protective legal measure. The call is simultaneously an intimate event and an object in the world, a cultural artifact. This reflects the belief, among the Washitaw, that they are under constant law enforcement surveillance; nothing is truly private, every moment is lived under the gaze of the state. Callers, when they join the line, are asked to announce themselves with a brief recording of their name, and some do, adding greetings to family, but most callers remain anonymous, a practice explicitly endorsed by the Dauphin. The number of callers is mentioned only on occasion, by the moderator, usually when many callers (over a hundred) or very few (sixteen) are on the line. Some nights callers shout over each other, the allotted hour a constant cacophony of conversation, debate. Some nights there is only silence. Callers are told, repeatedly, to keep their phones muted unless addressing the community, but often there is background noise, particularly the sounds of children—toddlers playing in the background, an infant in a lap.

A newborn cries, then is hushed and comforted by a mother or a father, a grandparent or an uncle, who usually offers an apology to the rest of the community, met with protests from the Dauphin that the interruption of children is a sound that should be cherished among the Washitaw.

On October 8, 2017—the week following the call just described—a widely beloved member of the community rejoins the call after an absence of several months. There has been much suffering in her life of late, she says, but she needed to hear the voices of the people she loves, her family, her nation, and remind them that "just because I'm not on here doesn't mean I don't love you."

Her voice quavering, she tells her community that she doesn't want to discuss her problems, only wants to share her joys. She tells them that she has just had a granddaughter born "under indigenous," meaning born to parents who proclaimed her authentic identity, a child who will be raised conscious of her ancestry as Washitaw and of her membership in the broader contemporary Washitaw community. Such identity matters, for many reasons, emotional and historical. It serves to orient the individual in relation to a distant past and a difficult present. But such identity also always matters—and foremost to the Washitaw—because it is believed to carry legal consequences. This baby is not African American; this baby is an indigenous Washitaw Mu'ur, a descendant of the Ancient Ones, a legal heir to Washitaw territory. As a Washitaw, this child will be raised to struggle, legally, for recognition and rights, but she will also grow up to have a unique relationship with law, divine law, being devoted to and focused upon this ideal, pursuing knowledge of true law, embodying true law in her behavior, feeling true law in her heart. The caller reminds the nation gathered over the phone line of the meaning of a Washitaw motto used by the movement's founding empress: "Love is law in Washitaw." The caller links this phrase to the movement's understanding of its mission: that individual members, as Washitaw, must work to bring society into alignment with true law. "We have to love one another," she says, "for the law to manifest as law," that is, for true law to manifest in this world. There are murmurs of agreement over the conference call, and expressions of gratitude for the sentiment, for the reminder of what it means to be Washitaw, to be part of the Washitaw community.

INTRODUCTION: "TO BE LAW-ABIDERS AND GOOD CITIZENS"

Drew Ali's "Divine and National Movement"

CITIZENSHIP AS SALVATION, UNDER LAW

IN ONE PHOTOGRAPH OF NOBLE DREW Ali (c. 1886–1929), founder of the Moorish Science Temple of America (MSTA), "the last prophet of these days" sits in a suit and tie, staring solemnly into the camera lens, holding in his hands two small flags.[1] Each the size of a handkerchief, these paired flags illustrate the central teaching of Ali's "divine and national movement," that *citizenship* was the *salvation* of his people.[2]

The two flags in Ali's hands offer a visual explanation of his theory of citizenship. Through the red banner in his right hand, the flag of Moorish tradition, the legal standing of citizenship in the United States, symbolized by the Stars and Stripes in his left hand, could be attained. Declaration of ancestral identity, what he called *nationality*, was a requirement of U.S. citizenship. Nationality implied and included religious belief and practice, rules of behavior, and means of conceptualizing the universal deity, "Our Father-God Allah."[3] All humanity was divided into nations, and each nation thus had its own culture and religion by which it must abide: "Every tongue," Ali wrote in his *Holy Koran of the Moorish Science Temple of America*, "must confess his own."[4] America, Ali argued, was composed of many such communities, and, thus, all citizens of the United States were holders of two flags. "All true American citizens are identified by national descent names," Ali argues, by their distinct religion and "descent flag of [their] forefathers."[5] The red Moorish flag simultaneously called attention to a distinct cultural heritage and served to reject incorrect labels previously ascribed to those who held it—namely that they were "negro, colored, or black."[6]

Ali introduced himself as the prophet of "the Great God Allah," tasked with communicating a universal message.[7] Allah's divine design for the world hinged on a multiplicity of nationalities and the human struggle of citizenship. Allah, Ali taught, had sent the religions of the world for each "nation" so that all might live together in peace and justice, one pluralistic body politic, a patchwork of communities each under its own "vine and fig tree." Ali taught his community to "honor all divine prophets" and all national religious traditions; he included all such prophets under his own universal religion, claiming to have "come to speak to all Nations."[8] Ali described the MSTA's goals as both "to help in the great program of uplifting fallen humanity" in general and to teach his nationality "those things necessary to make . . . [them] better citizens."[9] Ali understood citizenship as both a status and a process, a set of legal rights within the state and a set of "sacred obligations" to the work of transforming the state.[10]

As status, citizenship offered salvation because it meant that the people Ali called Moorish or Moors would be recognized by the state and by their fellow American citizens as equal in regard to rights, part and parcel of "We the People" of the United States. No longer would these people be misidentified, categorized under the incorrect legal labels of "negro, black, or colored"—all of which were titles indicating exclusion from the possibility of citizenship. What Ali called "Earthly Salvation as American Citizens," then, involved inclusion in the American experiment of popular sovereignty and democracy, equal standing under the legal system of the state, and state protection from the violence and discrimination of the state.[11] This salvific status could be achieved, according to Ali, by returning to—proclaiming and enacting—one's forgotten ancestral identity, one's nationality. Ali presented citizenship as the status of being recognized, by the state, as a *human being* as opposed to a slave, an object, or a legal fiction. Proclaiming one's nationality served as a way for Moors to transition "back into humanity."[12] The claim of a distinct nationality circumvented "the Negro problem," the social stigma and legal consequences of black identity, as MSTA members declared themselves to be *other than Negro*.[13]

Once recognized by the state as possessing the legal status of *citizens*, Moorish Americans would then be subject to the responsibilities of citizenship: "obedience to law, respect and loyalty to government, tolerance, and unity."[14] Ali's notion of citizenship as practice included the broadly ethical—such as devotion to truth and living a moral life—and the narrowly political—such as voting and campaigning, actively engaging in democracy. Citizenship as process serves as salvation not only for the community but for the country— "salvation of the nations," a means of restoring America to its founding ideals, its divine promise.[15] Ali presented civic practice as essential to an eschatology that anticipated an America made perfect through alignment of human society, including its varied legal and political systems, with the divine ideal of *law*—law understood as "love, truth, peace, freedom, and justice."[16] This "divine salvation" would mean the perfection of the social order in accord with divine design.[17] "In those days the United States will be one of the greatest civilized and prosperous governments of the world," Ali wrote.[18]

Aimed in particular at African Americans moving from the rural South to the urban centers of the North as part of the Great Migration, migrants who were confronted with social, economic, and political possibilities in these new landscapes—new roles and new rules, new systems of control and new tools for empowerment—Ali's "divine and national" movement collapsed the religious and the political, the spiritual and the civic, insisting that each aspect was inextricable from the other, framing both under the concept of law.[19] Salvation came only through law, in part because salvation involved, as both recognized status and ongoing civic struggle, negotiation with the undeniable power of the state.

Ali's MSTA spread rapidly across the America of the late 1920s. Thousands of African Americans joined the movement, forming temples in northern cities like New York and Detroit, Pittsburgh and Cleveland, as well as in southern cities such as Louisville, Kentucky, and Pine Bluff, Arkansas.[20] In the wake of Ali's death in 1929, the MSTA underwent the first of a series of schisms, and exists today in a highly fragmented, "multifarious" form.[21]

Ali's teachings outlived him, serving as the source material not only for a wide spectrum of communities and individual thinkers that identify themselves with the title of MSTA, but also for two other traditions, likewise diverse. The first of these, organized in the 1960s by Malachi York, eventually took the name United Nuwaubian Nation of Moors and the Yamassee Native American Moors of the Creek Nation (frequently self-identifying as

Nuwaubian Yamassee, the term used here, throughout). The second movement, the Washitaw de Dugdahmoundyah, was organized by a Louisiana
politician named Verdiacee Goston in the 1980s. (Washitaw, like Nuwaubian Yamassee, demarcates both the singular and plural forms of those who
identify with this tradition.)

While each of these movements consists of multiple communities, exhibiting a range of thoughts and practices, all three are best understood as
Aliite religion. I use this term to highlight the fact that these traditions are
indebted to and continually engage with the work of Noble Drew Ali. Ali's
thought frames a set of primary concerns within these traditions, namely a
focus on *citizenship*, an emphasis on *nationality* in relation to that goal, and
the theorization and practice of *law*.

ARGUMENTS AND STAKES OF *THE ALIITES*

Aliite religion represents a robustly creative yet largely overlooked lineage
of African American thought. In this book, I expand the three major unifying strands of Aliite religion—nationality, law, and citizenship—into three
basic arguments.

Aliite theories of *nationality* insist that the problem of racism is, on one
level, a legal problem, a problem of (mis-)identification. Racialization of
African Americans—a term frequently rejected by Aliites, along with the
more specific categories of "negro, black, and colored"—occurs through the
imposition of legal fictions, what Ali called "nicknames" that falsely label
Aliites, obfuscating their true nationality.[22] This amounts to an erasure of
culture, history, and inherited religion, but it also has real social results,
as the identity marked by these legal fictions is stigmatized, excluded, and
oppressed, stripped of rights and subjected to state violence, whether in the
period of chattel slavery or in today's era of mass incarceration and police
killings. Aliites argue that those who accept such oppressive nicknames are
responsible for their own fate, from slaves (who, Ali argued, had forgotten
their true identity) to Michael Brown (who, contemporary Aliites argue,
would not have been killed had he known and embodied his authentic nationality).[23] The Aliite solution to "the Negro problem" begins with rejection of such labels. The project Ali called the "uplift" of his nation, while
it requires state recognition, begins with the self, with individual initiative
and responsibility and pursuit of knowledge.

Law, as a concept in Aliite tradition, is understood to exist in two related forms. Law is understood as refracted through the *legal*—a system of historical practices and institutions, positive law, fallible and shifting human interpretations enforced by human states. Such contingent instantiations of the legal are secondary to *true law*—God's law, "Ultimate Law," natural law, divine law, and often explicitly law *as* God, phrased in one Aliite coinage as Allah as "All-Law," the Most High as "El Obey." True law is synonymous with the five canonical values of the MSTA: love, truth, peace, freedom, and justice, values that themselves are understood as names of Allah.[24] Understood as eternal and transcendent, true law offers a model for the perfected social order. Aliite faith is faith in true law, acknowledging the power of the state and the possibility of using the state's legal system as a means of reforming society, bringing society in alignment with Allah's plan for the world, with Allah's law.

Aliites, in identifying *citizenship* as salvation, explicitly sacralize the American political project. Ali reimagined American democracy as dependent upon strictly maintained cultural and religious differences determined by ancestry, a pluralistic vision he claimed was the direct design of the universal God Allah. America's social and political structure thus plays a privileged role in human history, as an example for the world. Despite a history of racist oppression and injustice, Aliites argue, America stands as a political, social, and legal experiment founded upon universal truths, with values and ideals expressed in the country's founding documents explicitly identified as values of Allah. Pursuing citizenship as a process of "earthly salvation" through, among other means, political and legal activism, Aliites engage the power of the state through recourse to true law and an understanding of law's relation to the legal, to state power, and to sovereignty that reimagines the possibilities and meanings of those concepts. Believing that a sense for true law is inherent in all humans, Aliites understand their own attempts to speak true law before representatives of the power of the state—judges, police officers, politicians—as underwritten by the metaphysical reality of law. Law, moreover, is understood as the ultimate level of sovereignty—with sovereignty understood as multiple and relational, always temporary, and the product of encounter and negotiation. Aliites appeal to the sovereignty of true law, which they believe all humans possess an innate desire for as a result of their divine creation. Aliites mobilize as a sovereign constituency of citizens, able to influence democratic politics in the United States, and Aliites experience sovereignty standing as individual citizens before the power of the state.

Members of Ali's original MSTA carried "nationality cards" with them at all times, versions of which are still carried by Aliites today. These cards declared the authentic identity of their holders and the legal consequence of that identity, expressed in the phrase at the bottom, written in large capital letters: "I AM A CITIZEN OF THE USA."[25] Like "I am a man" or "Black lives matter," this phrase offers an indictment by stating a truth denied by society, insisting upon a reality counter to state practices. Simultaneously, the phrase highlights the state-centered focus of Aliite religion, predicated as it is on recognition of status, engagement with the legal system, investment in the authority of and negotiation of the power of the state. It also expresses hope in a more perfect, future America. Aliite claims to American identity gesture toward a new America, reiterating American exceptionalism by locating the American experiment along a divinely guided trajectory, while, at the same time, taking exception to current American social realities.

The Aliites: Race and Law in the Religions of Noble Drew Ali intervenes in three academic conversations that, while too often isolated from each other, are inextricable in relation to Aliite religion: the study of African American religious history, the study of religion in America, and the study of law and society. By focusing on the MSTA, Nuwaubian Yamassee, and Washitaw movements as linked, part of a single lineage, and by tracing the emphasis, therein, on citizenship and law in relation to race, *The Aliites* corrects an oversight in scholarship on African American religious history. Academic attention to the Aliite religions has treated these traditions separately and failed to focus on the theory and practice of citizenship and law that predominates throughout all three.[26] This Aliite response to racialization and racism, approaching race as a "legal construction" and seeing racial labeling as legally consequential, anticipates the work of critical race theory in analyzing the naturalization and legitimation of race through law.[27] Aliite thinkers offer sophisticated reads on and responses to the situation of race in America. Their voices deserve to be heard and highlighted within broader African American religious history, just as Aliite history must be located within that broader African American context. Aliite enaction and display of true identity—nationality—involves what Derek Hicks describes as a key characteristic of African American religiosity: "symbolic embodiment of amendment" for the purposes of rejecting the diminutions of self imposed by a racist society, alongside insistent imagining of a "new identity" as "something more."[28] Such radical reinvention is at the heart of Aliite "uplift" discourse, which echoes wider African American uplift ideology in sidestepping structural oppression. Aliite thought's emphasis on "uplift" through personal responsibility places the "burden of race relations . . . squarely on the shoulders of Black Americans," even, in Ali's case, assigning to slaves the blame for slavery.[29] At the same time, Ali added an element of universalization to his theories, insisting that people of every nationality must seek "dignity and self-affirmation" through national (rather than racial or class) difference and stating that all nationalities had experienced slavery and could experience it again if they did not maintain their distinct identities.[30]

Even as Aliite thought rationalizes antiblack racism by placing the blame on those who experience it, thus placating potential Aliite outrage against racist injustice, such placation is consistently disrupted, in Aliite history, by the very structural racism it could otherwise allow. Aliites deny black identity, but they suffer, all the same, from being identified as black. And the problem of being identified as black within an antiblack society drives Aliite engagement with American political and legal history and mythology. Aliites turn to the sources of value as well as the voices of authority in America in order to make sense of what Frederick Douglass called America's "national inconsistencies." These range from the foundational paradox of a country devoted dually to freedom and slavery, to the ongoing reality of a legal system promising equal access while continuing a historical pattern of racial discrimination— and also to creative reinterpretation of socially authoritative sources often used to uphold oppressive hegemonic norms.[31] Aliite investment in the legal system as a means of salvation echoes Sally Merry's argument that the discourse and practice of law "contains both elements of domination and seeds of resistance."[32] Aliite creativity coopts and reimagines the language and protocol used to uphold the hegemony, a move akin to what other scholars of African American religion and history have described as exegetical "conjuration" or—making a verb from John Coltrane's name, in honor of his improvisational genius—"traneing," a radical reimagining of the legal.[33]

The examples of Aliite religion provide valuable case studies for academic work in American religious history generally, with the explicit sacralization, therein, of America and U.S. citizenship. Aliite religion reimagines American democracy, American pluralism, and the place of religion within American society, coopting secularism and disestablishment under the name of a universalizing religion, insisting that the political and the religious cannot be separated. The study of religion in America often focuses on how lived religion rubs against the confines of legal understandings of religion. Winnifred Fallers Sullivan has argued that "modern disestablishment, dependent as it is on a narrow and distinctively post-Reformation understanding of religion as appropriately limited to the voluntary association of like-minded individuals" led to a distorted view of religion created by legal judgments.[34] With Aliite religion, however, we have not only traditions innovated—and adapting—to match the legally privileged model, but also religions from which the claim is advanced that this model is, in fact, the eternal, universal, and divine model. Disestablishment does not result, in the Aliite view, in a distorted model of religion, but in a *true* model of religion, proprietary to a given nationality—offering grounding and justification for, but always subservient to, the shared civic project. Aliite religion conforms to the pattern of what Catherine Albanese has identified as "public Protestantism"; what Janet Jakobsen and Ann Pellegrini, flagging the purported neutrality and thus invisibility of such pervasive and legally recognizable religion, have termed "stealth Protestantism"; and what Robert Orsi calls "good religion," calling attention to the fact that such an implicitly Protestant model of "rational, word-centered, nonritualistic, middle class, unemotional [religion is] compatible with democracy and the liberal state."[35]

Ali actively pursued such conformity, embodying an understanding of religion as allowed by and fitting within the state and attributing Allah's design to this particular, legally recognizable model of religion. Aliite thinkers strive for their religion to be "good," "public," and even, in their understanding of universalized difference, invisible. Aliite reverence for—even attribution of divine design to—American democracy is part and parcel of this, a deference to the state out of, in part, desire for protection from the state. Aliite religion must be recognizable by the state as "civil religion," because it seeks salvation through the apparatus of the state, even as its eschatological hope is for the transformation of the state.[36] While in some ways—socially and economically, in relation to categories of race—Aliites serve as the sort of marginalized "outsider" communities that R. Laurence Moore has argued help highlight how Americanness is imagined and enacted, unlike so many of these communities Aliites are actively invested in theorizing and embodying such *Americanness*.[37] Moreover, Aliites engage in an explicit process of and rhetoric about *Americanization* that represents a melding and conscious presentation of "their religious ideals" as simultaneous with "the interests of the constitutional order," unlike the religious communities Eric Mazur analyzed in conflict, through the legal system, with the state.[38] Aliites claim the state as their own and themselves as representatives of its ideals and potential. Such state-centeredness emerges, in part, from a constant awareness of state power—not as a philosophical abstraction, but, rather, as a force ever-present in Aliite life, and a force determinative of life or death. Aliites raise the flag of the United States in order to seek protection, within the state, from agents and policies of the state that would, otherwise, be targeted against them as "negro, colored, or black." Aliite investment in citizenship must always be seen on this practical, everyday level, along with other practical concerns that permeate Aliite history, concerns for basic material welfare—employment, food. Aliite aspirations for political leverage, social reform, dignity, and respect cannot be divorced from these commonplace yet no less pressing desires. Aliites, as marginalized and often impoverished Americans deprived of equal resources and opportunities by a history of racist policies, institutions, and practices *de jure* and *de facto*, theorize citizenship as, first and foremost, a means of survival.

This leads to the contributions of *The Aliites* to law and society scholarship, particularly to work on legal consciousness, theories of sovereignty, and understanding of law's function as "religious." Sally Merry used the term *legal consciousness* for citizens' conceptions of what law is and how it works, understandings of "people's expectations of the law, their sense of legal entitlement, and their sense of rights."[39] Aliite legal consciousness, with its emphasis on a metaphysically real law, is in accord with mainstream American legal consciousness, wherein an ideal of law is contrasted to the positive law of the legal system. Aliites view the interpretations and judgments of a shifting, historically contingent, human judiciary as separate from true law, which is imagined as synonymous with justice. At the same time, Aliites understand society as arcing slowly, through the work of humans—the work of *citizenship*—toward an alignment with true law. The metaphysics, ethics, soteriology, and even eschatology of Aliite thought, while phrased in a distinct vocabulary, express more broadly held American faith in law. Susan S. Sibley has argued that "legal consciousness . . . is [not] . . . something that is individual or merely ideational; consciousness is construed as a type of social practice, in the sense that it both reflects and forms social structures."[40] For Aliites, conceptions of true law shape social practices both explicitly and implicitly legal, from choice of clothing and headwear (as markers of nationality) to *pro se* performances in courtrooms. Such explicit practice of law, demonstrating knowledge of true law to representatives of state power, is understood by Aliites, in turn, as a manifestation of the sovereignty of the citizen. Sovereignty is a complicated and contested notion in American politics, one constantly reinvented by interested parties, from political philosophers to indigenous rights advocates. The term has a range of meanings in contemporary discourse, describing at one end a position of absolute power and, at another, acts intended to elicit recognition of subaltern existence by the state. The sovereign, then, can have the ability to decide life and death or engage in such acts as the "refusal" to acknowledge borders or laws, described by Audra Simpson in her work on contemporary Mohawk practices of sovereignty.[41] Aliites understand sovereignty to be multiple and relational, a matter of encounter and negotiation with levels of power. Aliite theories of sovereignty, while reflecting a practical view of political power as always situational and negotiated, complicate reductive readings of sovereignty while, at the same time, maintaining a focus on the violence inherent in law as observed by theorists of sovereignty, such as Walter Benjamin and Giorgio Agamben. Indeed, in the variety of Aliite theories and practices of sovereignty through citizenship as underwritten by true law, we see an expression of hope for salvation as exemption from the status of "Negro," a variety of "bare life" considered inhuman and disposable in much of American history and—certainly from an Aliite point of view—continuing state practice, like police killings of black people.[42] Law—understood as from Allah and often synonymous with Allah or All-Law—becomes the means of escape from the tyranny of the legal just as it offers the template for the perfection of the currently unjust state. True law, as imagined by Aliites, structures daily existence and provides a motivating hope for the future. Such law serves as the key to "the imaginative construction of a complete worldview," which, as Paul Kahn has shown, means that attention to law allows for an understanding of the "self as a legal subject" and of that subject's relation to "time, space, community, and authority."[43] Law provides Aliites with "a way of being in the world," what Robert Cover famously calls "a *nomos*—a normative universe," a means of making one's reality and one's actions within that reality meaningful.[44] Cover goes on to say that law thus offers "a resource in signification that enables us to submit, rejoice, struggle, pervert, mock, disgrace, humiliate, or dignify."[45] This recognition of the expansive functions of law, functions that approach the label of *religious* by orienting life around a primary concern, leads Cover to describe "an eschatological schema" wherein "redemption" of this world is achieved through first contrast with and then replacement by the imagined ideal of law, a scheme that describes Aliite understandings of the work of citizenship.[46]

Race, American identity, and law are interwoven throughout Aliite thought and practice, just as nationality, citizenship, and law are inextricable from each other within the Aliite worldview. Scholarly conversations about such themes and questions should be connected, as well, and Aliite religion offers valuable examples for such study. One goal for *The Aliites* is that it prove useful across a spectrum of academic inquiry and, like Aliites themselves, build bridges between thinking about race, identity, community, and history; thinking about citizenship, about both the idea and the palpable effects of the state, about legal processes and practices; thinking about values and ideals, about an idea of law as an eternal and transcendent reality, and about an understanding of human existence as a struggle to align society with that notion of true law.

ALIITE PARADOXES:
STATE-CENTEREDNESS AND SOVEREIGNTY

The state-centeredness of Aliite thought and practice is, on the one hand, a survival strategy. Aliites seek protection from the power of the state through appeal to and inclusion within the state. In a hadith or saying of the prophet quoted by contemporary Moors, Noble Drew Ali says, "The only way out of the fire is through the fire."[47] Aliites simply see no way to confront the power of the state except by appeal to and negotiation with that power. Aliites seek to transform the state not radically, through revolutionary action, but incrementally, by persuading agents of the state to align their interpretations of the legal with Aliite teachings of true law.

Key to such Aliite negotiations of state power is the concept of sovereignty. Sovereignty represents a paradox in American legal and political thought, one directly engaged by Aliites as a source of hope for and an explanation of their project of engaging with the power of the state. In American legal consciousness, the sovereignty of the state is understood to coexist with the state as composed of "We the People," who exercise sovereignty as a collective while also retaining individual sovereignty *as citizens*. As Lazarus-Black and Hirsch have argued, attention to paradox in regard to social experience with and understanding of the law is a particularly productive mode of entry into the study of law in society more broadly.[48] In Aliite thought, especially as it developed after Ali's death and under surveillance by law enforcement, ideas about this paradoxical conception of sovereignty helped frame Aliite understandings of citizenship as salvation.

Sovereignty, for Aliites, is both an ideal—understood, in its ultimate form, as synonymous with true law—and a reality experienced by Aliites through political leverage within the state and individual encounters with its representatives. Law, likewise, is also known as both an ideal—true law, transcendent and eternal, synonymous with justice and the other Aliite values—and, through the legal, as a reality, manifest in palpable and undeniable forms, such as the right to a trial or the right to vote, social realities understood as linked to the sovereignty of the citizen. Aliite thought responds to the cognitive dissonance of a legacy of injustice from the legal system by insisting that true law is outside such a system, and, indeed, outside human history altogether, an eternal and transcendent ideal to which humans must commit themselves and for instantiation of which on earth humans must struggle. Aliites believe that "law shaped by the interests of the powerful is not law at all," as Vincent Lloyd says of the broader black tradition of natural law, but they also insist on the practical reality that a rule can be legal within the state while not being true to ideal law.[49] Aliites advance a wide range of legal interpretations of their own, voiced as true law in contrast to the contingent interpretations authorized and enforced by the institutions of the state, but they nonetheless maintain fidelity to Ali's advice for circumventing the violence of a racist power structure, to "be law-abiders and good citizens" by voicing such interpretations to the state, for recognition by the state.[50]

Moreover, Aliites privilege agents of the state, from police officers to clerks to judges, as a primary audience for Aliite arguments, seeking, from such representatives of state authority, recognition of Aliite claims. This stance emerges from an essential Aliite optimism that the legal system, however repeatedly unjust its rulings and processes, is nonetheless patterned on and swayed by the influence of the transcendent ideal that is true law. Aliite thought holds that all humans, as creatures of Allah, possess an innate ability to recognize true law, a persuasive power understood to underwrite Aliite arguments before representatives of the state. State authorities do not always agree with Aliite claims to the legality of their practices, but Aliite investment in the (at least imagined) legality of such practices reflects an overall focus on the state's legitimacy. Aliites, appearing before and invoking the authority of the U.S. legal system and American legal history, are dismissed as criminal "sovereign citizens," even as their understanding of that term is likewise rooted in direct citation of American legal precedent.

Previous scholarship has portrayed Aliite movements in a separatist light, with treatments of the MSTA in particular emphasizing Arna Bontemps and Jack Conroy's statement that early members in Chicago "were accosting the white enemy on the streets" with their nationality cards, declaring that "they had been emancipated from 'European' domination."[51] Yet Ali, in a dispatch entitled "Prophet Warns All Moslems," addresses the problem of

Moors "flashing your cards at Europeans," a practice that "causes confusion." His emphasis, in that context and across his written œuvre, was always on remaining law-abiding, even law-revering. Ali's was a civil and civic movement in which he urged avoidance of any "radical" action or speech among his followers, insisting that social transformation could only come about through the existing legal institutions of the state. As the original "Divine Constitution and By-laws" of the MSTA states, "All members must obey the laws of the government, because by being a Moorish American, you are a part and parcel of the government and must live the life accordingly." Also, "this organization of the Moorish Science Temple of America is not to cause any confusion or to overthrow the laws and constitution of the said government but to obey hereby."[52] "This religious organization is secured and safeguarded by the very constitution of the United States," said Ali, "for in reality it makes of the ordinary man or woman a better citizen for they realize what citizenship means. It teaches loyalty to the nation and the deepest respect for law and order."[53] The three Aliite religions under consideration in this book express a wide variety of thoughts and practices, from emphasis on esoteric initiations to practices for the transcendence of the bodily realm, but one unifying strand is engagement with Ali's teachings on citizenship and law, privileging engagement with the state and the state's legal system in order to achieve recognition and to transform society.

Aliite emphasis on citizenship, understood both as a struggle for recognition of status as citizen and as an ongoing process of social transformation through the practice of citizenship, has roots in an African American context where these aspects are realities. The obsession with state power and state recognition, the obsession with citizenship as a status and a practice, these reflect the fact that society has been closed to "negro, colored, and black" individuals. The prioritization of citizenship reflects exclusion from citizenship, while citizenship and the equal hearing before the state and equal rights under the state that citizenship entrails become a focus for Aliite reaction to broader inequalities and oppressions, exclusions, and violence suffered by Aliites.

Citizenship is palpable because the state, central to Aliite thought, is not merely a symbol or an abstraction but always a collection of concrete state effects, perpetrated by very specific and identifiable state agents, from the county clerk to the police officer. Inclusion in American democracy matters not simply because the idea (and ideals) are promising, but because the opposite—exclusion—becomes a focus for conceptualizing and discussing all other forms of oppression, from extra-juridical abuses like lynching and unfair treatment in job interviews or housing applications to unequal treatment under the law in the form of racial profiling or harsher sentencing. As Carl Schmitt wrote in 1923 in *The Crisis of Parliamentary Democracy,* "Every actual democracy rests on the principle that not only are equals equal but unequals will not be treated equally."[54] Aliites know what it means to be treated unequally; the centrality of citizenship emerges as an attempt to escape such treatment, to avoid further singling out by taking refuge within the pluralistic fold of citizenry. Citizenship is thus more than merely citizenship.

Citizenship serves as the focus for wide-ranging Aliite anxieties and frustrations, in part because citizenship is framed by specific protocol— such as the fact that state agents generally acknowledge those they engage with, a situation through which Aliites experience a mode of sovereignty, as examined in chapter 4. It is also a focus because Aliites can draw on foundational texts and the oft-repeated ideals of the American state to insist that the America into which they were born is not the America that was intended. Regardless of the fact that racist exclusion and discrimination has been the status quo in America since the beginning, Aliites insist that the nation is meant to be, should be, was once, and will be again aligned with truth, love, peace, freedom, and justice—that is, with Allah's true law.

This study, while focusing on a major strand of Aliite thought and practice, must not be read as reducing Aliite religion to *mere* legal theorizing or *mere* politics. This division (religion versus politics) is incomprehensible within the Aliite mindset (where "divine and national" are inextricable). Aliite "religion" is always also much more than Aliite thought and practice on law, citizenship, and race. The totality of Aliite religiosity involves an array of social interactions intimate and public, spectacular and banal. Yet citizenship, too, is always more than mere inclusion in the political life of the state, more even than access to "collective identity, privileges of political membership, and social rights and claims."[55] Citizenship involves a range of meanings, feelings, and values, as Nira Yuval-Davis and others have argued.[56] Aliite history is rife with examples of the everyday complexities of being religious and being a citizen. Consider, for instance, Sister Howell Bey, "crocheting an American flag," as reported in a 1943 issue of the *Moorish Voice,* planning to embark on a matching Moorish flag once her Stars and Stripes was complete.[57] Such displays of patriotism and insistence on inclusion, such rhetoric of "respect and loyalty to government" by those whom that government actively excludes, surveils, and brings violence down upon, are central paradoxes of Aliite tradition, examples of ingenuity in responding to a hostile reality, of resilient faith in a better world.

AUTHORIAL LOCATION
AND METHODOLOGICAL CAUTIONS

My own early education into Aliite religion could be characterized as a "mis-education," and my approach to this book seeks to correct the trends of these early encounters.[58] I first heard of Ali and the MSTA in graduate school, reading C. Eric Lincoln's work on the Nation of Islam, a movement in relation to which he located the MSTA as a mere ancestor. Lincoln's characterization of MSTA thought as "a mélange of Black Nationalism and Christian revivalism with an awkward, confused admixture of the teachings of the Prophet Muhammad" excused the scholar from serious engagement with it, regardless of the role such thinking played (and plays) in the lives of other human beings.[59] This dismissal continues to serve as a motivation for my desire, here, to attentively explicate Aliite logic.

The next time I heard about the MSTA was from Chicago police officers, students in a college program in which I taught after earning my Ph.D. Coming in off their shifts for night classes held in the police academy building, my police students regaled me with stories about MSTA practices that I heard at the time as primarily about breaking the law—refusing to use state-issued license plates or identification, refusing to pay taxes, mobilizing IRS forms or liens against adversaries, and claiming property by squatting and citing obscure historical treaties and passages from legal dictionaries in defense of their presence there. Even when Aliite engagement with and imagination of the law was foregrounded—as it frequently was in questions my students posed about the use of legal documents or the seeming need evinced by Aliites to persuade law enforcement authorities of their claims about the law—I heard stories about criminals. In this book, I follow the focus of Aliite thinkers themselves in considering law as central. Rather than countering Aliite reifications of law with counterreifications, debating true law, this study seeks to examine human claims about law, understanding law, foremost, as a product of the human imagination and an organizing worldview that gives meaning to existence.[60]

When I began researching Aliite movements, I encountered little critical scholarship and an excess of often irresponsible writing from watchdog organizations, chief among them the Southern Poverty Law Center, warning that these "cults" were likely to engage in violent crimes. This literature presented Aliites as, alternately, individual masterminds relying on charisma and false claims to religion to facilitate their selfish goals or gullible victims who surrendered all agency in their allegiance to such leaders. There is no mass hypnotism at work on Aliite communities, nor, in most cases, are Aliites caught in someone else's manipulative scheme. My research has revealed remarkably free-thinking individuals, within a broader system that encourages intellectual disagreement and innovative, original thought. In this study, I not only reject the derogatory label "cult" for these religious communities, I also decenter leaders from my focus.[61] Aliite religion is the work of individuals and grassroots communities. These movements involve myriad interpretive voices, expressed in discord and debate and yet with an underlying commitment to unity. Working primarily with texts, although I cite some prolific Aliite writers repeatedly, my interest remains with the text and the role of the text in Aliite communities rather than with the individual who wrote it. I largely eschew biography except when it is repeatedly cited within the community as relevant, as in the case of Kirkman Bey's military service, for instance. This book presents a story not of the rare person of exceptional accomplishment, but, rather, of the mass of seemingly everyday people who are exceptional in their thoughts and practices, like those Washitaw contributing to the "nation-building" Sunday-night conference call, the Nuwaubian Yamassee posting their ideas in response to memorial videos of the movement's achievement at Tama-Re, or the Moorish American spending her evening crocheting a giant U.S. flag.

Presenting my early work on Aliite religion at the national meeting of the American Academy of Religion, I found myself an accidental participant in a debate about whether Ali's teachings should be classified as "Islam." The policing of borders of religious categories is often an important religious act, but it is not the work of academic scholarship. Likewise, the rhetoric of authenticity is an important subject for the academic study of religion, but it should not be a mode within such study. I am attentive to the ways that claims of inauthenticity have been leveled against Aliites from the earliest days of the MSTA to the present. A 1929 *Chicago Tribune* article describing MSTA members as denying "their negro blood" and doing so "under cult oath" uses the same rhetoric as contemporary journalist Bill Osinski, whose 2007 book-length attack on Nuwaubian Yamassee movement founder Malachi York includes such lines as "York was a pompous, uneducated poseur. To call him a religious leader is to blaspheme the whole notion of religion as a force for good."[62] The linkage here of authentic religion with education, humility, and a universal good is thoughtless, at best. Religion is the work of human beings, whose intentions and inclinations vary wildly. Some are considerate and wise, some arrogant and ignorant, some violent, some compassionate. Religion, therefore, manifests in many ways, from the horrific to the heartwarming. My goal with this book is to cast light on some of the thoughts and practices of Aliites. As to York's sincerity, I'm unclear how such data could be ascertained outside of mind-reading, but, to state my stance plainly, I have no interest in whether York *believes* anything he wrote. I do, however, care a great deal that thousands of people use his words to help make sense of and navigate their lives. In short, this book offers an education into Aliite religion composed in stark opposition to my own early "learning" on the subject.

This is a book told through Aliite voices. My analysis is based on examination of cultural artifacts—books, newspapers, photographs, recorded lectures and performances, legal documents and court records, visual art, videos, websites, internet discussion boards, architecture, radio broadcasts, and public conference calls. It is a work of criticism rather than of ethnography, a close reading of texts and objects produced by Aliites to communicate Aliite thought. Too often dismissed as cultists and/or criminals, Aliites deserve a fair hearing on their own terms, with attention to their logic, their articulations, their desires. The subjects of this book are referred to throughout as *Aliite thinkers*, individual contributors to a broader Aliite system, organic intellectuals who, as Vincent Lloyd writes of his own subjects in *Black Natural Law*, are "*doing* theory, but in an expansive, powerful sense, involving the use of reason, emotion, and imagination, carefully staged for specific audiences."[63] *The Aliites*, organizing Aliite thought in relation to major concerns of and trends within the lineage, curates some of this prolific work of theory and imagination, rendering it accessible to a broader audience than that for which it was intended. Collecting Aliite voices from across the spectrum of MSTA, Nuwaubian Yamassee, and Washitaw thought likewise helps to highlight shared logic and both the influence and reinterpretation of Ali's example within these three, linked, movements.

THE STRUCTURE OF THIS BOOK

Aliites locate evidence of Moorish influence in the earliest symbols of America, giving particular interpretive attention to the Great Seal of the United States. Aliite thinkers offer myriad theories regarding the significance and secret origins of this seal. Some insist that the seal was a Moorish invention stolen by Europeans when they instituted slavery in America. Others hold that it was included by the founders as a homage to Moorish civilization, from which the founders borrowed many of their ideas, including representational democracy and the basis of the Constitution. The Great Seal's presence on the one-dollar bill is attributed by contemporary MSTA thinker Hakim Bey to Ali himself. Hakim Bey claims Ali commanded that the seal be printed on the dollar bill, rather than on rarer, higher denominations of currency, so that all Americans could "see it every day" and carry the lesson around with them in their pocket.[64] That the seal is printed symmetrically, front and back on either side of the bill, is said to echo the two flags held by Ali, that iconic image of how U.S. citizenship depends upon declaration of nationality.

As Aliites interpret the elements of this Great Seal to reference and thus reveal truths about Aliite claims, I use the seal to organize my engagement with Aliite arguments and actions, structuring this book around its mottos and images. Such use of the seal foregrounds the centrality of U.S. citizenship to Aliite thought and practice, while the individual chapters investigate Aliite engagement with key tensions in American society, politics, and law.

Chapter 1, "*E pluribus unum*: Drew Ali's Democratic Theology," roots Ali's notion of citizenship as salvation within the local context of Chicago, where his MSTA began, simultaneous with a turn by Mayor William Hale Thompson and his reigning Republican machine toward African American voters. Ali positioned his MSTA as an essential organization in local politics and sought to benefit from a patronage system that rewarded supporters with jobs and influence. Chicago also provided Ali with a vocabulary of Islam associated, through fraternal societies, with political power, and with the example of ethnic communities, simultaneously semiautonomous and functioning as constituencies within the local democracy. Such communities offered the model for Ali's conception of nationality, a reimagining of difference and identity that characterizes the two other Aliite movements introduced in this chapter, the Nuwaubian Yamassee and the Washitaw de Dugdahmoundyah. I conclude with consideration of Ali's theological vision of American democracy. Ali, insisting that religious and cultural difference was a requirement for American citizenship, universalized difference, identifying the state's system of secularism as Allah's plan for humanity. While secularism contains and manages religion, Ali insisted upon a model of religion—as proprietary, inherited, a mode of difference that all people must have in order to be citizens—in which such management was, again, claimed to be the plan of Allah.

Chapter 2, "Stars in Relation to Stars: Aliite Sovereignty in Politics and Law," argues that Aliites understand *sovereignty*, a central term in their discourse and practice, to be multiple and relational, a matter of encounter and negotiation. Such an understanding opens up possibilities for contesting and coexisting with radically unequal levels of power, a reality Aliites tie to the work of Ali's original MSTA in the local political scene of Chicago in the 1920s. Understanding citizens, united as a constituency, to be capable of exercising their own sovereignty within—and even against—the sovereignty of the American state, Aliites have continued to cite that example across the decades, using Ali's community as an inspiration for their own exertions of sovereignty through political organizing and public protest, as citizens. I turn, next, to the role of international law in Aliite thought and practice, focusing on the identification by Aliites of true law as the ultimate level of sovereignty. This location of ultimate sovereignty as outside history and thus beyond human machinations serves to bolster Aliite faith that, regardless of their lack of power or the overwhelming power of the state they seek to change, through appeal to and practice of true law, human effort can transform social reality.

Chapter 3, "*Annuit cœptis*: Recognition, Authority, and Law," examines the tension inherent in the fact that for a legal claim to have consequence in society, it must be recognized by the authority of the state. Examining both appeals for recognition and the citation of evidence thereof, this chapter considers Aliite use of the original MSTA's incorporation documents and of imagined legal precedent, mobilized as proof of governmental endorsement of Aliite claims. This chapter also examines Aliite reliance on the Supreme Court's 1857 *Dred Scott v. Sanford* decision as proof that "negroes" can never be citizens. While bureaucratic documents, legal decisions, and even (largely symbolic) governmental pronouncements are all held as official evidence of state recognition—and even endorsement—of Aliite claims, I argue that Aliite dealings with such texts should not be considered as "fetishistic" or "magical" in their logic. Rather, Aliite understandings of the power of the legal reflect widespread legal consciousness, rooted in an accurate understanding of the efficacy of legal texts. The chapter concludes by considering Aliite state-centeredness in relation to postcolonial theories about the politics of recognition, suggesting that Aliite examples productively complicate thinking about subaltern communities and their engagement with state power.

State power remains a central concern for chapter 4, "Beneath the Wings and the Shadow of the Eagle: Aliite Sovereignty and the Power of the

State." Focusing on the mode of sovereignty, the sovereignty of the citizen, experienced fleetingly by Aliites through practice of the law before representatives of the state—judges and police officers, primarily—this chapter examines how Aliite legal performance contrasts true law with false legal opinions while ultimately privileging the ability to be *heard* by the state, a right understood as guaranteed by law to all those who are recognized as citizens. Aliites understand true law to be compelling not only through logic but also because, as creatures of Allah, all human beings have an innate sense for true law, linked to Aliite theories of law as love and love's transformative power on the individual, communal, and universal level. This chapter examines specific Aliite performances in courts and on the streets through videos recorded and posted online, which, in turn, become sites for Aliite discussion and serve as pedagogical examples for future Aliite practice. Having established the importance of state authority for such Aliite practice of the law, I examine the term "sovereign citizen," used irresponsibly and overly broadly by watchdog groups to criminalize Aliites who exercise what they understand to be their rights as citizens within the state. The chapter concludes with consideration of the inequality and imbalance inherent in any *pro se* legal practice, noting the divide between rights enshrined in law and the legal system's dependence on resources and elite training.

Chapter 5, "The All-Seeing Eye: Display and Surveillance," links the essential Aliite dynamic of public display of identity with the history of law enforcement suspicion about and surveillance of these communities. Aliites see such surveillance as promising, the intimate proximity of state agents bringing with it the potential for recognition, and also dangerous, as such agents have the power to harm. Turning first to the importance of public display of Aliite nationality, this chapter examines early MSTA public performances, the shifting styles of clothing worn by the Nuwaubian Yamassee, and a passage involving masks and disguises from the Washitaw scripture, noting that Aliites face accusations of masquerade, of faking identity, in their attempts to be recognized as authentic. I argue for a concept of "masking," borrowed from Mardi Gras Indian tradition, to elucidate Aliite understanding of performing identity. Next, the chapter turns to an examination of Aliite responses to law enforcement surveillance, from the early decades of the MSTA to the Nuwaubian Yamassee Tama-Re period to contemporary Washitaw and their appeals to the FBI. Aliites across history have consistently coopted such surveillance for their own ends. As essential as the state is for the Aliite goal of citizenship, it remains a dangerous, even deadly force. This chapter concludes with a consideration of Aliite self-surveillance and the use of camera phones in an era marked by both ongoing state violence against African Americans and widespread self-surveillance practices by citizens.

Aliites are also invested in effectively communicating their claims in order to convince authorities of what they take to be true. Chapter 6, "The Unfinished Pyramid: Knowledge and the Legal," examines Aliite epistemology and knowledge practices, particularly the characteristic Aliite practice of "research," which simultaneously contests dominant narratives of history while arguing for a counternarrative "uncovered" within, and thus relying upon, the authority of accepted, mainstream sources. This practice of research provides a means of establishing and contesting authority among Aliite thinkers, and the focus on "evidentiary" facts—truth understood as framed such that it can be used in legal argumentation—shaped Aliite attitudes toward "religion," a term that is dismissed in favor of a language of objective fact ("science," "overstanding," "factology") while nonetheless mobilized as a means of gaining special rights and accommodations under the law. Aliites thus reject the term "religion" for its implications of belief rather than knowledge, while relying on the term to argue for "religious liberty" for themselves and their communities.

Chapter 7, "*Novus ordo seclorum*: Experiments in Reordering Society," approaches Aliite declarations of U.S. citizenship as declarations of investment in a struggle for a more ideal America. Aliites argue that such a transformed America must follow the patterns laid out in their own utopian social experiments. This chapter thus examines the Aliite imagination, through Aliite representation, of three such semiautonomous Aliite societies, spoken of in the present, past, and future tenses. Looking at the Moorish National Home of the 1940s as represented in the newspaper of the MSTA community that founded and ran it, online video memorialization by contemporary Nuwaubian Yamassee of the Tama-Re settlement (1993–2002), and Washitaw rhetoric expressing desire for a reservation imagined as paralleling Native American examples, I argue that Aliites understand such social experiments as radical alternatives to American society as it is. These utopian experiments, with Aliites living under their own "vine and fig tree," serve as projects of imagining an America yet to come.

Such an America is central to the book's conclusion, "Aliite Faith in American Citizenship," which uses a description of an MSTA "nationalization ceremony" to reflect on the claims about Aliite thought and practice assembled in, and the arguments advanced by, this book. Aliites understand this ritual as framing the official moment when individuals transition from noncitizens to citizens through proclamation of their true, inherited identity. By declaring their Moorish ancestry, these Aliites can also confidently declare a new legal status and, with it, rights and responsibilities in the ongoing process of perfecting America. Reciting in unison, as the climax of this ritual, the words on MSTA nationality cards, these Aliites reiterate the role of citizenship in Aliite religion as both status and process, legal standing and ongoing struggle. Their declaration expresses audacious hope both for immediate legal consequences and for the perfection of an America in which such a statement will generate no controversy but will simply be accepted as fact: "I AM A CITIZEN OF THE USA."

1

E PLURIBUS UNUM

Drew Ali's Democratic Theology

ONE OUT OF MANY:
ALI'S VISION OF DIVERSITY

ONE OF THE THREE TEXTS on the Great Seal of the United States, adopted by an Act of Congress in 1782, is the Latin phrase *e pluribus unum*: "out of many, one." Originally a statement on the union of the individual colonies into a single nation-state, the phrase has reverberated throughout the country's history as a reference to the defining characteristic of America as a country of immigrants—a country of multiple nationalities of people in the Aliite sense, its citizenry composed of the descendants of varied ancestries, inheritors of myriad cultures, practitioners of diverse religions.

Ali did not just affirm this conception of America, he claimed that Allah mandated it. To be an American citizen, Ali taught, one must proclaim one's nationality and practice that nationality's cultural inheritance as a predication for what he called "the sacred obligations of American Citizenship."[1] The flag of one's distinct ancestry must be displayed in order to announce one's legal access to the rights represented by the flag of the United States. Cultural and religious diversity, in this view, was not merely a feature of American society, it was a *requirement* for full participation in the American political system. Only by acknowledging (and supporting, living within, committing to) the "vine and fig tree" of one's own ancestral nationality could one be part of the broader civic project, of this country predicated on the notion of being a collection of "united" differences. Ali responded to problems of discrimination, bias, and hierarchies based on difference by reimagining American diversity and pluralism as elements upon which the democratic experiment depended.

At the same time, this system universalized difference and, thus, leveled it. All citizens of America, in Ali's understanding, were minorities. Moors, in proclaiming their nationality in order to have their "Divine rights" recognized and to be "unmolested by other citizens that they can cast a free national ballot at the polls," were just like everyone else. Such was, according to Ali, American protocol for all peoples: "If Italians, Greeks, English, Chinese, Japanese, Turks and Arabians are forced to proclaim their free national names and religion before the constitutional government of the United States of America, it is not more than right that the law be forced upon all American citizens alike."[2]

As a "Universal Prophet," Ali addressed "all nations of the earth," declaring that *his* was the only system that could bring peace. The universal Allah on whose behalf he spoke had sent a number of "true and divine prophets," each with a revelation to their own nation. Worship of Allah was different "in all lands," a singular religion split, as if through a prism, such that unique versions were revealed to each nationality, around the globe.[3] Ali, while focused on his own nation of people—those Moors who had long been unconscious of their true identity and lived in oppression as Negroes in America—preached to all peoples, urging them to follow the same instructions. Return to your ancestral tradition, your nationality, he said. This was his task as "the last prophet of these days."

Explicitly, he spoke of his prophetic mission, in part, as "returning Christianity to the Europeans," getting white people to embrace their difference, as well—and thus accept their role within a pluralistic society, not as superseding and colonizing, but as one nation among many out of which the United States of America was composed. As Sylvester Johnson has argued, Ali's "pluralizing ideology, asserting that particular peoples should possess particular religions," inverted "colonial ideas about universalism and particularity," rendering Christianity as particular to whites, rather than as universal, and declaring it destructive rather than salvific for the world's nonwhite peoples.[4]

Ali's eschatological vision imagined a future of harmonious pluralism that would balance a degree of national cultural autonomy with coexistence and equal participation in a shared, democratic body politic. The lion and the lamb, which Ali identified as the rich and the poor, would lie down together without rancor, and each "nation" would exist under its own "vine and fig tree," a utopian vision of American democracy that originated in the context of local Chicago politics.

This chapter examines the role of Chicago in shaping Ali's take on "Islamism" and "Moorish" nationality, and then expands the investigation to two other Aliite religions (the Nuwaubian Yamassee and the Washitaw de Dugdahmoundyah) and into the present. It analyzes Ali's model of religion—explicitly pluralistic and democratic, religion conceived in relation to the American state's secularism, explicitly sacralizing the notion of *e pluribus unum*.

For Ali, the United States, a country predicated on difference and unity across difference, was the product of Allah-God's plan and offered a unique opportunity for the instantiation of divine law. America, thus, offered the possibility of equal justice for all, under law (and thus under God), within a political system where diversity was both required and regulated, a mosaic of distinct "vine and fig trees" assembled under the U.S. flag. Ali saw an example of such *e pluribus unum* on the local level, in Chicago.

A THEOLOGY OF LOCAL DEMOCRACY:
ALI'S MSTA

Ali's vision developed in a specific time and place, the Chicago of the 1920s. Ali described this city as offering a unique model of God's plan for humanity. Chicago's local political scene made that city "closer to Islam" than any other city, Ali argued.[5] Chicago's political scene thus resembled the theology Ali laid out in his movement's central scriptural text, the *Holy Koran of the Moorish Science Temple of America*, also called the *Circle Seven Koran*, a text that presented Allah as a deity with a democratic nature, apportioning revelation on a representational basis, sending prophets to each of "the families of nations." This family included "Europeans," by which Ali designated a range of so-called white nationalities, as well as "Asiatics," his term for a spread of so-called brown and black peoples, from the inhabitants of Africa to those of South America and Asia. Allah had established for each nationality a distinct religion, conveyed by the divine prophet of that nationality.[6] Ali used the term "Islam" as the universal term for religion, distinct from both the specific "Islamism" he preached to his Moorish community and the Christianity of the "Europeans," or whites.[7] Islam in this sense was a divine design for pluralistic harmony and civic cooperation, parallel to an idealistic interpretation of Chicago's civic body as a tapestry of nationalities united, each with its own "vine and fig tree" and its own elected representative voicing its members' interests in City Hall. Ali insisted that this political system was exceptional. "There is but one Chicago," he wrote in one of the many short pieces published in the original MSTA newspaper, the *Moorish Guide*, and later canonized in *Moorish Literature* (*ML*), a compilation of Ali's writings studied, individually and communally, by Aliites.[8]

In "So This Is Chicago," Ali reiterated his sense that all of the earth's nations "are now being forced to contribute their share in this American life," and noted that while "some of the nations here are put at a disadvantage supposedly" because of the color of their skin, the real restraint is "a peculiar psychology designed to hold them in mental slavery." His system promised to supplant this poisonous psychology, replacing an identification with the category of Negro with a new identification with the true and empowering category of Moor. Chicago offered a particularly suitable venue for this project, as it was as unlike other American cities as America is unlike the other countries of the globe. What would happen among the Asiatics of the world would happen first in the United States of America, and this would happen first in Chicago, "the first cosmopolitan city of this nation"—the only American city, Ali told his Moorish community, "that has all features of this American life engaged in by our people. Aldermen seated in the council of the city. Men high in official affairs of the city generally. There is but one Chicago."[9]

Ali's vision of vines, fig trees, lions, and lambs, while borrowing language from biblical apocalypticism, was resolutely this-worldly and practical. Black migrants had long overlaid religious imagery onto the journey to the North. Ali saw this promised land as a place where one could exercise rights, under the law. While the salvation that would come with citizenship would lead, ultimately, to the transformation of society, in the meantime it had real material rewards. Among Ali's immediate hopes was the hope that his community would be granted patronage jobs in return for political activism and loyalty to the Republican Party machine of Mayor William Hale ("Big Bill") Thompson (1869–1944, mayor of Chicago 1915–23 and again, with Aliite help, 1927–31).

In what would become a hallmark of Aliite tradition, Ali offered evidence—objective proof—for his claims. Another famous early photograph, still cited by Aliites today as demonstrating the efficacy and achievability of Aliite claims, illustrates this. A group shot, this image frames Ali with men and women from his MSTA as well as special guests whose presence at a Moorish event the community wanted to preserve on film. Ali wears regalia befitting the title of prophet. He leans back in a chair garlanded with flowers, wearing a robe and sash along with a turban from which feathers extend at the crown. His fellow Moorish Americans likewise wear various forms of eye-catching headwear and garments that visually proclaim their nationality. The fez, the most iconic of male Moorish headwear, is here, as is the turban, the most popular Moorish headwear for women. There is some variation, as well, including one boldly striped pharaonic headdress.[10]

Flanking these Moorish Americans are representative political and economic leaders of the Chicago's so-called Black Belt. Among those paying their respects to Ali and the MSTA is Jesse Binga, founder of the first privately owned African American bank in Chicago; Louis Anderson, incumbent alderman (City Council representative) for the predominantly black Second Ward, up for reelection; and Oscar De Priest, candidate for U.S. Congress, soon to be the first African American elected to such an office since the early, fleeting days of Reconstruction. These last two are part of the slate of the Republican Party machine courted by Ali with promises of a sizeable Moorish American voting bloc and an even larger MSTA-led voter registration drive. These three figures remain particularly important in Aliite memory, with quotes from them, praising the MSTA, frequently repeated in Aliite texts—for example, De Priest stating that "I feel that with the help of the Moorish Americans in this city, that I have won."[11] The photograph serves as evidence of Ali's teachings and their efficacy. This event, with the MSTA hosting local power brokers, represents the culmination of the project of proclaiming "nationality," not merely citizenship as a status but citizenship as a practice, a process of political engagement that leads to social transformation.

Ali's movement was influenced by Marcus Garvey's Universal Negro Improvement Association (UNIA), so much so that Ali, and Aliites to this day, refer to Garvey as "the forerunner of the prophet."[12] Yet while Garvey called for global black unity and migration "back to Africa," Ali focused on the possibility of reforming America. Political engagement, *use* of the law, was and remains the hallmark of Ali's thought. Ali is said to have visited Garvey in federal prison in 1927, and shared the Jamaican thinker's focus on practical economic concerns, quest for political sovereignty through unity as a nation, and attention to the use of media, from newspapers to the framed copies of the MSTA "Divine Constitution and By-laws," which, as with parallel UNIA documents, were hung in MSTA meeting places.[13] Ali also echoed Garvey in drawing on the American religious movement of New Thought, with its emphasis on human perfectibility and individual responsibility for circumstances, individual attitude and action, as a path to new modes of being.[14]

Ali arrived at a fortuitous political moment for African Americans in Chicago's history. Mayor Thompson—whose name became synonymous with spoils politics and general corruption, "Thompsonism"—found himself in a closely contested reelection battle in 1927 and made a strategic decision to court votes in the "Black Metropolis" of the city's South Side. His "America First" slogan was expanded, as he later stated in a victory statement printed in the leading African American newspaper in Chicago, the *Chicago Defender*, to mean "I am for America and American citizens first, last and all the time, without any distinction of race, creed or color," a stance he, like Ali and his followers, linked directly to the Declaration of Independence, to American tradition, and to, if not the legal as interpreted and enforced by the state, then an idealized notion of values at the heart of U.S. law as represented in the rhetoric of its founding documents.[15] The move cost Thompson white votes and led to a public racist smear campaign— "palm cards of Thompson kissing a black child ('Thompson—Me Africa First' appeared on the reverse side)," for instance—but the Great Migration had been pumping new black voters into the city, and the move paid off.[16] Thompson was already familiar with racist hate mail and had already been rewarding loyal black Republicans with patronage jobs at a much higher rate than any previous mayor.[17] Such political moves represented pragmatic attempts to treat the black neighborhoods as what, in Chicago, they most resembled—the other "ethnic ghettoes" of immigrants who could be courted and then counted on for loyalty as bloc voters for a political machine that rewarded its own.

Ali, turning to claims of Moorish nationality as a way to guarantee American citizenship, struck upon the same logic as his fellow citizens "of foreign extraction" with their "realistic view of political patronage."[18] Such immigrant communities engaged in their own "politics of respectability," linking individual and community behavior to the possibility first of acceptance as equal participants in, and then for broad structural reform of, society.[19] But Ali's community, through its claims to nationality, sought to escape the "deeply rooted history of stigmatization" associated with black Americans. As Moors, they could expect to be treated like "recent immigrant groups," free of the stigma of "Negro" identity as well as the consequences of the legal category "Negro."[20] Coming together under the red Moorish flag, as a unified nationality group, Ali's MSTA engaged in "ethnic coalition politics," making a bid for recognition as a constituency group, voting in solidarity as a bloc of citizens.[21] Ali's MSTA thus resembled the myriad other "ethnic political clubs" started in Chicago by immigrant groups with an eye toward the quid pro quo of livelihoods in exchange for votes.[22] Even the language used to describe such politics reflects the level of material need to which it appealed: below the level of graft and payoffs for rich cronies, local political machines in Chicago were built on "bread and butter" strategies for building up a voter base, swapping something as basic as food for electoral support.[23]

Attention to "bread and butter" matters as much to Aliite history as attention to real political power. Ali laid out a "doctrine of economic security." Moorish Americans, he wrote, as part of their responsibility as citizens, ought "to *urge* that our business men and women build on the principle of service . . . [and] keep firmly in mind the necessity of keeping each dollar spent as much as possible within the spheres of our own activities where they will create further openings of business enterprises and wider opportunities for the men and women of our group to procure soundly remunerative employment."[24] Ali insisted that "*no other one thing is more needed among us at this time than greater economic power.*"[25] Ali's mission to his nation involving working for "social or material benefit," "for mutual improvement, for dispensing charity, for aiding the unfortunate, for protecting our civil rights, for aiding one another and for elevating the nation," as a post-Ali column in the MSTA's *Moorish Voice* put it.[26] Much of Aliite history is geared toward practical and immediate concerns—employment, food to eat, a communal economy wherein Aliites support each other. Early MSTA members started businesses, from laundries and cafeterias to grocery stores, while the organization itself ran a publishing company and newspaper as well as the Moorish Manufacturing Company, which sold cleaning products and health supplements.[27] Aliite political organization and Ali's theories of politics and law must be considered in light of this focus on practical economics as well.

The possibility of material rewards for exercising one's "sacred obligations" by voting (and getting out the vote) served to make citizenship—especially for Ali's original audience, largely rural blacks from the South who had been violently denied the right to participate in local politics—a means of existential survival, "salvation" on the level of basic material needs, the level of the physical body. Voting didn't just make you a member, in some abstract sense, of the polity, with a hand, however slight, in collective governance. Voting could lead to deliveries of food, to jobs with good pay and good pensions, to formal recognition and local fame, to what was read (and what continues to be read, by many Aliites) as official state endorsement of religious claims. The characteristics of Thompson's third term (1927–31)—patronage rewards for those loyal to the machine as well as "recognition of blacks and ethnic groups" upon which his reelection had depended—offered a profound opportunity for Ali to leverage his position as leader of a growing, and high-profile, MSTA community into an unofficial role as something like a ward sub-boss or precinct captain, a vote collector.[28]

Ali was explicit about—and publicized—the use value of his movement to the party machine, promising "three thousand" Moorish voters who followed his lead. His MSTA community, moreover, launched a campaign "to register every Man or Woman in order to take the lead for the various candidates whom they have been instructed to vote for," turning the MSTA into both a voting bloc and a campaign organization (though an unofficial one).[29] Ali's notion of "respect and loyalty to government" meant allegiance to a particular power structure and the expectation of acknowledgment in return. In Chicago, an unspoken agreement was understood to pervade arrangements such as Ali's get-out-the-vote campaign. Ali assured his audience that "your condition can be better," but first they all had to "take [their] place in the affairs of men," to function *as* citizens, exercising their right to vote and encouraging others to vote for those candidates endorsed by the MSTA organization.[30] Through political activism, Ali sought attention and respect from the Republican bosses, which he assumed would, in Chicago style, lead to "general relief for the economic good of all," with particular attention to those Moorish Americans whose work deserved patronage recompense. Citizenship offered salvation not in some abstract or otherworldly sense, but in practical and material rewards—power, employment, income— in this specific society and political scene, Chicago.

The local context here allows for politics in the sense articulated by Sheldon Wolin: "legitimized and public contestation, primarily by organized and unequal social powers, over access to the resources available to the public authorities of the collectivity."[31] Politics, thus understood, is a process, "continuous, ceaseless," that can blossom into democracy, or what Wolin terms "fugitive democracy" to mark his assertion that democracy is "an ephemeral phenomenon rather than a settled system." Aliite engagement with the local political machine is politics that, at moments, becomes an instance of such fugitive democracy. Always local—on the scale of the neighborhood, for instance, or the ward, the unit into which Chicago's political geography is divided—fugitive democracy is "protean and amorphous, embracing a wide range of possible forms and mutations that are responsive to grievances on the part of those who have no means of redress other than to risk collectivizing their small bits of power."[32] Citizenship is that which allows for such possibility of power, for what in the next chapter I will discuss in terms of *sovereignty*. Wolin's "fugitive democracy" is a doubly useful term for the Aliite case as it simultaneously describes and evokes. "Fugitive," with its implications of a covert, questionably legal quality, nicely resonates with, and calls for reconsideration of, that which has been so often dismissed simply as cronyism, corruption, or "Thompsonism." For even through circumstances arranged to facilitate one group's greed, another group can leverage real power, real rights, real dignity through the experience of democratic participation. Citizenship, as a salvific ideal, need not be pursued only in polite society. Or, to put it another way, democracy often occurs in and through messy and multivalent situations, many of which involve explicit negotiation of radically imbalanced power relations. Aliite utopian dreams of and for American democracy do not deny the existence of imbalance of power and resources. Aliites struggle, however, for equal standing before the law, a struggle undertaken through the work of citizenship.

A CITY "CLOSER TO ISLAM": DIFFERENCE AND POLITICAL POWER IN CHICAGO

The city of Chicago influenced Ali's movement in two other important ways, providing what Ali took to be a recognizable symbolic vocabulary of Islam and the Islamic as well as a model of society understood as consisting of ethnic communities at once semiautonomous and distinct, yet participating in a common democratic government—a practical, local example of *e pluribus unum*.

The religious vocabulary Ali adopted, the language of "Islam," was ubiquitous in Chicago. In very public venues, from fraternal society parades composed of civic leaders wearing fezzes to newspaper photos of orientalist and explicitly Islamic-identified symbolism as the marker of social prestige, a popularized version of Islam signified respectability and political power.[33] The presence and symbolic power of Islam in 1920s Chicago cannot be overstated. Islam was enshrined in the monumental Moorish Revival architecture of famous buildings such as the Medinah Temple—a center of political power via Freemasonry, featuring Arabic citations from the Qur'an over its Moorish-design doors and under its onion domes—and the Chicago Athletic Club, the minaret of which rose to the top of the city's skyline. Such coopted Islamic symbolism was resolutely associated with social and political power

via the fraternal societies, but for Ali surely there was an association of Islamic history with the continent of Africa (Moors, after all, were historically
both African and Muslim), as well as with a vision of racial equality. There
is no evidence he interacted directly with the Ahmadiyya missionaries sent
to Chicago's South Side, or read their English version of the Qur'an.[34] Indeed,
Ali called his religion "Islamism" to differentiate it from other forms of Islam, and noted that he himself had been called by Allah "to Americanize the
Oriental idea of Islam," noting that his particular, Americanized formulation
of Islam had as its "sole purpose" the aim "to save fallen humanity," and to
save America.[35] But for Ali, "Islam" signified a range of social goals his own
movement shared: political power, respectability, a glorious history in African civilization, and a denial of race prejudice.

In Chicago's thriving immigrant ethnic neighborhoods, communities
maintained their own "national" traditions, with their own flags, their own
newspapers, their own native dress, their own colorful celebrations of their
own holidays. Simultaneously, such communities asserted their belonging in
the broader civic culture and political power structure and offered a pattern
for Ali's vision of the ideal society. America, in Ali's theory, was composed of
various nationalities of peoples, each with its own distinct culture and traditions. MSTA members adopted "national" dress and took the surnames "El"
or "Bey," marking themselves in ways recognizably parallel to various immigrant ethnic communities in Chicago. The myriad functions of such identity
work cannot be reduced to the negotiation of legal categories or political
organizing, as essential as both were for Ali's MSTA. Moorish nationality
also offered a sense of heritage and values, a set of religious beliefs and practices, symbols with powerful emotional resonance. As in the case of other
ethnic communities, nationality, for MSTA members, represented a sense of
belonging and facilitated a degree of autonomy, a people gathered under a
flag with a shared sense of their past and shared hope for their future. Unlike
other ethnic groups, however, those of Moorish nationality understood their
identity to be first and foremost a *correction*; conversion to the MSTA was
a return to authentic ancestry and a rejection of oppressive and incorrect
labels foisted upon Moors by a racist society.

Sylvester Johnson has described Ali's adoption of an "ethnic heritage
paradigm"—his theory of nationality—as a way to break away from and refuse the concept of *race*.[36] Ali insisted (at points) that there was only one race,
the human race, and that all people, regardless of ancestry or "hue" of skin,
were of that race, including specifically "all inhabitants of Africa" historically
and into the present.[37] Ali's claims about racialization focused on the legal

nature—and effect—of such categories. The labels "negro, black, and colored" carried with them very real social and legal consequences, being used by the state to segregate and disenfranchise, discriminate, dehumanize. *Negro* is the most marked of such terms, with a history in American legal policy and juridical interpretation, most famously the 1857 Supreme Court decision *Dred Scott v. Sanford*, which declared that a Negro could not be a citizen.

Ali's turn to nationality explicitly identified the legal history and consequences associated with the labels "negro, black, and colored," and substituted an alternative term, one with a separate legal history—"Moorish." This had been a legal category from colonial times on signifying dark-skinned individuals who were distinct from slaves—foreigners afforded rights in an otherwise racially segregated America.[38] The linkage to Morocco, the first country to recognize the sovereignty of the United States, also bolstered the significance of this identity for Aliites, as will be discussed in chapter 2.

By rejecting "Negro" and adopting "Moorish," Ali rejected the consequences of a legal fiction by rejecting that legal fiction itself, understanding, as critical race theory has since argued in detail, "the centrality of law" in the social construction of race.[39] Conscious of what the terms "negro, black, and colored" implied—their legal status—Ali insisted upon an alternative identity as a means of avoiding those consequences. Ali's turn to nationality resembles other examples of "changing ethnicity" in response to social and legal incentives, such as "switching" from "black" to "colored" in apartheid-era South Africa or converting to Islam to escape the ethnic category of "Scheduled Caste Hindu" in India.[40]

While Ali argues in one text that the terms "negro, black, and colored" are mere "nicknames," fictitious labels designed to keep some humans in a state of legally sanctioned inequality and oppression, at other times in his writing Negro seems like an actual category of being in the world. In the traditions of thought that follow from his work, this category of Negro is widely reified, understood to be not a legal fiction but, first, a mode of behavior (people can become Negroes by acting like Negroes, as A. Hopkins-Bey argues in a contemporary MSTA sermon), and second, an actual ontology, a category into which one is born and which may or may not (depending on the given thinker) be understood as escapable.[41]

One result, then, of Ali's turn to a concept of nationality instead of a concept of race—his rejection of Negro in favor of Moorish—is that such thought manages to keep the category of Negro alive. Much Aliite thought reiterates antiblack racism as it attempts to free Moors from the label of blackness and, thus, from the direct effects of such racism. This trend begins in Chicago, with Ali telling his followers to gather and "hear the truth about your nationality and birthrights, because you are not negroes." His message offered a distinction between those who remain complicit in their own oppression through their confusion regarding who they are—those who think they are, who identify as, "negro, black, or colored"—and those who acknowledge an alternative history and cultural heritage as Moors, descendants of an industrious African empire who trace their roots back to the biblical Canaanites and Moabites.[42] Ali linked denial and amnesia about national identity and ancestry, in his narrative of American history, to the problem of slavery and ongoing Jim Crow laws.

The blame, then, was put on black-skinned people. Ali explains the tragedy of slavery in biblical tropes, that Moors of generations past had adopted the religion of Europe and abandoned their own true faith. Moors had forgotten who they were, lapsed in the enactment of their identity, and, thus, had become slaves, first in the system of chattel slavery and now in "mental" or "political slavery." Racist discrimination resulted from the *personal* failing of those who called themselves "negro, black or colored," individuals who had lapsed in their sacred civic duties, who had lost knowledge and thus love for self. Moors were not, Ali taught, alone in this failing. According to his *Holy Koran*, black chattel slavery is in no way a unique historical experience; due to "sin and disobedience every nation has suffered" a similar fate at some point in time.[43] Ali's historical narrative universalized slavery much as his notion of nationality universalized difference.

While nonblack audiences may have appreciated being let off the hook for America's racism, Ali's approach to slavery and racism, while counterintuitive, could also be empowering to his now-Moorish audience. Their rise as Moorish Americans, MSTA rhetoric insisted, would be facilitated by their own efforts and their willingness to take the initiative and act as citizens. Ali, by offering them their nationality, returning them to knowledge of the red flag, had freed them to determine their own future on their own. Ali's theory of nationality's relationship to citizenship relied upon a liberal notion of individual agency and responsibility, and was part of Ali's call for "uplift" through economic and political action, which similarly emphasized the individual as actor, as captain of his or her own fate.[44] This same emphasis on individual responsibility and agency characterizes the theology of Ali's *Holy Koran*, drawing on New Thought tradition, which insists that individuals can achieve God-ness through their own effort. Such thinking led to real-world effects in terms of Moorish entrepreneurism and business ventures. This emphasis on initiative and possibility led to opportunities for women in the MSTA organization. In the earliest years, women played prominent leadership roles, as founders and heads of temples (called "sheikesses" and "governesses"), as well as editors of the *Moorish Guide*, pursuing a logic that linked the limits of possible accomplishments to limits of initiative and effort.[45]

Racism, such logic claims, is a problem because black people, Negroes, those who *identify* with those terms, will suffer under it. Uplift—escape from the problems of racism—begins with a declaration of identity, understood as a legal declaration, one that should lead to recognition, by the state, of one's status as citizen. To be recognized as a citizen is, in turn, the first step in a process of active civic involvement. The voter registration drives run by Ali's MSTA were understood in this light, a practice of one of the duties of citizenship for both those registering and those running the registration. Both steps were seen as essential parts of *being* a citizen, essential elements of the "salvation" promised in MSTA thought.

As the responsibility for slavery fell on the individual and the community, so, too, did the responsibility for salvation. "Our plight will change when we change ourselves," Ali insisted.[46] Ali's system gave the voting franchise (and, for many members, the move from the rural South to the urban North) new historical, even mythic significance. Chicago was not just a different world from where they had been previously; for those who joined the MSTA, the ability to participate politically as citizens of Chicago allowed them to believe that they had become different people, had woken from mental and political slavery, liberated by Ali's teaching and their own efforts. Given the opportunity, in the North, to participate in the franchise of voting, one *had* to participate. "Anytime a Man or a Woman fails or refuses to cast a sacred ballot at the polls they separate themselves from all rights of an American citizen"—one was damned, cast back into slavery, "political slavery," by failing to engage in civic responsibilities. One must play an active "part in the affairs of the nation," organizing and campaigning, getting out votes as well as voting as an individual, in order to *be* a Moor.[47]

FROM ALI TO ALIITE: THE MSTA, THE NUWAUBIAN YAMASSEE, AND THE WASHITAW DE DUGDAHMOUNDYAH

With Ali's death in 1929, the MSTA began to splinter. This set the stage for a contemporary scene in which "Moorish Science" and "Moorish Science

Temple of America" are terms used and contested by hundreds of organiza-
tions and far more individual thinkers, representing diverse interpretations of
Ali's thought but all sharing a focus on the legal consequences of proclaiming
Moorish nationality. As contemporary Moorish thinker Hopkins-Bey says,
"If you don't have a nationality you have no political rights nor status."[48]
The responsibilities inherent in citizenship status—the work of community
organizing, voting, protesting, undertaking economic projects, and engaging
in courtroom legal performance—are likewise seen, across the spectrum of
communities influenced by Ali's work, as effective and salvific responses to
practical social and political problems, such as "rampant unemployment, few
business resources and limited retail store power," in Moorish communities.[49]
Following Ali, contemporary Moors understand citizenship as the means to
solve such problems, by working to align society's understanding and institutions of the legal with Allah's Ultimate Law.

These key characteristics of Ali's thought are found not only across the
range of MSTA organizations and individuals, but also across two other
Aliite movements, the Nuwaubian Yamassee and the Washitaw de Dugdahmoundyah. Both these movements likewise involve a variety of organized
communities and an array of independent thinkers. There is also interaction and movement between, and occasionally dual or triple identification
as, Moor, Nuwaubian Yamassee, and Washitaw. The three movements share
a focus on Ali's thought and writings, and involve interpretation and contestation of each other's distinctive vocabularies and teachings. All three
movements are predicated on Ali's theory of nationality, on the legal consequences of proclaiming national identity and the responsibilities of citizenship that follow recognition of status by the state. While each movement has
its own specific narratives of history and its own ultimate, eschatological
goals, law remains a central concern across all three, as does citizenship,
understood both as legal status and as a process of transforming society.

The Yamassee Native American Moors of the Creek Nation is the latest name and iteration of a movement founded by Malachi Z. York (born
c. 1945) in Brooklyn in the 1960s, most famously known as the United
Nuwaubian Nation of Moors. Members of this movement, called throughout this book by the popular contemporary usage Nuwaubian Yamassee,
link identity to legal status in two ways, both as Moors or Mu'urs, in a manner parallel to the MSTA, where the identity means something distinct
from "black" and therefore outside the legal exclusions historically imposed

upon blacks. The Nuwaubian Yamassee also insist upon another form of identity, popular across the spectrum of Aliite religion, that of "indigenous" or "aboriginal," a status resulting from the community's claim to deep history in the land of America. Indigenous status is also understood as a legal status, which, when recognized by the state, comes with its own set of legal privileges and accommodations.[50]

Explicit engagement in the rhetoric and practices of citizenship and law has increased, among the Nuwaubian Yamassee, since York led many of the movement away from New York and to Putnam County, Georgia, in 1993, to found a settlement on 476 acres of land, called the Golden City of Tama-Re. Tama-Re was a target for local law enforcement from its beginnings, ultimately leading to its destruction following a joint federal and local raid in 2002, yet parallel to this the Nuwaubian Yamassee began speaking openly of their rights as part of "We the People," demonstrating their citizenship through the staging of public protests, the filing of lawsuits, and the act of carrying copies of the U.S. Constitution. In such practices, Nuwaubian Yamassee mobilized a notion of ideal law in contrast to the unjust treatment of their community and their leader (who is now serving a 135-year federal prison sentence) by and within the legal system of the United States.

First as the Ansar Pure Sufi movement, then later as the Nubians, the Nubian Islamic Hebrews, the Ansaar Allah, the Holy Tabernacle of the Most High, then as the United Nuwaubian Nation of Moors (UNNM), this movement has adopted and discarded symbol systems, styles of dress, and the vocabulary of other, existing religious traditions. There have been distinctly Islamic, Jewish, and Christian phases, for instance, though in recent iterations Moorish identity and some linkage to MSTA legacy have been foregrounded and survived transition from one phase to another. Nuwaubian Yamassee generally identify as Moors. The author of an important early monograph on Ali and the MSTA, York includes quotes from and images of Ali in his books.

Known variously throughout his career by such appellations as Dwight York, Rabboni Y'shua Bar El Haady, As Sayyid Al Imaam Isa Al Haadi Al Mahdi, Pharoah Neter A'aferti Atum-Re, Chief Black Thunderbird Eagle, Maku, and the Master Teacher, York claims authorship of hundreds of Nuwaubian Yamassee publications, in addition to sermons and lectures distributed in recorded form, that articulate the values and elaborate cosmology of the group.[51] This cosmology includes claims of a superhuman, extraterrestrial origin for Nuwaubian Yamassee, a subhuman origin for "Caucasians," and the belief that multiple species of aliens live and have lived on earth, some of them covertly. The ancestors of the Nuwaubian Yamassee fell into slavery—chattel

slavery and ongoing mental slavery—due to a lack of self-knowledge aug-
mented by the physical removal of an organ the community believes to be
necessary for full consciousness, the "barathary gland." Gathered by York,
the community embarked, beginning in the 1960s, on a process of increasing self-knowledge and self-realization that led them through iterations of
other, known religions and ultimately into York's mature system, a worldview
drawing on a range of sources, from ancient Mesopotamian texts to modern
ufology, the primary scripture of which is *The Holy Tablets*, a sprawling text
that serves as a synthetic culmination of the movement's many phases.[52]

While Nuwaubian Yamassee reject the word "religion" as signifying false-
hood, the movement nonetheless reiterates the universalism of Ali, believing the religious traditions of the world to all offer forms of the one truth.[53]
This truth is synonymous with law, called at times by the Nuwaubian Yamassee the "Fundamental Laws of Nature," understood as the ideal behind
such ethical values and political goals as "Justice, Liberty, Freedom, Domestic
Tranquility, General Welfare, and Common Defense."[54] Nuwaubian Yamassee thought is understood as a developing trajectory, moving toward more
complicated revelations of truth, and the movement itself follows a trajectory
across its history—largely in response to pressure from law enforcement—
of increasing engagement with representatives of the state and increasing
practice of Nuwaubian Yamassee understandings of true law.

The Washitaw de Dugdahmoundyah identify as "the oldest sovereign nation known to humanity," descendants of the original settlers of the land of
North America, who built mounds and earthworks (hence the name "dug-
dah-mound-yah") marking the expanse of their former empire, which was
also the first civilization.[55] Washitaw, as members of the movement are
called (less frequently, Washitawans, though also identifying simply as indigenous *mound-builders*), share a name with the land they insist is legally
theirs, generally identified with the Louisiana Purchase of 1803, occasionally identified as most or all of the New World, but with its center point the
"holy land" of "Washitaw Proper," a section of northern Louisiana that includes Ouachita Parish, through which the Washitaw River runs. This area
contains several important archaic American sites, including the Watson
Brake mounds and the UNESCO World Heritage Site called Poverty Point,
usually identified as the ancient religious and legal center for the ancestral
Washitaw, called the Ancient Ones. The remains of this "Ancient Imperial
Court of Justice" was "mis-named 'Poverty Point,'" Washitaw contend, to

"whitewash" their history, part of a conspiracy of racist U.S. governmental authorities to erase the memory of these dark-skinned, woolly-haired indigenous people from the land in order to illegally claim that land for the United States. Washitaw refer to the site by such names as Old Mecca, Our Mecca, and Prosperity Point.

Prehistoric mound sites, many of them recognized now by state-run parks and museums, offer evidence, the Washitaw insist, for their claims of history and identity. Such claims, in keeping with the tradition of Ali, are seen as having direct legal consequences. Most important, to come to consciousness of the truth of one's identity as Washitaw requires the individual to take action for Washitaw rights and reparations, particularly the project of "getting the land back." The central, shared goal of the Washitaw movement is acquiring control over at least part of the land that was once the empire of the Ancient Ones. Getting the land back is seen, moreover, as an explicitly legal project, dependent upon the power of the state to recognize and accommodate Washitaw claims. As part of their work of citizenship, the Washitaw today submit petitions and letters to elected officials as part of a broader effort to publicize their community's narrative of pro-Washitaw Supreme Court jurisprudence. The Washitaw emphasize the potential persuasive power of international legal and political bodies, such as the European Court of Human Rights, Interpol, the International Criminal Court at The Hague, and the United Nations, calling upon such bodies to influence the legal decision of the U.S. government. Another legal tactic, though one contested within the wider Washitaw community, is approaching the Bureau of Indian Affairs for federal recognition as a Native American tribe.[56]

The movement was founded in the 1980s by Verdiacee Goston (1927–2014), former mayor (and legal founder) of Richwood, Louisiana, a majority-black town bordering the city of Monroe in Ouachita Parish.[57] Proclaiming herself Empress Verdiacee "Tiara" Washitaw-Turner Goston El-Bey of the Ancient Ones, Goston linked herself by genealogy to Drew Ali.[58] Teaching that Ali had prophesied her coming, Goston declared all Washitaw to also be Moors, though in the movement the preferred spelling is Mu'urs, understood as also linking Washitaw ancestry to the legendary lost continent of Mu. Settlers from Mu arrived in what is now Louisiana by the year 3000 BCE, Goston wrote in the movement's scriptural text, *Return of the Ancient Ones* (1993). At times Goston identified the religion of the Washitaw as "Moorish Science," and she built alliances with Moors that, from the beginning, involved contestation over whose account of history and whose use of terms such as "Moorish" were authentic and correct. This debate continues in contemporary Washitaw circles; some Washitawans identify as Moors, and some reject the designation. Ali is understood to be of the imperial Washitaw bloodline and a forerunner of Goston. His birthday is celebrated by some—but not all—Washitaw as a holiday, and his writings are frequently cited by Washitaw thinkers. In many Washitaw images, he is paired with Goston, the two being understood as progenitors of the Washitaw movement.[59] Some contemporary Washitaw, moreover, claim miraculous posthumous encounters with Drew Ali, as when Washitaw thinker Brother Red Hawk describes Ali appearing in the cab of his truck, a vision that launched Red Hawk's quest for true identity and a narrative of which helps to establish his authority in Aliite circles.[60]

The Washitaw movement was the subject of an FBI raid in 2000, following several moves by Goston that raised the suspicion of that agency: namely, her alliance, via treaty, with two communities claiming sovereignty outside the legal jurisdiction of the United States, the Republic of Texas and the Kingdom of Hawaii. While the major prosecutions following the raid were of lieutenants involved in various financial frauds (including a scam involving online sale of collectable Beanie Baby toys), the raid significantly altered the position of the group within Louisiana, where Goston had amassed both political and financial power. The Washitaw generally believe that the stress of the raid led to Goston's quickly declining health, which resulted in a decision, by her son, to place her in an assisted living facility near his home in California, where she was kept out of contact with the wider Washitaw community.

Fragmented into several communities and multiple individual interpretations, the Washitaw movement's best known organization is the Empire Washitaw, led by Goston's son, Fredrix Joe Washington. This nationwide group communicates primarily via a series of weekly telephone conference calls (as described in the preface), though yearly "family reunions" are also held, with varying levels of attendance. The Empire Washitaw continue Goston's appeal to law, with particular attention to the legality of their own actions. Washington has forbidden the printing or use of any sort of identification card or even the maintenance of a roster of "members," until he can be sure that such paperwork will be legally recognized by the state. This group's major public outreach is in the form of letters to elected representatives and online petitions, seizing their power as citizens to protest for their legal rights. As Washington, called the Emperor or the Dauphin, declares, any strategy for Washitaw, going forward, must have "detailed reference to the law."[61]

"ONE NATION UNDER GOD"

E pluribus unum functions as an unofficial motto for the American state—used on currency, for instance, as well as on all imprints and reproductions of the Great Seal itself, on all U.S. passports, and on those flags used for governmental purposes, including military and diplomatic identification. It is not the official motto of the United States, however. That, via belated bureaucratic procedure, was not selected until 1956, at a moment of increased attention to the role of theological rhetoric in American national life. Two years after the phrase "under God" was added to the Pledge of Allegiance flag ritual, Congress resolved that the motto of the United States of America would be "in God we trust."[62] This multiplicity of mottos tells us something about America, flagging a tendency to overlay the divine onto the political, despite discourse about disestablishment or a wall of separation between spheres imagined as "church" and "state."

Aliite thought on democratic citizenship offers an avenue into the lived complications of disestablishment as a legal means of conceiving of and policing religion. Aliite thought approaches and theorizes the concept of secularism, showing—as recent scholarship on the topic has argued—that phenomenon to be "a process of defining, managing, and intervening into religious life and sensibility," one enmeshed in the sovereignty of the state and the rule of law.[63] A secular regime thus remakes "religious subjectivities . . . render[ing] them compliant with liberal political rule," as Saba Mahmood puts it.[64] Rather than an alternative to religion or mark of religion's absence, secularism is thus "a historically evolving, normative project of government that entails the administrative intervention into and transformations of what are called, retroactively, religious traditions, institutions, and sensibilities," such that what gets to be called religion is, itself, "an effect of secularism."[65] Secularism is the "political doctrine" that, as Talal Asad has argued, "transcend[s] the different identities" of a population, unifying them under an overarching, secular identity.[66]

While secularism restricts the scope of religious ambition—limiting claims to religious authority and power, subordinating religious truth to the political and legal truth-claims of the state—it also contributes to the creation of new forms of religion, suited to, and making sense out of, assigning significance to, such secular conditions. One American result is often described as a kind of vague-edged, nonsectarian "civil religion," a sense of shared religiosity existing alongside, and thus restricting the aspirations of, more particular religious commitment, what Sidney Mead has described as a system in which "no religious sect must aspire to be anything more than equal with all the others." American society is thus united under a civil religious framework "melding many diverse sectarianisms into one cosmopolitan religion."[67] Yet in such systems, the norm remains white Christianity, the categories Vincent Lloyd has argued as "unmarked" within American society.[68] Ali's system defies that association of secularism with whiteness—and with Christianity—by denying the possibility of an "unmarked" category, insisting that the only norm is difference. Ali's engagement with "colonial ideas about universalism" involves seizing those ideas, breaking them free from privileging whiteness by breaking them free from hierarchical "particularity" in general.[69] Difference becomes the norm.

W. Clark Gilpin, indebted to the work of Harvey Cox, speaks of "religious secularism," not merely the state's shaping and policing of religion but, indeed, a mode of religiosity that results from what Cox called "the cosmopolitan confrontations of city living": pragmatically focused on social problems, this-worldly, and seeing in social transformation the fulfillment of a divine plan.[70] "Religious secularism" represents the reclamation, under the name of religion, of a model of the secular understood as policing and restricting religion. Charles Taylor described secularism as "a necessity for the democratic life of religiously diverse societies"; Aliite theology does not contest this stance, but reframes that diversity as divinely mandated, reimagining democracy as *religious*.[71] Aliite religion, "cosmopolitan religion" simultaneously universal and pluralistic, stands as an example of "religious secularism" that has sacralized the demands of the disestablished state, the political ideals and practical realities of democracy, and has prioritized citizenship. Aliite thought is simultaneously "divine and national." As contemporary MSTA thinker Denham El has argued, "The Secular could not exist without the Spiritual."[72]

Ali's system represents an "institution of the universal," as Balibar describes *laïcité*, only here the common ground is religious difference.[73] Aliite tradition embraces the position of religion assigned by the secular state, while sacralizing the secular model of society, requiring existing religious communities to conform to restrictions in order to count as valid (legal) religion. Within Ali's universal theology the world is parceled into nations, each with its own version of divine truth—all valid, but all likewise already assigned to a given people by inheritance. Only by all citizens strictly maintaining their inherited, ancestral religions can civic harmony be achieved.[74] Religion remains proprietary to a given nationality; the borders of religious communities must thus remain sealed. As Ali makes clear, adopting a religion other than one's own leads to suffering, to catastrophic consequences like slavery.[75] Thus, like other markers of difference within the distinction that is nationality, religion is a form of difference all citizens must have but none can select. One is born what one is. As Ali writes in his *Holy Koran*: "What your ancient forefathers were, you are today without doubt or contradiction. There is no one who is able to change man from the descendant nature of his forefathers; unless his power extends beyond the great universal Creator Allah Himself."[76]

Aliite theology offers an alternative origin myth for American democracy, insisting on *e pluribus unum* not as the result of historical circumstance but as divine design. Difference is not merely a requirement for equal participation in American citizenship, difference of nationality forms the common basis of American identity. This model is strikingly similar to that articulated by Mayanthi L. Fernando, who argues that French Muslims' claims to "Muslim French" identity reframe difference "not as deviation but as variation," such that there is no "fixed, normative center" of French identity; rather, French identity is a matter of "equally different differences."[77] Ali has the advantage of advancing his theory in and on a country already associated with pluralism and a population marked by difference. Ali insists that, despite the popular metaphor of the melting pot, the ineluctable *plurality* of difference within the *unum* of the state must never melt away but must be proclaimed, displayed, and enacted. It is not only difference of nationality that is presented as necessary in Ali's system. In his vision of the eschaton, class differences remain as well. The rich and poor coexist in harmony, part of a social tapestry of multiple "vines and fig trees," yet there is no sense that such a form of difference is inherently unjust. Rather, difference in terms of class and resources is another form of universal difference, a difference all citizens have in common.

Equality, while valued as a social goal within Aliite thought, is understood as that which citizenship should—must—provide, an equality of status under, and access to, the law, an equality of rights within the state and fair hearing from the state. It is worth noting that the five ideals associated with true law—love, truth, peace, freedom, and justice—do not include equality, nor, in Aliite thought, is any of those ideals predicated on equality in general. Equal justice as equal access to, and acknowledgment by, the legal system is a far cry from full equality. While Aliite thought is resolutely opposed to inequality under the current legal system, it accepts financial inequality as a given. Ali's commitment to economic uplift for his community did not preclude the continuance of poverty in society at large, resulting in an ambivalence about money and its pursuit that permeated Aliite tradition. Expanding on Ali's statement that "money doesn't make the man," contemporary MSTA thinker Love El, for instance, contrasts wealth with the real value of citizenship, insisting that "it doesn't matter how much money you have," if you are one of "those who are considered as negroes, black people, colored folks, [then you] are not truly being received and respected as a nation of people" and will be excluded from the status and practice of citizenship.[78]

Ali insisted that difference was ordained by God and grounded in true law. As difference is required for citizenship, so, too, in the Aliite system difference is required for understanding the nature of true law because true law is characterized by equal justice across differences. Difference is likewise seen by Aliites as essential to democracy. There can be no *unum* without the *pluribus*, no American *state* without citizens who know and enact their distinct nationalities. True law makes sense only in relation to a polity that contains difference; otherwise, its equalizing function—arguably its most impressive, defining characteristic—would be meaningless. As Sylvester Johnson has argued, Ali and the MSTA can be read as internally colonized populations responding to empire, but Aliites enact the ideology of empire that Julie Stephens describes as "defin[ing] colonial legitimacy in terms of a universal regime of rights and limits on government despotism."[79] While imperialism can impose a new culture on the colonized, forcing them to accept a lesser status and to adapt to new ways of being in keeping with the ruling hegemony, Stephens argues that this is not the only way empire is experienced by the colonized. Colonized minorities can seize and coopt the empire's rhetoric and stated ideals and rule of law, bolstering difference rather than seeking to eliminate it. Ali's movement offers an example of such a move, insisting that ideals of the state are Allah's ideals and that the work of citizenship is perfecting the state, into alignment with a universal understanding of law identified not as that of the colonizer but as that of the creator.

Ali insisted that his teaching applied to all people, all nationalities, a religion modeled on and responding to the conditions of the "secular city" with its social, political, and legal demands. Those demands became, to a large part, the focus of the religion, understood as "citizenship," a struggle to transform society and align it with the transcendent true law of God. "True religion," as contemporary Aliite thinkers Matthews-El insists, is "a means to an end, a journey, way of living, it is a process not an event."[80]

When Aliites wave the U.S. flag, they are also offering their own claims about the nature of the American experiment and how difference relates to citizenship. They are reimagining the *e pluribus unum* of America—and the notion of an exceptional state "under God"—in their own terms, imagining America as theirs in order to secure a place within it.

STARS IN RELATION TO STARS

Aliite Sovereignty in Politics and Law

RELATIONAL SOVEREIGNTY AND THE
SOVEREIGNTY OF LAW

APPEARING AS A GLORY TOWARD THE TOP of the Great Seal of the United States, above the bald eagle with its talons grasping arrows and olive branches, is a star-shaped constellation of thirteen individual stars, the seal's representation of American sovereignty. This star made out of stars denotes, as designer Charles Thomas wrote, "a new State taking its place and rank among other sovereign powers."[1] A visual proclamation of a political claim—America as sovereign—this image also functions as an illustration of a political theory, of what sovereignty means within and for America.

Toggling in perception first as a field of stars, then as a star composed of star-shaped pixels, this picture represents a concept complicated in lived reality by claims of multiplicity and relationality. Sovereignty is here understood not as a singular location but, rather, as something that is always divided and multiple, existing only in relation to other—sometimes more powerful—levels of sovereignty. The Great Seal's image of sovereignty reflects a practical understanding of the negotiation of power, of sovereignty as a position of and for negotiation. As Jessica Cattelino has written, the "connections and interdependencies of the modern world deny the possibility of a self-contained, unfettered sovereign, but limited sovereignties exist all around us": multiple levels of *sovereignties* ranging from the Westphalian sovereignty of a nation-state in relation to other nation-states, the union of sovereign states maintaining some degree of autonomy and self-determination within the United States, and that democratic republic locating sovereignty in "We the People" as a collective, as well as, on an individual level, what the Supreme Court has called the "great and glorious principle, that the people are the sovereigns of this country"—sovereignties grounded in and guaranteed by law.[2]

These layers of *sovereignties* exist in tense, ever-shifting relations with each other, just as this notion of a multiplicity of sovereignties exists in tension with dominant academic conceptions of the term, following the work of Carl Schmitt. In his 1922 *Political Theology*, Schmitt articulates a theory of sovereignty as singular, as "he who decides on the exception," a power *above* the law.[3] Contra Schmitt's ideal, the Great Seal's image serves as introduction to a lived American conception of the sovereign as one who negotiates relationships with other sovereigns.[4] Such an understanding of sovereignty as multiple, asserted "through interactions with others," is at the core of varied Aliite claims about and to sovereignty.[5] Sovereignty "is derived from NATIONALITY," as one contemporary MSTA thinker insists. A Washitaw thinker, Fayola Modupe, cautions that while the concept is much debated, sovereignty "does not mean you doing whatever you wish" like the tyrants of history (she cites King George by name); rather "Sovereignty comes with responsibility," with layers of commitments to those with whom one is in relation.[6] "No man lives unto himself, for every living thing is bound by cords to every other living thing," as Ali's *Holy Koran* puts it.[7] Sovereignty is a matter of relation, exchange, negotiation, existing always as a result of encounter. Every individual holds the capacity to be sovereign, but such sovereignty depends on recognition by other sovereigns, other layers of sovereignty, and is not unilaterally achieved. Moreover, sovereignty as a concept and experience is grounded in and patterned on the ultimate level of sovereignty, that eternal and transcendent sovereign that is the true law.

In a system of multiple sovereignties, the power of any given sovereign is qualified. Such an understanding of sovereignty holds great appeal to Aliites, who often cite, as a model of how sovereignty is multiple and relational, the fact that the sovereignty of the fledgling United States came about not through declaration of independence but through legal procedures and the agreement of recognition in the 1786 "Treaty of Peace and Friendship" between America and Morocco. Sovereignty in this understanding requires recognition by other sovereigns and is the product of encounter and appeal. Such relational sovereignty is encountered in "multiple and layered forms" that can be thought of, in terms of their power relations with each other, as "nesting," like Russian dolls.[8] Theories of sovereignty serve as means of conceptualizing and coping with power and its imbalance. For Aliites, sovereignty becomes a way to imagine the power of the state as something that can be contested, as fleeting and incomplete, and—most important—as never outside the law (even when in violation of the legal), but, rather, as the result of recognition and relation, facilitated and framed by means of law.

Aliites identify law—ideal law—as the ultimate level of sovereignty within a lived reality of layered and negotiated sovereignties. In this view, law is always above the legal, to paraphrase Schmitt. True law's relation to the legal serves as that "sovereign power both inside and above" the legal that William Connolly describes as essential to rule of law in a democracy; the sovereignty of true law is a law above, yet inherent in and always possible for, the legal.[9] Law, in this understanding, simultaneously structures and serves as a check on all forms of human power; it underwrites and limits all earthly sovereignties. Such a view of law as potential equalizer of differences in power reflects the Aliite desire for justice. This model of sovereignty, moreover, represents Aliite hope that power can be checked, redirected, and transformed. Such an approach is not naïve about power—particularly the sovereign power of the state, and the violence through which such power can manifest—yet it insists that such power is only ever temporary, while true law is eternal. State exercise of sovereignty can, in Aliite understanding as well as experience, trample on the (tenuous, because always relational, negotiated) sovereignty of the citizen and violate true law. The legal is always a matter of power, and recognition and enforcement of legal precedent is likewise always a matter of the power held by the moment's legal establishment. Thus, while Aliite thinkers insist that "the concept of the Sovereignty of the people is well supported by court cases, presidential quotes, a book published by the United States Congress and other sources," which they are quick to cite, they are as quick to note that sovereignty on the level of state and local governments has a history of infringing upon such popular sovereignty.[10] Moorish thinker Kinda El, for example, cites the example of violence delivered by state agents to civil rights protesters on the Edmund Pettus Bridge in 1965, an event immortalized in the film *Selma*, which he urges all Moors to watch as a lesson in injustice justified by the legal system of the sovereign nation-state but in blatant violation of true law.[11] While sovereignty may take "double exception from human and divine law," Aliite thought counters that *true law*, eternal and transcendent, nonetheless remains as a moral check on such power.[12] That sovereignties can take exception to the true law is intrinsic to their nature, but true law is only ever disobeyed, never suspended; it never ceases to exist, and this belief that true law serves as eternal and ultimate sovereign underwrites Aliites' hope in their struggles to reform society, their work of citizenship. While the authority of sovereignty may be "grounded in violence," the concept of sovereignty is grounded in the ideal of true law.[13] While human sovereignties may act in violation of such true law, they are never really outside of it, Aliites insist, as true law permeates all creation and all humans are understood to have a natural sense for such true law, a product of their divine creation (see chapter 4).

Aliite understanding of the violence of earthly forms of sovereignty—whether the nation-state or the individual—defuses something of the terror of such threats by emphasizing their transience. This may sound like cold comfort, especially in the face of brutal, state-sponsored and legally endorsed violence (as in Selma), but herein lies the core of Aliite faith in law: All-Law is eternal and unchanging, and will, with the work—and sacrifice—of humans, be brought into alignment with all forms of human sovereignty. The relational, multiple, always-in-negotation and thus temporary sovereignties of this world are, according to Aliite thought, patterned on, and existing in the shadow of, the ultimate sovereignty of (ideal) law. True law cannot be compromised, hence its sovereignty as a sovereignty above all negotiation. Sovereign citizens may find themselves without power to have their claims recognized, the sovereign state may find itself similarly unrecognized and thus occupied, ended as a political project, but the law cannot, in its ineluctable reality, ever be subverted. Law remains, eternal and true.

As Anne Kornhauser has written, one "corollary of seeing law as a constraint on political power was to view the legal system as different from other political and social institutions by virtue of qualities intrinsic to law itself."[14] Aliite religion offers an example of this: these movements in which thinkers attribute to "law" an eternal metaphysical reality and an identity synonymous with ideal values like "justice." Aliites are such partisans of, and even evangelists for, the rule of law and the ideal of law in part because they understand law—and its fallible instantiations in the legal—as offering them real protection from the violence of the state. Not only is law understood as that which grants a status beyond bare life, it is the only defense these communities have in a radically asymmetrical imbalance of power with the state. We have no weapons, Aliites frequently declare, only "universal law."[15] If Aliite religion is excessively focused on the state, even venerating the state's authority, this is because Aliites have no other option. Structures characterized as fallible, as frequently corrupt and unjust, nonetheless offer the means by which true law will manifest in the world. The legal allows for recourse to ideal law.

This chapter examines Aliite theories of and claims to sovereignty, focusing first on the sovereignty that is manifest through law by collective political negotiation as citizens, then turning to Aliite imagination of and appeal to international law. Both of these valences echo conceptions of sovereignty represented in the stars on the Great Seal, and they reveal an Aliite theory of sovereignty at once practical and hopeful. First, Aliites understand democratic politics to favor those citizens who link together, individual stars amplifying their own luminosity by joining into a constellation, a constituency, able to better negotiate with and influence both elected leaders and fellow voters. Second, aware that the sovereign stars that are nation-states only possess such status as the result of recognition from other stars in the firmament of nation-states, Aliites imagine international legal bodies and legal documents as having occasional bearing on the legal systems of nation-states. International law, in Aliite understanding, is effective and enforceable only when recognized as valid by a given state. Yet even when it lacks immediate legal consequence, international law is often approached by Aliites as bearing witness to true law, a prophetic and aspirational phrasing of God's law in legal discourse.[16]

Aliite claims about the sovereignty of true law help not only to negotiate the multiple, contradictory claims about sovereignty made in U.S. law and politics but also to balance faith in "rule of law" with an often unjust and oppressive rule of the legal, using theories of sovereignty to maintain hope in a transformative trajectory of law on and through the legal institutions of the state, such that America, through Aliite effort, can be perfected into a society of equal justice for all citizens.

"ALL REGISTERING": ALI'S MSTA AND LOCAL DEMOCRACY

Drew Ali's "divine and national" project appealed largely to those who, like himself, had migrated from the rural South to northern cities in the early waves of the Great Migration. His project of communal "uplift" was rooted in the new economic, social, and political possibilities of this milieu. One of myriad African American religions offering comfort, hope, and community, the MSTA was explicit from the beginning in linking "salvation" from race-based oppression to the work of citizenship, and, most specifically, to the political leverage that would result from local mobilization as a political unit. Ali's theories of citizenship and nationality emerged from a context where ethnic coalitions were recognized and courted, and a time in which the ruling Chicago Republican machine adopted an election-changing strategy of courting black votes, with particular attention to the votes of new migrants. In the early days of the MSTA, the community was a precinct-level, voter-registering, campaigning, and vote-delivering force for the Republican Party machine, which, in turn, was happy to recognize Ali's community as citizens with the "power to participate in the establishment or administration of government."[17]

In this context, active *citizenship* came with the promise of rewards. In the wake of his hard-fought reelection in 1927, Mayor Thompson inaugurated the golden age of Chicago patronage politics, rewarding supporters for their active citizenship. Supporters of the machine were rewarded in material as well as political ways.

This is often presented as a dubious legacy, one of corruption and graft, but such relational politics opened spaces of possibilities for communities like the MSTA. The system of power, the organization that ran the city, offered a relational role for Ali and his organization. That role was filled by other organizations but needed expansion, particularly into the Black Belt. Ali's "divine and national movement" responded to Thompson's need, in the 1927 election, for black street-level operatives, extra precinct workers. In turn, the MSTA brought to this opportunity interpretations of the work that fused the political with the religious, identifying the legal and metaphysical. Ali wrote, in the *Moorish Guide* article now canonized as part of the *Moorish Literature*, "All Registering":

> The three thousand Moslems of The Grand Temple and The West Side Temple are making ready to register every Man or Woman in order to take the lead for the various candidates whom they have been instructed to vote for. Alderman Louis B Anderson, Hon. George W. Blackwell, Hon. Oscar DePriest, Hon. H. Jackson, all working through the regular Republican Organizations of which The Hon. Daniel M. Jackson is our matchless leader all know the whole situation and have their own way and time to give the order to go. The Moslems will be ready.

As a central document of Aliite thought and a foundational statement for ongoing debates about and theories of sovereignty within Aliite communities, this small text deserves detailed reading. Ali here declares his local organization—under two temples—to include a certain number of recognized citizens who, moreover, understand their responsibilities as citizens to involve both registering others (non-Moors, so-called blacks) from their neighborhoods and voting (and encouraging those they register to vote) for the Republican machine's slate. This slate, as listed here, includes only the African American candidates—and one African American party operative, entrepreneur Daniel Jackson, "possibly the most powerful African American in the state."[18]

Ali is thus taking upon himself the role of precinct captain, an essential role in the Chicago machine system. As Marco Domico says in the oral history of Chicago politics *We Don't Want Nobody Nobody Sent*, the mark of a good precinct captain is "good registration. Registration, that's your election, the most important thing of all. When you register your new voters, you have many, many people."[19] When Ali used his movement's newspaper to declare—on his own authority as "Prophet" of the universal creator God—"Vote Anderson," for Second Ward alderman, he was extending his hand not only to support the "uplift" of a politician he identified as Moorish but also to receive payment for the civic work of his community.

Registering, campaigning, voting, and delivering votes: these were "sacred obligations of American citizenship," and citizenship, in Ali's formulation, was the opposite of "political slavery." But the *freedom* that came from them was not merely the freedom the individual citizen experienced in the poll, but the freedom that came as a reward for successfully delivering on these tasks. Voting led to freedom in the most material, practical sense. Support the machine in power, experience the benefits of power. Ali phrases this in a higher register: "Before there can be general relief for the economic good of all, all forms of political slavery must be abolished and every citizen must take his part in the affairs of the nation."[20] Paraphrase should not sully the sentiment here, but, rather, highlight its practical radicality. Ali is saying, vote and get paid. Only from a position of privilege can this be dismissed as mere "corruption."

For Ali's community, unifying as a constituency to leverage power in negotiation with other levels of sovereign political power represented the promise of American democracy—and Allah's design for a world of nationalities united as one civic body. Local politics, at its most corrupt, offered early Aliites the promise of achieving full human identity, existentially and socially, politically and economically, spiritually and materially.

CONTEMPORARY ALIITE SOVEREIGNTY THROUGH CITIZENSHIP: POLITICS AND PROTEST

The role of Ali's MSTA in the local politics of 1920s Chicago is frequently discussed across the spectrum of contemporary Aliite religion. While Aliite communities have never claimed the same level of success they attribute to Ali, political organizing and bloc voting are recurrent, both on the level of idea and discussion and on the level of practical action. Contemporary MSTA thinker Sharif A. Bey insists that the divine and national movement must "organize, mobilize, and politicize" as a unified constituency.[21] Mahdi L. McCoy El writes that what "we as a people MUST realize is that ALL politics are local," a fact he claims that no one understood better than Drew Ali. "During the roaring twenties the Moorish Science Temple of America was one of the most influential organizations in the country, but primarily its heaviest influence was in the State of Illinois and in the city of Chicago."

> What many may be asking is how did Drew Ali manage to obtain such great influence over these local, state, and national politicians? How did he manage to have 2 Governors coming to him to ask for his assistance? How did he manage to almost single-handedly influence the outcome of elections? It is simple: He galvanized and organized the people, and he controlled their vote with his influence. In other words, no Moor voted until the Prophet told them which way to vote, and when he told them which way to vote then they voted as a unit and as a single weapon took charge of their own destiny. You see while voting is the right of each individual, without a collective effort you are simply wasting your greatest political power. Together we are a force, but individually we are weaklings led around by our noses by politicians who should be at our beacon [sic] call. The politicians only fear one thing, and that is our unity.[22]

Championing the idea of functioning as a "voting bloc"—of exercising the sovereignty of the constituency—McCoy El lamented that Moors have failed, in recent years, to exercise the same kind of political unity (and thus failed to reap the kind of economic rewards) that the unified "Jews, Catholics, and even the Gay Community" have managed. He continues:

> Let us galvanize our force in the local school board elections, city council races, and state and local Mayoral and Governors races. We must change things so that we are represented, and we can direct our tax dollars. The politicians will come once we are galvanized. We have a working Model in Noble Drew Ali and the Moorish Science Temple of America. Learn about their/our successes, and let us reproduce it once again. Let us Moors and Asiatics (So-called Blacks, African-Americans, Negro, Colored etc.) Rock the Vote back in our direction. The power of the vote is that we influence the direction of this great nation one election at a time. Let us take back our power.[23]

Sharif A. Bey offers a hypothetical, in proposing his own, new Aliite activist movement, Operation Proclamation: "control of 15,000 votes can turn and sometimes OWN an election," he writes, adding, "please reference our Prophet's/MSTA very public political campaign for our own Oscar De-Priest [sic]," a reference to the 1928 election, in which the African American De Priest was sent to the House of Representatives from Illinois as part of Mayor Thompson's Republican Party ticket.[24]

Aliites link such unified political action to sovereignty, understanding it as a mode of sovereignty that I term "the sovereignty of the constituency." Uniting as an identifiable part and parcel of the diverse "we" that is "the people," the "we" of a select constituency group is able to exercise sovereignty through negotiation and relation.[25] Sovereignty of the constituency represents the Aliite understanding that political power comes first and foremost from unity within a representative democratic milieu, a possibility open, of course, only to citizens, with citizenship, in turn, underwritten by knowledge, proclamation, and official recognition of nationality.

Outreach to political officials by Aliites is also an attempt to use this model of sovereignty, seeking recognition of Aliite claims and official action from elected officials. The Empire Washitaws' letter-writing campaign for the return of their land (through recognition of their identity and claims about legal history) explicitly invokes the idea of a popular sovereignty of the citizenry, with the Washitaw insisting on their role as part of "We the People" and their power to sway government officials through their united "national" community. One MSTA group has reached out to what they call

the "so called" Congressional Black Caucus, urging these politicians to research Aliite claims. The letter expresses confidence that once members of
that caucus have "sufficiently researched this matter," they will recognize
that abandonment of the language of blackness and embrace of national
identity are "the legally correct path to remedy the condition under which
our people suffer." That letter concludes with a prayer that "the ALL CREATOR
strengthen your resolve and fortify your Spirits of Determination in immediately bringing this matter to the floor of Congress in Session and seeing
the process through to fulfillment."[26] Such a request for inquiry and action
is a standard technique of democratic citizenship, here imbued with the
specific hopes of Aliites, that true law will sway the opinions and behaviors of these elected officials, once they are prompted by recognition that a
group of their own constituents is invested in such action.

The work of citizenship, in Aliite understanding, also includes protest.
Such protest can be economic, an exercise of what Audra Simpson calls
the sovereignty of refusal, or it can be a matter of public performance designed to raise awareness of a complaint among a broader section of the
citizenry.[27] "Boycotts are very effective tools used in transforming conditions peacefully," writes Bandele El-Amin.[28] Public protests by Aliites reflect
more caution, as Aliites are always aware of the dominance—the power, the
potential for violence—of the state. Patterns of other protests are studied by
Aliite thinkers to offer models. McCoy El, for instance, cites both the gay
rights movement and the Tea Party as examples of effective citizen protest
that Moors should follow. Sharif A. Bey insists that mobilization of a constituency bloc can lead, though media attention as well as direct action, to
"social and economic power."[29]

The Nuwaubian Yamassee, since the arrest of Malachi York in 2002,
have been particularly prominent in public protests. Such protests are generally eye-catching, with a mainstream or even platitudinous message foregrounded. For instance, in a 2002 photo-op with Georgia governor Roy
Barnes, members of the community dressed as friendly-looking clowns
(long part of Shriner tradition, to which the Nuwaubian Yamassee, like all
Aliites, make explicit reference).[30] These clowns held signs that proclaimed
"Hate is nothing to Clown With," "Violence is No Joke," and "Smile when
Children get Educated."[31] Although more truisms of civil society than pro-
vocative political statements, these slogans offered a rebuke of charges of
child abuse at Tama-Re and by York, thus subtly rejecting the stated justification for law enforcement action against the community.[32] This protest

reframed the legal plight of the Nuwaubian Yamassee as one in which the community were victims of hate, not for hurting children, but for wanting to educate their own children and instill in them pride and self-respect. That outsiders might not share the frame of reference here is inconsequential to the extent that being viewed as another child-focused religious charity is already a public relations win for the group. For those who understand the context from which the community was speaking, these are protest signs, but utterly uncontroversial on their face.

The turn toward a rhetoric of "torture" in relation to York's imprison-ment is also in keeping with foregrounding a noncontroversial claim. Op-position to torture is a mainstream human rights issue. Nuwaubian Ya-massee protesters tap into such mainstream opinion by dressing in orange jumpsuits reminiscent of those worn by prisoners at Guantanamo Bay. Arranging themselves sometimes around and sometimes inside a cell or cage set up in the street, such protesters often carry signs with similarly mainstream quotes from civil rights and human rights leaders such as Gan-dhi and Martin Luther King, Jr. Yet the real focus of these protests is not opposition to torture in general, but advancing the claim that York is being tortured, that such torture characterizes the perversion of justice involved in his case, and that, therefore, he should be freed.[33] This final point is made more explicitly, though again not without some degree of subtle double valence, by small signs held by Nuwaubian Yamassee that say, in large print, "FREE," and in much smaller print, "Dr. Malachi K. York." Signs explicitly linking "Dr. York" to Dr. King, and even staging of such protests on Martin Luther King Day, accentuate this mainstreaming—both of the topic and of protest, for protest carried out under the banner of Martin Luther King has a kind of sacrosanct legitimacy in the American scene. Such associa-tion implies, as well, another important Nuwaubian Yamassee claim: that they are nonviolent fellow citizens using legal and peaceful means to fight for justice.[34]

Protest, here, is presented as an essential feature of democracy, a means of drawing attention to injustice and demanding redress through political and legal reform.[35] Acts of protest, moreover, normalize the community, not merely through the way they protest but also simply *because* they pro-test. Protest serves as a public performance of American citizenship. As with the civic participation of voting, a sovereignty is seen to reside in the unity of Aliites as a bloc, a constituency acting as one at the ballot box or in protests on the street.

"GOING TO GENEVA": SOVEREIGNTY
AND INTERNATIONAL LAW

———————

As the sovereignty of the individual nation-state must be recognized by other sovereign nation-states, relational sovereignty is understood to have an international scale. Nation-states thus hold a degree of influence over each other. Aliites imagine the international negotiation of sovereignty not merely as an issue of nation-states negotiating via their own power; they understand international law, as well, to be as an influencing factor. International law can function in two ways, according to Aliite thought. First, some international legal decisions are accepted as having bearing within the legal system of a given nation-state. Second, international law is understood as phrasing, on a high-profile level, the ideals of true law. Even when rejected and therefore unenforceable, international law offers another testimony of true law and represents the work of citizenship, in aligning legal systems with such law on a global scale.

The form of international law considered by Aliites to be most consequential within the legal system of the nation-state is the treaty. Treaties, a particularly privileged genre in Aliite thought, are understood as documentary evidence of recognition by multiple parties. Treaties thus offer proof, in Aliite understanding, that at least two sovereign states (the signatories) recognize and grant their authority to the claims made in or linked to the treaty. Many Aliites insist that "according to Article VI of the United States Constitution, 'Treaties are the Supreme law of the land.'"[36] Treaties also play a special role in Aliite history as the 1786 "Treaty of Peace and Friendship" between the United States and Morocco not only served the essential function of recognizing the sovereignty of the fledgling United States but also granted special legal privileges to "Moors."

The "Treaty of Peace and Friendship" is reproduced in multiple Aliite publications, and various interpretations are offered of its historical and contemporary relevance.[37] For many Aliites, this treaty stands not only as evidence of the rich and conjoined history of Moors and U.S. government and law (much like the use of what Aliites claim to be originally Moorish symbols on the Great Seal), but also as legal guarantee of Moorish American rights, notably that Moors "are not to be made Slaves" and that, as Moroccan citizens, Moors are understood to have "equal Justice" to U.S. citizens as persons before the law.[38]

Washitaw communities, who are especially active in theorizing and engaging international law as part of their claims to indigenous rights to their land, have a particular history of drawing up their own treaties as well as invoking historical ones. Empress Goston, for instance, in addition to soliciting endorsement of her claims from the United Nations, also took the initiative of entering into the "international" arena by signing treaties of recognition with what she took to be sovereign nation-states, the Republic of Texas and the Kingdom of Hawaii—a move that led to increased FBI scrutiny of, and eventually a law enforcement raid against, the Washitaw.[39]

Treaties are understood to be legal, hence their citation in court cases, even where Aliites are accused of breaking U.S. law.[40] In 2016 a group identified as the Washitaw de Dugdahmoundyah Empire of Mu'urs claimed property in the New Orleans neighborhood of Bywater by moving into a house and posting signs around the property citing international law. Understanding themselves, in keeping with broader Washitaw claims, to be descendants of the original settlers of the land that become the Louisiana Purchase and thus that territory's rightful heirs, these occupiers publicly announced and defended their occupation as legal by citing "international treaties"—including the "Treaty of Peace and Friendship"—as well as "the United Nations Declaration on the Rights of Indigenous Peoples," as international law accepted as authoritative by the American state.[41] As part of their claim, members of the New Orleans Washitaw group posted signs publicly declaring their occupied house to be "Washitah Mu'ur" property; the wording of the signs included—in quotation marks indicative of citation of the law—the phrase "Federal Offense to Ignore."[42]

Similar claims are made by Aliites regarding diplomatic status. When Malachi York claimed diplomatic status via Liberia, during his fourteen-day trial in 2004, it was a claim to legal rights *outside* the norms of the U.S. state *through* accepted legal norms of the U.S. state; the authority York invoked was not Liberian, but, as in the case of the New Orleans Washitaw group, federal law recognizing international legal precedent.[43]

The other Aliite approach to international law, understanding it not as consequential within American law but, nonetheless, as a phrasing of true law, able to influence American legal interpretation, can be located within a deeper tradition of African American internationalism. Appeals to international institutions, like W. E. B. Du Bois's 1947 appeal to the United Nations or the 1952 "We Charge Genocide" petition to that same body, express the same logic, the same hope that international legal influence might sway American legal realities. Such moves share the logic of Malcolm X's distinction between "civil rights" as an appeal for "right" treatment from the federal government versus "human rights" as natural, "something you were born with. Human rights are your God-given rights . . . And anytime anyone violates your human rights, you can take them to the world court."[44] Indeed, this statement, aligning the idea of an international legal body with jurisprudence on natural, God-given rights, parallels Aliite understanding, as does the insistence here that American (legal) injustice can be appealed by means of international law. Aliites often specifically list the international bodies through which they hope to get eventual rulings—the International Criminal Court, the International Court of Human Rights, and the United Nations, for instance—knowing that such rulings will not necessarily be immediately enforceable but that they may, all the same, push American legal authorities to reconsider and rightly decide American legal interpretations that Aliites see as blatantly at odds with true law.[45] Moreover, Aliites privilege texts issued by such bodies, like the *Declaration of Human Rights* or the *Declaration on the Rights of the Indigenous Person*, as expressions of authentic, divinely given rights, true law phrased in a recognizably legal form. Aliites understand international law as a form of translation of divine law, such that it can be comprehended by the legal authorities of various nation-states.[46]

In the most dramatic Aliite instance of appealing to international legal bodies in the hopes of persuading U.S. legal authorities of Aliite claims, Verdiacee Goston, the founding Empress of the Washitaw de Dugdahmoundyah, made a "pilgrimage" in 1996, in the company of other Washitaw leaders, to Geneva to represent the Washitaw people at the United Nations Economic and Social Council, Commission on Human Rights Sub-Committee on Prevention of Discrimination and Protection of Minorities, Working Group on Indigenous Populations. A Washitaw representative briefly addressed this body.[47] The name of Washitaw was listed in the program, along with an identification number, "215/93." This number is frequently cited as proof of official recognition of Washitaw claims to indigenous status, much as registration with Cook County was cited as authority by the early MSTA. Moreover, Goston insisted that the United Nations, in 1996, "declared" the Washitaw to be the "oldest indigenous people on earth," which, indeed, was entered into the official U.N. record—the program of the conference—because it was included as part of the Washitaw organization's name for the purposes of that program. Such participation is cited by the Washitaw as official recognition, by the United Nations, of Washitaw claims, citation of which, in turn, is believed to have the potential to change

American attitudes toward the Washitaw and influence American legal interpretations in that people's favor.

THE SOVEREIGNTY OF TRUE LAW

Winnifred Sullivan has analyzed the "tremendous ambiguity" in the phrase "rule of law," noting that

> in its strongest form, the rule of law has a powerful substantive quality making it akin to the foundational claims of natural law at their most expansive. In this version, law is singular, uniquely rational, self-evident, universal, and autonomous. When the rule of law is achieved, the implication goes, the lion will lie down with the lamb. Crime and violence and poverty will no longer exist.

This is in keeping with Aliite conceptions of true law and its eventual eschatological alignment with the legal, down to the lion and the lamb harmoniously cohabitating. But Sullivan goes on to observe that "rule of law" has a "more modest" or "weaker sense," one that seeks "some minimal conditions for a just society," such as "equality before the law for all" including the "sovereign" power of the state. While not synonymous with a universal ideal of justice or freedom, this second conception of "rule of law" nonetheless motivates "reform" of the legal system on multiple levels.[48] Aliite faith in the first conception of law undergirds Aliite dedication to this second conception, the practice of seeking, through the legal system, a means of checking power, invoking the ideal of law as a means of clarifying, negotiating, and simply surviving within the state as it currently exists. True law, for Aliites, is eternal and transcendent, a metaphysical reality synonymous with ethical ideals like justice and truth. As the ultimate form of sovereignty, in addition, true law is understood not only as existing beyond all human instantiations of the legal but also as constituting the true grounds for instantiations of sovereignty in this world where sovereignty is multiple, relational, always negotiated. Sovereignties, as experienced in this world, may still be enforced by power or violence, but such human power is only ever temporary, an act of human rebellion against the true law imprinted in all of creation by its Creator.

Aliites theorize a model of political and legal reality that simultaneously recognizes and reduces the power of the state, submitting to and coopting such power. Aliite thought maintains faith in law as transcendent of history and yet imbues action in this world with sacred significance as part of a process of transforming the world into alignment with true law, particularly by, in Sullivan's words, "training" those in positions of authority within American legal institutions as to that true law. Aware of the profound injustice perpetrated by and through the legal system, Aliites nonetheless recognize on a practical level that their salvation can only come through the grace of the state, and they insist on a metaphysical level that agents of the state can be swayed not merely by raw power (even the power of a democratic constituency) but also by true law, knowledge of which is innate in all humans due to their creation by Allah. With their eyes focused on law as divine and eternal, Aliites are equally invested in a "more modest" "rule of law" project as a practical step toward the eventual perfection of America. If, for instance, members of the Congressional Black Caucus can accept their own authentic nationality, or if citizens of Georgia can understand that the Nuwaubian Yamassee remain focused on the welfare of children, these are major accomplishments, even if far short of the broader goal of an eschatological "rule of law" in which all human legal institutions are aligned with divine justice.

Aliites, after all, operate always in awareness of the profoundly asymmetrical power relations between the state and Aliite individuals and communities. Aliites also remain conscious of the deep, historically constant divide between the American state's use of power through the legal system and that state's founding ideals as enshrined in written laws as well as, of course, the true law. Washitaw Empress Verdiacee Goston's phrase, much repeated in Washitaw circles, "I have no bombs, no bullets, no threats, no war. Just common sense and universal law," speaks to this understanding of Aliite sovereignty in relation to the sovereign power of the state.[49] Like many other Aliites, she was willing to—and did—challenge the authority of the U.S. government, but only by insisting that the interpretation of law held and enforced by that government (what the state claims as *legal*) was incorrect and, thus, turning an authority already recognized by the state back against the state.

Aliite appeal to true law in the face of unjust legal policy echoes acts of resistance, through law, of other marginalized, minority religious groups, from the Jehovah's Witnesses to the contemporary Christian Patriot movement.[50] Law—imagined and real, transcendent and localized as legal interpretation—is often turned to as a tool, even a weapon, for those who otherwise would be powerless against the state. Such a notion is enshrined in the American legal consciousness, what Sally Merry has called the "mythic vision" of the rule of law.[51] That this mythic vision focuses on the structures of power that justify and continue racist oppression is in keeping with the creative resistance of colonized communities around the world. As Thomas Blom Hansen writes, "The imagining of free selves was always shaped by the specific structure of unfreedom they arose from."[52] Aliite recourse to legal precedent can be read as an embrace of the structures (epistemological as well as behavioral) that constitute the power of "civil society" in the sense described by Achille Mbembe, that structure which replaced the "raw physical violence" and "vulgar brute force" of colonial regimes with a framework of rationality that served as a technology of control. In postcolonial societies, Mbembe associates such a framework with "the transformation of behavior, respect for binding agreements, and control of conduct," though Aliites perceive this very technology of civil governance, the bureaucratic framework of the legal system, as a potential arena for their own power.[53] Although the state and its legal system perpetuated slavery, then Jim Crow, and contemporary mass incarceration and police brutality to so-called blacks, Aliites nonetheless identify the state and its legal system as necessary for their "salvation." In so doing, Aliites distinguish between historical state practices and the eternal ideals of the state, between the legal and the true law, the contingently human and the universally moral.[54] Aliites thus reimagine the state in light of their own ideals, thinking of the state not in terms of its past violations of true law but in terms of its past declarations of allegiance to true law and its future possibility as an instantiation of that law. "Citizenship," for Aliites, is more than either status or practice—it is an abiding belief in values, in eschatology, a system of "identifications and emotional attachments" between true law and the legal system of the United States of America.[55] To be a "citizen of the United States" is to believe in a possible future America, a state of many nationalities, equal under true law.

Aliite identification of true law as the ground for infinite, multiple, and relational sovereignties serves as a (hopeful) solution to two distinct problems in American political and legal history. First, Aliite thought imposes a coherence on the seemingly contradictory claims about sovereignty advanced in American law and politics. The sovereignty attributed to the citizen clearly clashes with lived reality, yet the Supreme Court, with its seemingly sovereign power to judge the constitutionality of laws, represents a "countermajoritarian problem" beyond that, already, of elected officials to whom popular sovereignty is supposedly transferred and yet who are ultimately their own deciders.[56] Ali's system imposes order on this disorder, accepting sovereignty as existing on multiple levels and in multiple modes, but always grounded by, and under the ultimate sovereignty of, law. Instead of viewing sovereignty in America as a paradox, a mess of entangled and contradictory claims, Aliites rationalize a multiplicity of sovereigns by recourse to "rule of law," seeing that notion as "both an expression of the ideal of popular sovereignty and a denial of popular sovereignty as absolute," for in Aliite understanding *all* sovereignty other than that of true law is necessarily less than absolute while, at the same time, what makes sovereignty possible *is* such true law.[57] Ali's system of sovereignty as multiple and relational, with law as the ultimate sovereign, likewise embraces the myriad "alternative forms of sovereignty" facilitated by American populism (political and religious) while accepting Marianne Constable's characterization of U.S. citizens as "minisovereigns"—indeed, judges and politicians, tyrants and kings are all only ever "minisovereigns" in a system where the role of ultimate sovereignty is attributed to true law.[58] Contemporary Aliite thinker Kudjo Adwo El's commentary on the famous frontispiece to Thomas Hobbes's *Leviathan* speaks to this. He describes the image "depicting the Sovereign as a massive body . . . composed of many individual people," as a portrait of the ultimate sovereign, Ultimate Law/Allah. This picture reveals the deity's multivalent, multinational, and essentially democratic nature, an idea "resurrected in America by Prophet Noble Drew Ali."[59] In Aliite thought, true law is that sovereignty which "survives" all transitions between rulers and even political systems, as described by Justice Sutherland in a 1936 case, *United States v. Curtiss-Wright Export Corporation*: "Rulers come and go; governments end and forms of government change; but sovereignty survives. . . . Sovereignty is never held in suspense."[60] Sovereignty in this understanding is, as Mateo Taussig-Rubbo has written, "not merely as a state of exception to the normal order, but also as a creative, foundational force, a constituent power," a kind of displacement of the sovereign will of "the long-dead members of a democratic assembly" onto the laws they wrote, thus allowing those laws to serve as an extension of the sovereignty of the people back into history.[61] Such foundational sovereignty, however, also displaces sovereignty in another way, essential to Aliite desires, imbuing the notion of law as ultimate sovereign with the hope of disenfranchised, marginalized, and relatively powerless people for a sovereignty that is synonymous with justice.[62]

A second solution offered by Aliite theories of sovereignty is in relation to the deep history of (legal) injustice in the United States. Aliite attribution of ultimate sovereignty to true law allows for a reorientation of history as a long arc toward justice, underwritten by Allah. As history is understood as tilting toward justice rather than following the caprices of power, so, too, the *legal*, in Aliite understanding, is seen as simultaneously limited by and grounded in true law. At times, of course, the legal can become a tool for the temporary tyrant, but despite the centuries of unjust legality, the fallible human legal is nonetheless patterned on and grounded in the true law. The legal—the same legal system that facilitated slavery, that imposed segregation, that deals out racially imbalanced prison sentences, that allows state agents to go unpunished for the murder of dark-skinned citizens—nonetheless must and will serve as the means of redeeming America, through engagement with those devoted to and possessing knowledge of true law. The ultimate sovereignty Aliites attribute to law thus bolsters their own claims to sovereignty, as when they engage, as sovereign citizens, with the powerful sovereignty of the state—encounters understood as consisting of recognition and negotiation between sovereignties (see chapter 4).

Aliite claims about sovereignty emerge from and represent close readings of sovereignty as it is imagined, discussed, and engaged in the mainstream society. When Aliites discuss the sovereignty negotiated by treaties, the sovereignty of the citizen as theorized by the U.S. Supreme Court, or the sovereignty associated with theological descriptions of the divine, they are never thinking in a vacuum but always engaging with a range of sources understood widely in America as being authoritative. This chapter began with the stars on the Great Seal because this canonical illustration of sovereignty as multiple and relational speaks to on-the-ground engagements with, and claims to sovereignty by, people whose goal is not rulership but, rather, coexistence, not deciding the exception to the law but being recognized in equal access to it. If human society is understood as consisting of multiple sovereigns existing alongside each other, the means by which they are able to communicate and agree, keep peace and take note of each other's sovereignties, becomes not only logically paramount but also presents itself as the location where ultimate sovereignty lies.

Aliite understandings of sovereignty acknowledge the power of the state while seeking to negotiate such power through a higher sovereignty, that of law. This is done in what Aliites take to be practical and efficacious ways, through engagement in democratic politics as a constituency and through appeal to international law, both moves understood as mobilizing sovereign power (of the constituency, of international law and legal bodies) to influence sovereign U.S. legal institutions. Citizenship and law offer Aliites the promise of their own sovereignty—their own self-determination, communal autonomy, and political power. As stars coming together as stars and seeking recognition from other stars in the firmament, Aliites see sovereignty as always a matter of negotiating with other levels of sovereignty. Aliites live in a world of powerful forces, in relation to which they have recourse to law as simultaneously the most powerful force and one entirely dependent upon human effort and existing institutions. Aliites must hope for—and must work to acquire—recognition from the state, from its agents in authoritative positions within legal and political institutions. Aliites need recognition of their claims to identity and the legal consequences thereof, but then, as citizens, they must struggle for the state to recognize and accept their claims about true law.

ANNUIT CŒPTIS

Recognition, Authority, and Law

SEEKING THE FAVOR OF RECOGNITION

ANNUIT CŒPTIS, THE THIRTEEN-LETTER PHRASE on the reverse of the Great Seal, is more ambiguously phrased than the earlier candidate for its position, William Barton's suggested *Deo favente*, or "God willing." The phrase that was ultimately chosen, *Annuit cœptis* "Favor [our] undertakings" or "[He] has favored [our] undertakings"—leaves direct identification of its subject, that which has favored or will favor these undertakings, unnamed. The centrality of *favor*, however, is unavoidable. We have already seen the necessity of approval and authorization, of *recognition*, within an interdependent, relational model of sovereignty. In this chapter, following the double valence of *Annuit cœptis* as implicitly pleading for favor and explicitly offering assurance of having already received such favor, I examine instances of Aliite engagement with recognized sources of state authority and the ways Aliites court favor by claiming—and offering evidence of—past recognition.

Aliite claims about national identity are understood as legal claims and, as such, must be recognized by the institutional authority of the state in order to have legal consequence within the state. Even as Aliites believe that true law is a transcendent, metaphysical reality, they hold that such power manifests in the world only through human action and human institutions, institutions that are patterned on the model of true law but can only become actualizations of it through human effort. True law's manifestation in this world is limited by institutions, by power. The power of the state is undeniable and overwhelming in relation to Aliites. Yet Aliites respond by courting this power, seeking the favor of representatives of institutional power, and citing instances of such recognition in the past—real or imagined—as precedent to sway decisions on Aliite claims in the present.

Aliites acknowledge, revere, seek out, and sometimes appropriate the authority of official state legal and political institutions. Interactions between Aliites and state power are tense not only because Aliites realize their claims have no legal consequences without state approval but also because the same institutions Aliites seek recognition from are often those responsible for and associated with unjust and oppressive legal interpretations. The state can convict Aliites and sentence them to prison, can arrest and even kill them on the street, can demand payment of taxes and impose fees. In seeking the favor of recognition, Aliites must proceed cautiously, attempting to convince representatives of this potentially deadly power that Aliite claims are true. To do so, Aliites have recourse to legal texts, documents that, they claim, offer evidence of previous recognition of Aliite claims by state officials.

This chapter analyzes the frequent Aliite citation of texts understood as offering such evidence of state recognition. The registration paperwork of Ali's original MSTA serves as the first example, a bureaucratic document revered as "Our Authority," as proof of state recognition and endorsement of his mission. This document plays a central role in Aliite religion, being read as authorization, from the state, for Ali's work as prophet and for the ongoing work of citizenship pursued by Aliites. Next, this chapter considers Aliite claims to legal precedents, with attention to Washitaw citation of an imagined precedent, what Washitaw call "the 1848 Supreme Court Case," *United States v. Henry Turner's Heirs*. The Supreme Court heard *United States v. Turner*, involving land disputes related to the Louisiana Purchase, in 1850; Washitaw refer to, and reproduce, the district court ruling that preceded—and was reversed by—that decision. The counterfactual nature of Washitaw claims highlights Aliite dependence upon official recognition and the need for legal precedent as part of Aliite argumentation for claims.[1] After consideration of Aliite emphasis on the Supreme Court's actual decision in *Dred Scott v. Sanford*, which is widely read by Aliites as authorizing the ongoing legal exclusion of "Negroes" from citizenship in the United States, the chapter concludes with a caution about describing Aliite use of legal texts as "magical" and consideration of how Aliite examples can contribute to contemporary academic criticism of the politics of recognition.

"OUR AUTHORITY": LOCAL
INSTITUTIONAL RECOGNITION

In one oft-told Aliite legend of recognition, Ali, early in his career as a prophet, traveled to the White House to demand that the president return the red banner of the Moors.[2] The story goes that this banner had flown in the presence of U.S. political authority as a mark of legal recognition of Moors and their rights, but that it had been "chopped down" by George Washington. This event was preserved in the popular legend of the cherry tree, Aliite thinkers claim, but there never was such a tree; rather, Washington, a slave owner, severed the legal agreements with and recognition of the Moors in order to enslave them as "negro, black, and colored" people. When President Woodrow Wilson (or, in some versions, presidents Calvin Coolidge or Herbert Hoover) met Ali at the door of the White House, he immediately understood the request, went into an archive, and returned with the red Moorish flag. MSTA thinkers today still cite this event as one of recognition: "President Woodrow Wilson officially recognized the Moorish Science Temple of America (MSTA) as a legal incorporated entity and accepted the Moorish Americans as a legitimate nationality bound by the rights and privileges bestowed to other independent people of the earth."[3]

This is not only an origin myth for the red flag displayed beside the Stars and Stripes in the famous photograph of Drew Ali discussed in the introduction. This is also a myth about recognition by state power—a narrative that reiterates the necessity of engagement with and recognition by the state. We see here how institutions of recognized power—and their representatives, ranging from police officers and clerks to judges and elected officeholders, including the president of the United States—can acknowledge and recognize the legal claims of, can *favor the undertaking of*, those before them. In this story, the flag itself serves the role of an artifact of recognition. Its return equates to a treaty agreed to (or restored), one sovereign recognizing the sovereignty of another. The Moorish flag, as evidence of such recognition, continues to be so used by Aliites today, read as marker not merely of nationality required for citizenship but of a particular nationality denied and occluded by the American state, retrieved by the prophet, and revitalized today by those conscious of their heritage and the rights and responsibilities thus entailed.

Ali stated that the most important issue before his people was "to be recognized by this government."[4] Contemporary Moors insist that recognition was "the reason [Drew Ali] was sent."[5] Recognition by the institutions of power is of such importance that Aliites may hold up even mundane forms of interaction with local government, as evidence of such recognition. Bureaucratic offices can thus play a central role in Aliite rhetoric of recognition. One of the earliest instances of this practice is Ali's citation of his movement's registration as a civic organization with the state of Illinois in 1926, and as a religious corporation with Cook County in 1928, documents of which were reproduced in copies of the Moorish newspaper, *The Moorish Guide*, as evidence of "Our Authority."[6] Reprinted in newspapers, books, and websites; read aloud in sermons, over radio broadcasts, and on conference calls; held aloft at religious services and even placed "in the back of the casket" for a funeral—"Our Authority" is engaged, within Aliite religion, as an object as much as a text.[7] Aliites call it a "religious affidavit of organization," reproducing it and displaying it for the purposes of establishing that the authority of the state has endorsed the MSTA and its claims.

As Ali wrote, the MSTA had been recognized by being "incorporated in this government," a legal fact of such consequence that now the movement could be considered as "recognized by all other nations of the world."[8] Declaredly a "copy" of an archived legal form, "Our Authority" exemplifies characteristic Aliite understandings of law's universal, transcendent, and transformative power as granted by the favor of the state, as manifest at the will of institutions of power. As the presence of local power brokers and politicians at an early Moorish event (see chapter 1) was read as granting legitimacy—the recognition of those in established positions of authority—to Ali's position as prophet, so, too, the process of filing for legal recognition with state and county officials was read as granting legitimacy to Ali's claims, so much so that he declared:

> You who doubt whether I, the Prophet, and my principles are right for the redemption of my people, go to those that know law, in the City Hall and among the officials in your government and ask them under an intelligent tone, and they will be glad to render you a favorable reply, for they are glad to see me bring you out of darkness into light.[9]

Here bureaucratic paperwork offers more than a record—however "rich and complex"—of religious life.[10] Such paperwork, filed and registered with an authoritative state institution, is incorporated into, and understood as authorizing and communicating, religious claims. The bureaucratic document becomes religious object, evidence of state recognition of Aliite truth.

At the same time, as a historical document, "Our Authority" serves to reiterate the importance of Ali's specific context for the development of his thought. His theology (of a universal deity manifesting via prophets and gospels, paralleling City Hall's representative system of aldermen and wards); his ethics (of cooperation with the machine, of the expectation of rewards by means of a system of divinely ordained patronage); and even his eschatology (of rich and poor from diverse nationalities living together in tolerant civility, "each under his own vine and fig tree") were all rooted in the same context that gave jobs to the two non-Moors whose names are now enshrined in Aliite tradition: Salomes Jasconowskic and Roberta W. Counull. These names, that of the court recorder and the notary public who notarized this document, are enshrined in Aliite tradition. Like the name of Arthur C. Lueder, Chicago's postmaster from 1922 to 1934, they reveal an essential dynamic within the Aliite lineage.[11]

Ali, as prophet of the universal Allah, met with Lueder in an attempt to leverage what traction he had gained by delivering a bloc of voters to the Republican machine into postal jobs for his Moorish American community. As Susan Nance has pointed out, "In 1928, one quarter of the city's postal employees were black," and the expectation among political leaders was that "blacks would continue to hold a large proportion of post office jobs and that such positions would be handed out in return for black votes."[12] While it is unclear whether Ali's community achieved any of these positions as a reward for their political work, the fact that others did is already, from an Aliite point of view, proof of Ali's soteriology in action, "salvation" through the *quid pro quo* of the Republican machine.

Ali and his early MSTA publicized instances of acknowledgment by political authorities, conflating such acknowledgment with endorsement of the claims and project of the MSTA. When Ali's community staged a parade through the streets of Chicago's Second Ward in 1928, for instance, escorted by police officers in keeping with the parade license obtained through the city, the presence of such uniformed agents of the state was read as evidence of state support for the MSTA.[13] Other official gestures were read similarly, such as Ali and an MSTA delegation attending, as invited guests, the 1929 Illinois gubernatorial inauguration of Louis L. Emmerson, or even birthday telegrams from elected officials, sent to Ali and reproduced in the *Moorish Guide*. Yet the power of the official document, on file and certified with stamps of authoritative acknowledgment, remains paramount.[14]

The bureaucratic document, as Naynika Mathur and Matthew S. Hull have argued, is both text and object.[15] Marked with the signatures, titles, and stamps of state authority, archived in official collections, the bureaucratic document as material artifact is understood as conveying real power—by functioning as a "protective shield," for instance. The power such a textual object conveys is the power of the state. What bureaucratic documents do is remind the state—which, after all, exists not as a thing but as a variety of effects, existing in relationships and processes—of the state's own stance in relation to a given issue or person. A driver's license offers evidence that a given citizen has been judged able, by the state, to operate a motor vehicle; an inspection certificate provides proof of official examination and approval for the operation of an elevator. Both "Our Authority" and Aliite nationalization cards are understood, by Aliites, as functioning in this way. While merely "flimsy pieces of cheap paper," these items are understood as offering evidence to state officials of state recognition of status, privilege, and rights.[16]

"OBEY YOUR OWN LAWS": WASHITAW
CLAIMS TO LEGAL PRECEDENT

Aliite claims are legal claims, and arguments for such claims are understood to be legal arguments, advanced in terms of legal discourse as a universal mode of communicating a transcendent truth and embedded in legal history. Such claims reference the dependence Aliites acknowledge on institutions of power and the lineage of interpretations of the legal offered up and recognized by such institutions. Aliite claims thus cite legal precedent, turning to case law as evidence of past recognition in order to ensure recognition in the present, what one Empire Washitaw leader has called "documented court cases that prove who we are."[17] The most frequently cited such case is central to Washitaw arguments regarding legal ownership of the territory they claim to be their ancestral inheritance. The Washitaw cite interpretations of what they refer to as "the 1848 Supreme Court Case United States v. Henry Turner's Heirs" in defense of their claims to the land. The historical case revolved around property rights to the Louisiana Purchase, and, specifically, whether the Spanish government had granted possession of a parcel of that land in what is now northern Louisiana to the Marquis de Maison Rouge, who had been sent on a mission to mark this territory "out by certain and definite boundaries and limits." The Turner family argued that the Marquis had legally been given this land and, later, had sold it to them. The U.S. Supreme Court held, in a five-four ruling, that the said Turner heirs did not have a legal claim to the land in question, as the Marquis was merely an agent of the Spanish Crown, demarcating land for settlement by colonists. The "grant" of land in question was never the possession of the Marquis but was merely marked out by him for "those who were disposed to come," "emigrants who should accept the conditions" of the Spanish government.[18]

This case matters for the Washitaw because, first, they insist that the Turner family in question is the family of the movement's founder, Verdiacee Goston. The Turner family is the Washitaw royal family, "the imperial bloodline," which includes both Drew Ali and the young woman nominally considered to be the current empress (Goston's granddaughter, who has eschewed any public leadership role but is still mentioned in Washitaw prayer and conversation). Reliance on this case allowed Goston, and now allows her son Fredrix Joe Washington, to insist that their family—"the family" or "the Throne"—is uniquely situated to lead the Washitaw movement as they have distinct legal rights. Second, this case matters to the Washitaw because they interpret it to mean that the Turners were given, by the U.S. Supreme Court, recognition of rights of ownership to the land. "We own the title," Washington has said, to "the Land." The Turner land is the 68,883-acre territory called "Washitaw Proper" within the movement, understood to be the administrative heart of the empire of the Ancient Ones. This is, the Washitaw insist, a settled legal decision, one that need only be recognized and complied with by the power of the state. The authority here is the state's own: the Supreme Court.

The divide between Washitaw claims about this case and actual facts is notable. The historic "Turner's Heirs" case was not heard by the Supreme Court until 1850. The 1848 text identified as a U.S. Supreme Court decision in Washitaw discourse is the district court decision that was later appealed to the Supreme Court.[19] Goston's scriptural text, *Return of the Ancient Ones*, devotes some eighty-three pages to reproductions of documents from the *United States v. Turner* case, but all these documents are merely those that were submitted on appeal *to* the Supreme Court.[20] Although it may seem baffling, within a movement that presents itself as based in "research" and deeply engaged in textual study, I have found no Washitaw or Aliite who mentions the disparity between Washitaw claims about the Supreme Court decision and the actual decision. This lack of attention to the actual text can also be seen as characteristic of Aliite engagement with precedent. Other important Aliite legal precedents, such as the 1786 "Treaty of Peace and

Friendship" between Morocco and the United States, likewise need not be read so much as cited, and even "Our Authority," reproduced and reproduced, need not so much be *read* as possessed, gestured toward—as object more than text. Context—and relevance of the actual document or legal decision to the situation at hand—does not necessarily matter for Aliite invocation of precedent. The precedent is imagined as past recognition of Aliite claims, and this serves as its summary and primary use. This imagined recognition, by the highest court in the land, of Washitaw claims is mentioned in Washitaw prayers and discussed in publications and lectures. It is commemorated in the movement's major holiday, "Our Juneteenth," when "Washitaw families gather to celebrate the return of the land."[21] This holiday conflates the broader African American commemoration of the emancipation of the last chattel slaves (as news of the end of the Civil War reached the last outpost of the Confederacy in Texas) with the date, June 19, of the "Turner's Heirs" decision.[22]

The Washitaw insist that they have indisputable evidence of the official recognition that they desire, a U.S. Supreme Court decision in their favor. The power of this imagined precedent resides in the fact that the authority is recognizable to and synonymous with the American state—the Supreme Court is the law of the land, and Washitaw claims about the "Turner's Heirs" case is understood as equalizing the radical imbalance of power between Washitaw and the state by having the state speak on behalf of, endorsing and defending, Washitaw claims. Citation of this case is part of Washitaw efforts to correct the mistake of past and continuing American legal interpretations. As with the appeal to international law and legal bodies discussed in chapter 2, the Washitaw want to alert American legal authorities to the ways their interpretations have departed from actual law, and, in the case of the "Turner's Heirs" case, what the Washitaw take to be established American legal precedent that aligns with true law. A popular Washitaw motto, a rhetorical question, addresses American political and legal authorities: "Are you going to obey your own laws?" This captures the Washitaw sense that their strongest argument is an appeal to U.S. authorities to return to the truth already enshrined in and witnessed by decisions of the country's legal system. Washitaw citation of "Henry Turner's Heirs" holds authority over the government and courts, an authority understood not only to come from them but, indeed, to be their own. It is their authority that they must answer to—with Washitaw activists serving as reminders, mouthpieces, ventriloquizing what they claim to be American legal precedent, the American state's own authority.[23] Even while insisting upon the ultimate sovereignty of true law, Goston repeatedly acknowledged the authority of human law and the legal system, describing herself as "a firm believer in law and order."[24] Her insistence that the Louisiana Purchase was "illegal" is perhaps the most obvious and recurring example of this. While she argues that, in addition, the purchase was morally wrong and exploitative, the illegality of it hinges on interpretations of human laws, most notably "the United States Constitution," which, she says, "does not permit buying land or purchasing a country." She approvingly quotes Thomas Jefferson's comments that with the Louisiana Purchase, "[w]e [the U.S. government] are stretching the constitution to its breaking point" and that "[if] in some future date, we find that our actions have done harm to anyone, I hope that the United States will have the good sense to correct the mistake that we make here." Indeed, in her book Goston argues for a corrective to the "mistake" of the illegal seizure of Washitaw land, an argument she advances through citation of authoritative legal interpretations from the state.[25] *Return of the Ancient Ones*, a compilation of historical and legal texts, can be read as an assemblage of American arguments for Washitaw claims, an anthology of American legal interpretations that the Washitaw call to be recognized, for just as the Washitaw claim that, in terms of the territory of the United States, they were here first, so Washitaw legal argumentation relies upon the fact that, in terms of legal argumentation for Washitaw claims, other American authorities were there first. The state need not listen to Goston herself; the state should heed its own ancestral leaders and judicial bodies, from Thomas Jefferson to the Supreme Court. Central to Washitaw argumentation is the insistence that those American authorities have already sided with the Washitaw.

DRED SCOTT AND CONSTITUTIONAL RECOGNITION OF ALIITE CLAIMS

The most basic Aliite claim is to an identity distinct from "negro, black, or colored" and, thereby, a claim to legal rights of citizenship. Suffrage, Aliites insist, has been denied "negroes," but "Moorish" is a distinct category in American legal history, one never subject to the restrictions imposed upon the former. Moors, according to Aliite logic, have always—when their identity has been proclaimed and recognized as Moorish—been respected by the U.S. government and laws. Only when Moorish identity ceased to be recognized—which, as Ali frames it in the history chapters of his *Holy Koran*, resulted from Moorish infidelity to ancestral identity, the "sin" of abandoning Moorish tradition and straying "after the Gods of Europe"[26]— did Moors fall into the catastrophe of slavery. Forgetting who they were, these Moors accepted the label of "Negro" as an identity.

While Ali is often read as insisting that there is only one race, the human race, he also used the term "race" to describe nationalities of people, even urging "Asiatics" to join the MSTA if they "have race pride and love [their] race."[27] Contemporary Aliites take different stances, from insisting that "race" is a meaningless social construct to arguing, as Sharif Anael-Bey does in one text, that "Noble Drew Ali did forward a racial categorization, but one that is much more scientifically sound; he taught that there is but one race—the Human Race, yet subdivided into Asiatic and European."[28] Other Aliites insist specifically that "Negro" signifies an actual ontology in the world. Ali's narrative of history—placing the responsibility for slavery firmly on the shoulders of slaves and insisting, likewise, that those so-called blacks today who remain "political slaves" do so thanks to their own inaction or incorrect actions—aids in this perpetuation of antiblackness. Those who behave as Negroes, Ali taught, bear the blame for their fate. In contemporary Aliite thought, the concept of "Negro" survives not only as a fictive category but also as a real mode of being in contrast to which Moors define themselves and their uplift. The concept of Negro is reified in such thinking, and the existence of Negroes becomes something on which the claim to be Moorish depends. While Moorish citizenship follows a pattern and promise parallel to and open to other "nationalities," each with its own flag, traditions, and version of divine revelation from the universal Allah, "Negroes" have no nationality. Negroes are civically dead, political slaves, a status reinforced by their self-identification with that term or its corollaries ("colored" or "black"). The practical political and economic change Ali's MSTA strove for do not apply to Negroes—they are only for "Moorish Americans."

Such logic—the insistence on the existence of Negroes, outside the possibility of inclusion in civic participation—raises significant interpretive problems when considering American judicial and political history. Notably, the Reformation Amendments, in the wake of the Civil War, explicitly extend such rights to African Americans under the Constitution. Ali was aware of this issue, and he addressed it in a speech in Chicago, written for both a European (nonblack) and Moorish audience, and published as a pamphlet:

The 14th and 15th Amendments brought the North and South in unit, placing the Southerners who were at that time without power, with the constitutional body of power. And at that time, 1865, the free national constitutional law that was enforced since 1774 declared all men equal and free, and if all men are declared by the free national constitution to be free and equal since that constitution has never been changed, there is no need for the application of the 14th and 15th Amendments for the salvation of our people and citizens.[29]

Ali states here that there was no need for two major changes to a document that is rarely changed, the central legal document of the American state. This claim is echoed by many Aliite thinkers throughout history. The Fourteenth Amendment, in particular, is dismissed as illegitimate, as "NOT a part of the Organic American Constitution."[30] Aliite thinkers go so far as to say that even the assumption of legality for this text constitutes "a disgrace to free government and [the possibility of] a 'government of law.' "[31]

If accepted as current American legal interpretation, the Fourteenth Amendment undermines the basic Aliite claim that "Negroes" can never be citizens. The necessary correlation between nationality and citizenship central to Aliite religion, then, would be called into question, as would the aura of the Constitution, believed widely to be, in its original and authentic form, an expression of true law—declaring, specifically, "all *men* free and equal," a line Aliite thinkers read as excluding those without nationality and therefore without full humanity—that is, *Negroes*.[32] Exclusion of Negroes from the possibility of citizenship not only helps make sense of a history of legal racial discrimination in the United States, it also serves as a way for Aliite thinkers to revere the Constitution without attributing any of the taint of such racist legal policy to that document. While Aliites are not blind to the history of legal racism, discrimination, and exclusion, their insistence on differentiating between legal injustice to Moors and legal exclusion of Negroes allows for a more hopeful reading, not only of contemporary relations to the state, but also of the history of legal racist oppression.

Sharif A. Bey states, "As Prophet Drew Ali taught us, since the free national constitution of 1774 declared all men free and equal, and that law has not been changed, then there is no need for any special amendments for the salvation of our people."[33] Those dark-skinned people excluded from civil life, he argues, did not and never could count toward the "all *men*" who are endowed by their Creator with equal rights and declared as "free and equal" in the Constitution. Turning, as he often does, to the precise language at stake in the question, A. Bey asks: "Can a MAN be a negro, black, colored or Ethiopian?" or is that term—signifying humanity itself—exclusive of those categories?[34] To be fully human one must know and declare one's nationality, and only the fully human can be citizens.

Aliite thinkers thus insist that the 1857 *Dred Scott v. Sandford* opinion, which held that African Americans could not claim U.S. citizenship, articulates the accurate and current interpretation of the Constitution. With this decision serving as a gloss on the Constitution, the Fourteenth Amendment becomes meaningless, and Aliite claims to identity and its legal consequences still make sense. As Paul Kahn has observed, "All law remains available at every moment. Indeed, even law that has been overruled and seems dead can return to life. What has been taken for true can come to appear as error, just as error can come to be seen as truth." Kahn goes on to express his confidence that we will not see "arguments . . . to recover the 'true' Constitution, of which *Dred Scott* was the 'correct' interpretation," yet this is precisely the argument advanced by many Aliite thinkers.[35] Kudjo Adwo El writes that, since the U.S. Supreme Court "has never overturned" the *Scott* decision, "so it stands at Law that Negroes can never be citizens."[36] The Constitution of the UNNM features a lengthy analysis of the *Scott* case, staking a claim for the Yamassee as part of the "We the People" that is the U.S. citizenry on their non-Negro status.[37] The Washitaw, too, make reference to the essential legal categorization of "Negro" in the *Scott* decision.[38] Bandele El-Amin argues, in his interpretation of the *Scott* decision, that under the U.S. Constitution a "black person is [either] a Moorish American or a certified Negro from the city and state that they live in. Either you are a Moorish American under the Constitution or the property of the State," a literal slave, owned by corporate interests.[39]

Even those Aliites who dismiss "Negro" as signifying a real category of being do not dismiss it as an appropriate label for behavior. Sharif Anael-Bey has described *Scott* as "one of the worst court decisions in the history of the United States," both because of a "morality deficit" in the decision and because of the chaos of "civic ambiguity" for people of color that results from the decision. He follows Ali in dismissing "Negroes" as a legal fiction (there is no need for that category of person to have rights, because that is a false category) and in stating that there are people who live *as* Negroes, exhibiting a "general apathetic attitude" toward citizenship, which, in turn, he blames on the *Scott* decision.[40] In this, Anael-Bey at least holds open the possibility of salvation for those who currently act like and believe themselves to be Negroes.

Aliite reliance on the *Dred Scott* decision does not prevent dismay at the prevalence of antiblack racism in American society, but it does reiterate such antiblack racism. In so doing, Aliite *Dred Scott* discourse reiterates, as well, an emphasis on individual agency—and responsibility—that leads easily to political quietism, locating racism as the result of so-called blacks not proclaiming their true identity and ignoring the deep structural entrenchment of such discrimination.[41] A 2015 article in the *Moorish Oakland Star*, for instance, cites the murders by police of Michael Brown and Eric Garner as proof that "being black (as a political status)" means "we have no rights . . . we are seen as property, not human beings . . . we have no protection from any government." The solution to this, however, is for the blacks in question to change *their* status, to realize and proclaim their nationality. By doing *this* one can, as Ali taught, become recognized as a full citizen. The not-too-subtle implication is that if only Brown and Garner had declared themselves to be Moorish, they would not have been killed by representatives of the state.[42] The music video for "Moor Lives Matter" by the band Al Moroccans takes a more conciliatory tone, coopting the famous slogan while insisting that in America "Moor lives matter, because it seems like black lives don't matter," and that education and political unity through the MSTA will ensure "your inalienable rights, the insatiable delight of knowing yourself and bring all injustice to light."[43] Righteous anger at inequality and injustice is thus channeled toward proselytization, and recognition of Aliite identity by the state is held up as salvation from the very power of the state.

LEGAL RECOGNITION AS POWER FROM THE STATE

Just as the law only bears consequences in society when recognized as legal by the power of the state, so, too, Aliite understanding of sovereignty emphasizes that sovereignty is tenuous and temporary, the outcome of instances of recognition. Sovereignty exists when recognized by other examples of sovereignty. Hence the importance of documents cited as evidence of recognition, as evidence of state authorization and endorsement of Aliite claims and the Aliite mission of citizenship.

Bureaucratic documents and legal decisions are not the only texts that can function as evidence of recognition; Aliites ascribe a similar importance to official governmental correspondence and proclamations. Copies of such proclamations are often reproduced as credentials in Aliite texts, as Azeem Hopkins-Bey does with a 2001 proclamation from the city of Philadelphia, declaring July 20 to be "Moorish American Independence Day"; as Menora Bey does with a similar proclamation of "Moorish American Week" around January 8 in the city of Memphis; or as Joseph Jeffries-El does with a letter awarding his Moorish Mosque the Periclean Prize for "outstanding and devoted service to the life and people of New York City" and inviting him to a "Citizens' Luncheon" with Mayor John Lindsay at Gracie Mansion. Washitaw Empress Verdiacee Goston reproduces, in *Return of the Ancient Ones*, an invitation she received to a Pan-Indian event and a letter from the Louisiana Historical Society acknowledging her work in its archives, both serving as official recognition of her claims—to indigenous identity and to historical knowledge.[44] Shabazz Bey mails, to those who purchase copies of *We Are the Washitaw*, a photocopy of a letter he received from Julian Burger, secretary of the U.N. Working Group on Indigenous Populations, thanking Shabazz Bey for "the information which you sent to the Secretary General," which has now been "placed for reference in our permanent library," proof of interaction with, recognition by, and interest from this international legal body.[45] Some of these documents allow for more detailed reading as sources of recognition than others: a 2011 proclamation for the city of Chicago, signed by Mayor Rahm Emanuel, states that "the Moorish Americans, being aboriginal to the territories of North, Central, and South Americas, have formed a sovereign Theocratic Government guided by the command principles of love, truth, peace, freedom, and justice through virtue of the universal right to self-determination as well as the Declaration on the Rights of Indigenous Peoples guaranteed in the Charter."[46]

While concepts such as John Comaroff's "fetishism of the law" or Catherine Wessinger's categorization of such practices as "magical" call attention to the dynamic at play here, use of such language risks exoticizing Aliite legal consciousness, making it appear as aberrant, rather than in keeping with mainstream American legal consciousness.[47]

Comaroff turns to "fetishism" to discuss the historical influence of religion on law, the "sacred underpinnings" to social understandings of and relations to law that Comaroff describes as "*legal* theology," following Carl Schmitt's use of "political theology" to describe the fact that "all significant concepts of the modern theory of the state are secularized theological concepts."[48] While recognizing that religious conceptions exist as traces in modern politics and law, and that modern politics and law continue to be imbued with religious functions, Comaroff uses the concept of "fetishism" to exoticize and marginalize those who understand law as metaphysical, transcendent, and universal. Law, like an object attributed with sentience and intercessory agency by human worshippers, is "ascribed a life force of its own, and attributed the mythic, numinous capacity to configure relations and transactions in its own image" through what Comaroff calls "fetishism." Associating such approaches to law with identity politics and "multiculturalism," Comaroff links legal "fetishism" with racial, ethnic, and religious "others."[49] Reiterating such otherness, Comaroff claims that "the fetishism of the law" is related to "the judicialization of politics," the use of law and the legal systems as "the secular instrument by which civil society is to be remade in the image of the sacred."[50]

"Fetish," as William Pietz has shown, is a term with a "sinister pedigree."[51] Rooted in a dichotomy of the material versus the spiritual, the idolatrous and false versus the true, superstition versus religion, savage primitivism versus rational civilization, "fetish" brings with it a legacy of racism and racialization. Sylvester Johnson argues that the term, in its various academic uses, emerged directly from "materialist, fetish theory of religion . . . [that] rendered intelligible and justifiable European conquest wars, the trans-Atlantic slave trade, and the forced displacement of indigenous peoples."[52] Comaroff's use of fetish discourse—like the deep history of fetish discourse in the West—is predicated upon and used to defend an idealized notion of the purity of that to which it stands in opposition, here, law as "secular" in the sense of free of religious "underpinnings" and understandings. Comaroff's use of "fetish," as a term, allows him to insist upon a distinction between legal theories and practices, and religious beliefs and actions, a distinction he recognizes as nonexistent in the world but seeks to segregate, such that "legal theology" is that which others do, those who do not truly know the law (which seems as reified by Comaroff's theory as by those legal theologians he describes). The language of fetish is also a way to discount the call, by those others, to align the "civil" with the "sacred"— categories that Comaroff likewise reifies, by protesting their mixing. Talk about fetishism functions to police the boundaries around, and insist upon an ideal of, its opposite, "secular" civilization and a notion of law untainted by religious conceptions and desires.

Catherine Wessinger, in her analysis of the theory and practice of law by Montana Freemen, argues that such approaches to law can be best understood "in terms of magic," with legal action seen as so many "rituals (often involving speaking or writing words of power) that are believed to have the power to effect changes in the physical world."[53] The legal dynamics Wessinger analyzes are, indeed, strikingly similar to contemporary ritual magic.[54] My concern with the term "magic," however, rests in the category's valence as stigmatized, antisocial, and concealed, the hidden practice of a marginal underground. Use of the term "magic," as Kelly Hayes observed in her study of religion and power relations in Brazil, "tends to be a discourse of accusation rather than self-affirmation," with magic assigned the role of religion's marginal and "potentially maleficent" other.[55] While "magic" has a particular African American history—offering a sense of "control, power, and security" in tenuous social circumstances, as Yvonne Chireau has elucidated in her work on conjure—in African American contexts, too, the term signifies not merely practical efficacy but also individual practice as opposed to collective work, covert as opposed to public, personal as opposed to social.[56] Moreover, "accusations of magic typically function as markers of social difference that marginalize the efforts of socially subordinate or 'deviant' actors to obtain or exert power while masking the forms of control exercised by the dominant classes."[57] The practice of magic is not just antisocial, it is coded as the opposite of those practices that are socially acceptable and recognized to be socially powerful.

Wessinger's observation about the Montana Freemen—like mine about Aliites—is ultimately that their approach to the law recognizes and speaks to ways the law is understood as actually effecting change. The legal consciousness of Freemen and Aliites matters, not because it is an exotic alternative to mainstream American legal consciousness, but because it serves as a particularly privileged—both dramatically highlighted and explicitly theorized—representation of such legal consciousness. Use of the term "magic" obscures the important conclusion: that most citizens see legal texts and actions as being *like magic*. This point was made decades ago, in reference to legal professionals, by Jerome Frank.[58] Faith in the transformative power of the legal system, treatment of legal documents as consequential in relation to social dealings and social reality, even a hopeful insistence on proximity to power as equaling endorsement—these are not marginal ways of making sense of the power of the legal and political systems, and the role of citizens in relation to them, but, rather, characteristics of American faith in law. It may be *like* magic, but the greater takeaway from that comparison is that we are *all like magicians* in our understandings and engagements with law. Rather than performing some strange mystification of law, Freemen, like Aliites, enact and theorize widespread American concepts of law as transcendent force and transformative ideal.

Aliites show us not merely their own thoughts on law, but also something basic to the way law is understood in America more broadly. Such legal consciousness is replicated even by critics of the movement, as exemplified in coverage of an early Aliite crisis. In September 1929, in the wake of Ali's death, the MSTA splintered into three major factions—one led by Edward Mealy El, one led by Charles Kirkman Bey, and one led by John Givens El. At the annual convention on September 19, Givens El had declared himself to be the reincarnation of Ali and departed, presumably with some followers. Mealy El, taking the title of Chairman for himself, offered Kirkman Bey the title of Grand Advisor, presumably as an attempt to placate Kirkman Bey's supporters and Kirkman Bey's own ambition for leadership.

The fear of general schism—and anarchy—was pronounced enough for Mealy El's Supreme Business Manager, Chicago attorney Aaron Payne, to leave the assembly, taking with him "the Moorish Charter" (presumably the original "Our Authority" document), either for safekeeping or for political purposes. Four days later, on September 23, four gunmen arrived at Payne's house, demanding the paperwork. Police responded quickly, Payne was not harmed, and a police guard was stationed at his home.

On September 25 a group of four Moors, led by Ira Johnson Bey, abducted Kirkman Bey from his breakfast table at gunpoint. Johnson's goal was "seizing Kirkman's certificate, which had the signatures of the twenty-one governors of the various temples," a document offering evidence of authority and leadership.[59] Having been notified of the situation by his distraught wife, police rescued Kirkman Bey in a shootout, using a tear gas bomb and liberating Kirkman Bey, ultimately, with axes and ladders borrowed from the local fire station. One police officer died on the scene, as did one Moor; another officer succumbed later to his wounds. The event represents a watershed in Aliite history. "A general order to round up every member of the cult and every person who knew anything about the shooting was issued" by the chief of police, leading to sixty-two arrests, including those Payne and Mealy El.[60]

Lest this story be read as a case of marginal "fetishization" or exotic "magical" understanding, the commonplace nature of Aliite conceptions of law is reflected in the fact that the *Chicago Defender* echoed such conceptions when, in describing how police discovered "dozens or more rifles and automatic pistols" during this action, the newspaper that had previously celebrated the MSTA for its civic virtues now labeled it a threat and called for the revocation of Moorish "authority." Such deauthorizing was to come, according to the *Defender*, through official derecognition by the state. "Every effort will be made to have the state of Illinois revoke the license of the

Moorish Science Temple of America," a piece in the newspaper said, thus presenting the license as proof of legal status and—just as Aliites do—as evidence of a level of official endorsement, via recognition.[61]

Aliites exist in tenuous relation to state power. Citizenship, that status which serves as predication for any political negotiation within the state, does not exist without state recognition. While understanding the sovereignty of the people in a democracy to be real, Aliites also take it to be—like all forms of sovereignty short of the ultimate sovereignty of true law—always situational, fleeting, and dependent upon recognition by the sovereign state. Thus, Aliites appeal to, revere, coopt, and cite evidence of such recognition—real or imagined—as a means of acquiring the authority of the state for themselves. This dynamic of locating and publicizing recognition relates to Aliite experience of sovereignty through legal practice (discussed in chapter 4), Aliite engagement in public display (the topic of chapter 5), and Aliite knowledge practices, involving the mobilization of evidentiary facts via "research" (the subject of chapter 6). The array of Aliite responses to state power, and the constant focus thereon, emphasizes negotiation with the state as a non-negotiable reality, as the only possible path forward for Aliite communities.

The centrality of state recognition as a goal for marginalized communities has been widely criticized by postcolonial theorists as, itself, a continuation of colonial authority and control. As Maldonado-Torres puts it, "the struggle for recognition is fated to leave untouched the basic structure of the oppressive system."[62] Patchen Markell has argued that those who equate justice with the achievement of state recognition "may simultaneously make it more difficult to comprehend and confront unjust social and political relations."[63] The Aliite politics of recognition not only reaffirms the authority of the state but also insists that "recognition" is always already happening, a ubiquitous state practice and "state-effect."[64] Racialization, after all, is a form of recognition, and Ali insisted, as Charles Taylor later argued, that "a person or group of people can suffer real damage, real distortion, if the people or the society around them mirror back to them a confining or demeaning or contemptible picture of themselves."[65] Ali's push for recognition, after all, was framed as a corrective to *mis*-recognition, a desire for the acknowledgment of claims to authentic identity, with all the legal consequences pertaining thereto, and a desire to cease being incorrectly identified as "negro, black, and colored."

In one of the most comprehensive and compelling critiques of the politics of recognition, Glen Sean Coulthard argues that "when delegated exchanges of recognition occur in real world contexts of domination the terms of accommodation usually end up being determined by and in the interests of the hegemonic partner in the relationship."[66] Drawing on Frantz Fanon, Coulthard holds that in such situations the (colonizing) state projects its own values onto those populations seeking recognition, granting rights to citizens that are, in Fanon's words, "white liberty and white justice," values imposed by colonial oppressors.[67]

Aliite thought offers a useful example to consider in light of these critiques. Aliites deny that the values they hold are "white" values, insisting, instead, that the values they associate with American democracy and citizenship are part and parcel of true law rather than the creations of a given state or culture. These are divine values, values universal for and natural to all humanity. Such a stance, key to Ali's theory of citizenship, reflects power dynamics, as I have argued. Aliites see the power of the state as overwhelming. They *recognize* that their only hope—first for survival, then for achieving social change—involves protection from the state by the state, and that state recognition is, as Coulthard puts it, "profoundly *asymmetrical* and *nonreciprocal* . . . either imposed on or granted to" minorities by the state.[68] By laying claim to ideals that are, in turn, recognized by the state as the state's own ideals, Aliites accomplish a kind of intellectual *aikido*, using the strength of the state against the state. Aliites seek salvation through inclusion in the state, but they also struggle for the salvation *of* the state by working to align the state with what they insist are its original ideals. Aliites insist that America is predicated on ideals synonymous with true law, but in order to advance that claim, Aliites must first be recognized as citizens.

In this, Aliite politics of recognition departs from the Hegelian "master/slave" model which Coulthard—again, following Fanon—locates at the core of most politics of recognition. As Fanon wrote, in such a relation, "the master laughs at the consciousness of the slave. What he wants from the slave is not recognition but work."[69] Aliite thought, however, insists that legal recognition comes with palpable effects. There *is* a difference between a slave and a citizen, and recognition by the state is what brings about that difference—this is precisely the difference between a Negro and a Moor.

While Aliites also emphasize the need for what Coulthard calls "*self-affirmative* cultural practices" and empowerment from within the community, even these never exist in full separation from the power of the state and the necessity, for Aliite survival, of its favor. Likewise, such practices of self-affirmation—namely, the emphasis on a concept of divine love that begins with self-love and radiates out to include all humanity (discussed in chapter 4), and the pleasures, pride, and experience of the truth of identity that occur in Aliite social experiments predicated on self-determination and a degree of remove from wider society (the topic of chapter 7)—are understood by Aliites as part of the larger project of citizenship, the transformation of society through true law. Even the most seemingly private, intimately personal Aliite act—affirming self-love in front of a mirror, as described by Sharif A. Bey (see chapter 4)—is explicitly located within a society defined by state power *and* as part of an Aliite ethics and eschatology in which self-love must be understood, by the individual, as the starting point of a broader project of civic transformation.

Rather than, as Coulthard urges, engaging in self-affirmation as a political practice, in contrast "to relying too heavily on the subjectifying apparatus of the state or other dominant institutions of power to do this for them," Aliites insist that, above and beyond all practices of self-affirmation, they must still rely on the state.[70] Such necessity is understood not only in terms of practical awareness of state power and potential, brutal, violent force, but is also explained, in Aliite thought, by the belief that such state apparatuses and institutions are the means by which humans can bring about Allah's plan for the perfection of the world. The legal systems of the state are the way humans can work to align the world with true law.

To insist that one is not a slave is never enough. One must be recognized as other than a slave by the power of the state in order to escape—to achieve a degree of "salvation"—from the status of slavery. But, in Ali's worldview, one must also engage in the work of citizenship, exercising that status as other-than-slave, *being* a Moor. To be a Moor can involve momentary experiences of sovereignty, the display of authentic identity, and both self- and communal affirmation, but never is the power of the state absent from such events. In Aliite understanding, there is no self-determination completely outside the state, the favor of which is understood as essential for any Aliite undertaking—indeed, for Aliite survival.

4

BENEATH THE WINGS AND THE SHADOW OF THE EAGLE

Aliite Sovereignty and the Power of the State

THE EAGLE'S TWO FISTS

BENEATH THE STARS OF SOVEREIGNTY, the Great Seal features the bald eagle, the animal symbol of the United States. Wings displayed, its feet are spread, its breast covered in a heraldic crest the red, white, and blue of the country's flag. Clutched in the talons of its left foot, the eagle holds a bundle of thirteen arrows representing the United States as an unbreakable union of individual states, as well as the martial might of the country. A predator of remarkable speed and precision, armed here with a set of projectiles, the eagle signifies the power—the potential violence—of the state. Yet the bird's head is facing what its other foot holds: an olive branch (with thirteen leaves and thirteen olives), indicating an inclination for peace, a peace guaranteed by the weapons at the ready, the widespread wings, and the protective shield. At once a metaphor for U.S. tactical and military dominance, internal intelligence apparatuses and armed agents, the eagle is also a symbol of a peaceful political system. The state, as represented here, offers both threat and stability. Aliites, once recognized as citizens, see themselves as under the shelter of the eagle's wings. As Dingle-El says, with Ali's teachings of Moorish identity, "the great eagle spread her wings over the new foundation [of citizenship through proclamation of nationality] and vowed to protect" the MSTA community.[1] The danger inherent in the eagle's talons and arrows, however, remains a constant fact of Aliite existence.

This chapter considers the power of the state, a ubiquitous concern for Aliite thought, in relation to a particular kind of Aliite practice of law— direct encounter with and argumentation before representatives of the power of the state. This type of Aliite practice involves argumentation for Aliite legal knowledge and protocol in courtrooms and on the street, be- fore judges and police officers. The stakes of such exchanges are high, for these officials represent state power. These agents of the state personify the threatening might of the American eagle, able to do harm to those whom they encounter, sending them to prison, imposing fines, unleashing raw violence—beatings, even death—against them. Yet, in keeping with Aliite understandings of citizenship as salvation, of the state as protection from the state, Aliites use such encounters to attempt to convert and compel state agents to accept true law. To be a citizen, in Aliite understanding, is to be part of the collective body of this fierce bird of the state, to take refuge be- hind its shield. To be a citizen is to have a hand in determining the future of the state. Legal performances in courtrooms and on the streets serve as essential aspects of the struggle of citizenship, to align America with All- Law's law.

When Dingle-El speaks of the American eagle, he does so in the context of that Aliite origin tale of recognition of Moorish identity (and endorse- ment of the Aliite mission) by the authority of the state:

In 1912, the Prophet Noble Drew Ali appeared in Washington D.C., at the nation's capital, and asked President Woodrow Wilson for his people and the return of our flag (the proverbial Cherry Tree), chopped down by General George Washington, 1776. The President states that he wouldn't know where to find the Moorish flag since it has been stored away for so long. The Prophet told him that he knew where to find it, if given per- mission to enter the storage room. Prophet Noble Drew Ali went and re- trieved our flag, the Moorish flag. He then asked Mr. Wilson why did the government record the Asiatic as Moors on official record, and in actual practice label them Negro, Black, Colored and Ethiopians? Mr. Wilson's reply was that we know nothing of our national descent and birthright, and it would not be in the interest of the American people to wake us up to the truth about ourselves. Prophet Noble Drew Ali asked for the right to teach us the truth about ourselves and our Divine Creed. Mr. Wilson told the Prophet that we would not accept him or his teaching because he was of the same pigmentation of skin as we were and we would not accept our own. To prove his point he told our Prophet to go out and get 5,000 to follow him. He was so sure he could not get anyone to follow him, he reduced the figure to 50. Prophet Noble Drew Ali went out and sounded the trumpet and began to teach the everlasting Gospel to the lost tribes of Isra-el. Ten thousand answer the call. With this, the Prophet returned to Washington and was given authorization to teach Islam and to return our nationality to us. At this commitment by the government of the United States, the former slaves were finally acknowledged as a separate nation of people and the fact accepted that they were the true owner of this land called America. The great eagle spread her wings over the new foundation and vowed to protect it.[2]

This richly detailed account demonstrates the way Aliite religion incorporates aspects of varied traditions. There are echoes in this narrative of traditional Islamic accounts of the *mir'aj*, or Night Journey, wherein the Prophet Muhammad travels from Mecca to Jerusalem and up to the highest level of heaven. In that narrative tradition, the Prophet meets with Islamic luminaries, such as Jesus and Moses, and receives from Allah himself instructions on the daily prayers, which, as in this story, were reduced from an original number of fifty down to a mere five after negotiation between the Prophet and the sovereign deity. In describing the Moorish people as the "lost tribes of Isra-el," Dingle-El references strands of Hebrew Israelite thought within Aliite religion.[3] In calling Moors "the true owner of this land called America," he references Moorish claims to indigenous status. In this narrative's assertion, from the character of President Wilson, that African Americans will not accept the authority of one of their own, there is a reminder of the brainwashing and related self-loathing instilled, Aliites say, with the concept of "race" and its historical application in slavery and segregation.

In this telling, notably, President Wilson is opposed to Ali's mission, insisting that "it would not be in the interest of the American people" for Moors to come into consciousness of their true identity (and legal status). Wilson's resistance, however, is ultimately overwritten by the throng of "former slaves" rejecting their false Negro identity and proclaiming their authentic nationality. Against this tide of people speaking the true law, "the government of the United States" has no choice but to accept Moorish claims. Then the American state, symbolized by the eagle, does not cease to exist, but rather "spread[s] her wings" over her Moorish children. They *are* American now, a "separate nation" within a mosaic of other nationalities, and they are now—as

"true owners" of the American project, the people of the universal prophet—
America, "the new foundation" of what the state can and must become.

Ali, confronting the president of the United States, "stood his square,"
standing firm and fast in truth. A popular term in Aliite thought, to "stand
one's square" means to face state representatives "with just your word,"
speaking true law to legal authority.[4] Ali, in this moment, was sovereign in
his status as citizen and his exercise of citizenship. He instantiated a mode
of sovereignty Aliites identify as existing through legal encounters between
themselves and representatives of state power. A fleeting experience facilitated by one's status as a citizen, a status that allows for being heard by representatives of the state, this mode of sovereignty occurs through practice
of true law and is understood as the sovereignty of the citizen, a concept
discussed throughout American legal and political history. Aliites locate
such sovereignty in the tacit acknowledgment granted the citizen by legal
protocol, which they read as recognition by state power. Through such recognition, Aliites experience a temporary sovereignty "as citizens," sheltered
under, even empowered by, the wings of the American eagle.[5] This mode
of sovereignty is related to, but separate from, that of citizens united into a
constituency and thus, as a bloc, negotiating with the power of the state, as
well as from the ultimate sovereignty attributed by Aliites to true law itself.

Likewise important to the Aliite confrontations with agents of the
state—in courts and on the street—is Aliite faith in true law's persuasive
potential, an extension of the notion that knowledge of and desire for such
true law is innate and natural to all human beings, a result of their creation
by Allah. "All men desire at heart, freedom, justice, and equality."[6] People
of all nationalities share a tendency toward this desire, however concealed
or forgotten it may currently be, and accessing this knowledge is easiest
through experience of love, understood as an attribute of and synonym for
true law and Allah. "Allah is love," as Ali wrote in the MSTA "Divine Constitution and By-laws."[7] Self-love, inextricable from authentic knowledge of
identity, leads, in the Aliite schema, to love of community, which then extends to a universal love of all people, in keeping with Ali's vision of democracy. Yet in keeping with that vision of society as a patchwork of different
nations and lions lying down with lambs, love, as that valence of law felt in
the individual "heart," is understood within Aliite thought as a challenge
to the power of the state and the means by which Aliites accept the status
quo. The individual citizen can confront the power of the American eagle
through love of/as law, but in the perfected society, the rich and poor will lie
down together in harmony because they will both have been granted equal

access to such representatives of power, equal hearing, and equal justice, if not full equality.

This chapter begins with Aliite understandings of love and its link to knowledge of true law and Ali's eschatological vision for society, moving next to specific instances of Aliite practice of law that have been recorded and published online, where they serve as popular instructional tools within Aliite communities and as examples to be celebrated of Aliites bravely facing off against the state, armed only with true law. In such instances, respectful acknowledgment by representatives of the state is read, by Aliites, as recognition, regardless of the outcome of such encounters. This lack of concern for outcome—as well as the idiosyncratic use of legal vocabulary—confuses agents of the state, one reason Aliites are so often categorized as "sovereign citizens," a reductive and criminalizing label. After an examination of the use of this term, particularly by watchdog organizations that blatantly misrepresent Aliite communities, I conclude the chapter with comparative thoughts on what Aliite practice of the law reveals about subaltern communities and their ability to coexist with and navigate the nearly infinite power of the state from a position that claims to have no power *but* the power of law.

"LOVE IS THE LAW": TRUE LAW AS COMPELLING POWER

For Aliites, law is metaphysically real, universal, and transcendent; it is an eternal ideal, outside human history, yet capable of being appealed to and invoked in order to change human history. Aliites believe true law has a particular compelling power because the ability to know true law is inherent in all humans as creations of Allah. While rational arguments—and evidentiary data—are important to Aliite legal discourse, true law also resonates with something essential and innate within human consciousness. Humans can recognize and have a natural desire to accept true law, a principle of faith assuring that the Aliite struggle of citizenship will not, ultimately, be futile. People of every nationality contain their own "virtue or godlike quality," a trace of the divine within that, according to Aliite thought, can be cultivated and increased.[8] This ability to ascertain truth is understood as a quality of "heart," operating through what Mungin Bey calls "the Law of Learning." The transformative power of law is exemplified through love,

love that increases with personal development along a trajectory beginning with acceptance of authentic identity and love of self.[9] Aliites identify true law as synonymous with the ideals of love, truth, peace, freedom, and justice; of these, law *as love* is most frequently linked to the sense of natural, innate knowledge within humans. "Divine Love" unlocks the "secrets of Divine Law," one contemporary Aliite text argues. Love allows for perception of true law, and those who "cannot see" such law "have not experienced Love."[10] Love's centrality in the uplift of society was described by Ali himself, who called it "the remedy for the ills of today . . . all turning about the pivot of Love—love for humanity."[11]

In one articulation of this theory, Sharif A. Bey describes love as a phenomenon that radiates outward in concentric circles, accompanied by waves of responsibility. Love begins with the individual's acceptance of his or her authentic identity, extends to the national community, and finally becomes universal. Speaking in favor of the radical "empowerment" that comes with knowledge of one's correct "cultural heritage" and nationality, A. Bey frames such empowerment as always also dependent on being "recognized and respected" within society, by the power of the state. Love cannot exist in a vacuum from society but is naturally linked to social responsibility. To realize that one is a Moor and not a Negro "puts you on equal footing with everyone else" if that nationality is recognized. The dependence on recognition here, however, does not discount the internal mental transformations that occur and the behavioral changes that follow from such transformations. A. Bey insists that only when we "change our self-perspective," or "start with proper identification" can the view that others hold change.

A. Bey argues that a Moor no longer approaches "the world as an adversary" the way "blacks" do. Moors no longer see society as "alien" and thus are not bound to stay "in the hood," trapped—by their own lack of knowledge—in what A. Bey calls "a concentration camp with no walls, socially, politically, and economically." Self-knowledge and the self-love that follows from it, the pride in and love of nationality that result from realizing one's true identity, all this offers an individual a "place in the world," and both allows and requires that the Moor become "a productive member of society"—a citizen, in other words.

Rather than offering the practice of love as an alternative to the politics of recognition discussed in chapter 3 (the sort of alternative Coulthard theorizes in his work), A. Bey locates his system within the shadow of state power. He sets his example of love in action in a jail, within the carceral system of the state—a locale, moreover, with which he assumes his audience will be familiar. "When 'black people,' 'African Americans,' go to jail, we're like a cat in a room full of rocking chairs." "Blacks"—those unconscious of or rejecting their true Moorish heritage—posture and front and fight with their "own" people, approaching jail as a place of competition, hostility, threat, an environment where lashing out at other "blacks" is the natural reaction. They suffer from their own self-image, and they suffer because self-image shapes how people see the world. In contrast to this, A. Bey talks about the way Puerto Rican prisoners act. Instead of fighting, they "surround and embrace" and support each other, enacting unity and compassion. This is because Puerto Ricans embrace, recognize, and love their nationality.

> [They] are very proud of their heritage. When a Puerto Rican looks at himself in the mirror every morning, he's not just looking at him, he's looking at the *Boricua* heritage. It makes him so proud. . . . So when he sees himself, he loves himself. So when he sees his fellow man, and he sees himself, it's love on its face, it's love on sight.[12]

The "black" prisoners are imprisoned mentally as well as physically, trapped in ignorance just as they are caged by the legal system, refusing to accept their own humanity. Their lack of love is linked to lack of knowledge of nationality, lack of knowledge of true law, while the Puerto Ricans, who cultivate love of self, come to know—and enact—love for nationality, humanity, and true law. Reiterating Ali's stance that slaves were responsible for their own enslavement, MSTA thinker Amen A. El elaborates on this Aliite theory of love, describing the absence of love of nationality as "feelings of self-loathing, guilt or inferiority," as the source of "our aggressiveness, our violence, our paranoia, and our sometimes downright obnoxious social behaviors" as "a fallen community" corrupted by accepting a false identity.[13] In contrast to this, the experience of love for one's authentic self is inextricable from knowledge of law. "*Self-realization* consists in establishing oneself confidently in the awareness, which asserts that man is part and parcel of Allah" and Allah's plan.[14] Love of one's true identity thus becomes the first stage in the uplift of fallen humanity, the "'*great work*' of reintegration or synthesis."[15] This great work begins in the heart, with love that acts as a bridge between self, nationality, divine law, and the world-transforming work of citizenship.

When the Washitaw declare that "love is law," they are flagging the privileged, intimate, affective reality of love as a form of human knowledge and a means of connection between the self, the community, God, society, law, and salvific mission. Love can function this way for all humans, and Aliites see this as the persuasive power of true law. Thus, speaking true law to representatives of the state hinges, also, on love, as Aliites are not just arguing with logic and evidence but also appealing to the knowledge of true law that all humans have inherent within them as creations of Allah. The judges or police officers who insist upon interpretations of the legal that conflict with the true law can be "corrected" in their understanding, just as Aliites can correct their status by coming to knowledge of their true identity. In both cases, knowledge is inextricable from love: love of ancestry and self and community for the Aliite; love of true law and the divine design inherent in the world in the case of the agent of the state. When Aliites express confidence that representatives of the legal system are "lovers of truth," they are holding to a faith that those people have hearts that can be changed, hearts naturally inclined to recognize and desire true law.[16]

THE SOVEREIGNTY OF THE
CITIZEN PRACTICING LAW

Standing before state authorities and performing true law is understood by many Aliites as a responsibility, an essential aspect of the work of citizenship, a religious duty, and a direct experience of the transcendence that is true law. Much of Aliite literature and media is thus devoted to instructing Aliites on such practice of law—not merely "learning law" and learning "constitutional rights" but also learning the specific skills of *propia persona, pro se,* or self-representing, legal practice.[17] The protocol for Aliite practice of law does not always resemble that expected or even accepted by the legal system; rather, the citizen's responsibility to speak true law is prioritized. Aliite texts emphasize this, such as T. King Connally-Bey's *Enter Nationalnomics (The King-dom of Divine Free-dom): The Moorish Code,* which frames its advice on courtroom behavior as practical: address the judge with respect but speak to the authorities of "the name of law, Truth and justice."[18]

Aliites believe that through their invocation of true law within legal discourse, within encounters with authorities of the legal interpretation of the state, they experience a mode of sovereignty. They become what Marianne Constable calls "minisovereigns," a reality understood in terms of the concept of the citizen as sovereign, as advanced in American legal history.[19] Aliites insist that citizens "are sovereign, not subjects," in the American system.[20] Simultaneously having awareness of, standing against, and drawing upon the power and authority of the state, Aliite thinkers cite judicial opinions to bolster their own claims to sovereignty in relation to the sovereign state.[21] This sovereignty of the citizen is always fleeting and temporary, instantiated and experienced through the "legal proceeding" itself—that contest or "encounter," as Lawrence Rosen puts it, "between contending parties seeking confirmation of their respective claims, [that] carefully staged ritual aimed at the exorcism of potential chaos, [that] life-threatening confrontation with the manifest power of the state."[22]

One locale where Aliites experience sovereignty through legal performance is in the courtroom. Courts stand as "important sites for public performance of resistance by individuals and groups," as Hirsch and Lazarus-Black have argued.[23] "Subordinated peoples [do not] come to courts only as victims or supplicants," they come to argue for their own interpretations of law and the legal, to exert their own authority, and to use "their words and actions" to contest and claim both "power and law" as represented by the courts.[24] The courtroom, as Richard Sherwin has argued, becomes a site of spectacle, "an arena in which purification of deep cultural meanings may occur."[25] As Aliites insist upon a contrast between law, as ideal, and those legal interpretations generated and enforced by the courts, courts necessarily become sites of contestation for Aliites. For them, courts are public venues for testimony about and appeal to true law. Appearing before representatives of the political and legal establishment, demanding recognition of their identity and claims, Aliites use the courts to perform acts of resistance, even refusal, critique, and public education aimed not only at the audience (present in the courtroom and, through posting of videos of such performances, at home) but also at the judge.

Aliites generally appear in court as *pro se* litigants, enacting their authentic identity and the knowledge of true law understood as inherent in that identity. By standing in the courtroom, speaking truth to power, Aliites enter into a sovereign state in the temporal sense: not an "institutionalized political order" but, rather, a "condition of being" that follows from and manifests "new ways of thinking about law and power."[26] Sovereignty is thus experienced in what Georges Bataille calls "miraculous moments," which, in their visceral power, reaffirm rational claims.[27] For Aliites, the sovereignty experienced in the courtroom is a matter of subjectivity, an essential Aliite form of selfhood through law. As Hirsch and Lazarus-Black write:

The making of subjectivity through law is a particularly intimate locus
for the operation of hegemony and resistance. Contestations over the
"states of being" of individuals also implicate social struggles involving
political "states." In transforming people and polities, hegemonic processes and oppositional practices—and the contested states that they
produce—are inextricably linked to law.[28]

For Aliites, practice of the law offers an intimate experience of the power
of law as law's true form manifests in the fallible human legal system. Legal
institutions open a space for a discussion of the difference between ideal
law and the legal as socially interpreted and enforced. Aliite practice of law
in such settings is not merely a display of identity, akin to wearing a fez, but
is understood as a moment of recognition by the power of the state, akin to
the "Our Authority" document.

Like that document, Aliite courtroom performances are held up by Aliites as evidence of such recognition. Such performances are, when possible,
distributed, usually in video form (but sometimes merely in covertly recorded audio form) on the internet, where they become the center of discussions of Aliite claims and serve as models for future Aliite legal practice. This is the case regardless of whether the Aliite in question "won" or
"lost" his or her case; what matters is the performance, the act of speaking
law within the very institution devoted to, but—woefully, from an Aliite
standpoint—ignorant of, true law. The outcome or result of the appearance,
the decision by the judge, does not alter the sovereignty experienced within
the encounter itself, the affirmation of citizenship status offered by the opportunity to speak to representatives of the power of the state, to be heard
and even addressed by one's chosen, Aliite name. Chastisement from the
bench or even a prison sentence cannot take away from such an experience.
The same emphasis on tacit acknowledgment as recognition, on presence
before state authorities as recognition, can be seen in the *Murakush Jurisprudence: Case Law* series compiled by Shyaam Al Muharrir. These com-
pilations of Moorish legal decisions serve as a counterhistory of Moorish
jurisprudence and a series of precedents to be cited in future Aliite legal arguments, even though Moors lost all of the cases these books compile.[29] No
analysis is offered in Al Muharrir's books. All of the text included in these
(rather expensive) print-on-demand books is publicly available, yet collected as a book (and a series of books), the text serves as material evidence
of state recognition of Aliite sovereignty. As Mathur argued regarding the
material artifacts of bureaucracy, these artifacts of jurisprudence also "open

themselves up to multiple interpretations," offering proof of recognition of Aliite legal claims and the temporary sovereignty instantiated by Moorish *pro se* litigants.[30] The notion that a claimant to sovereignty can see the state as *endorsing* claims made in conflict with it simply by *acknowledging* them is central to Audra Simpson's work on Mohawk practices of sovereignty. For the Mohawk, and for the Aliites, sovereignty is used to describe actions undertaken by those who, while resolutely not in the position of unfettered power described by Carl Schmitt, nonetheless *can* engage in behaviors that *feel* like exceptionally decisive strokes of sovereignty—primarily because such moves thrust the actor into a position where she or he is negotiating directly with another sovereign. When a Mohawk refuses to produce a passport at the Canada/United States border, for instance, the claim of sovereignty made via this act of refusal is countered by the crossing guard, as an official representative of the power of the sovereign American nation-state. Yet simply by *engaging* in this encounter, that representative has tacitly acknowledged what the Mohawk interprets as her or his own sovereignty. The same is true for Aliites, with what happens after that moment of sovereignty being, in one sense, inconsequential, just as, for the Mohawks in Simpson's book, denial of passage can be seen as separate from the act of acknowledging the sovereign claim.

This dynamic—that the courtroom appearance itself, the performance, can be the goal for Aliites, rather than "winning" a case—leads to confusion for judges and lawyers who do not share this attitude or understand the logic behind what may appear to them to be a counterintuitive stance. Judges cite procedures and precedents at odds with the procedures and precedents similarly insisted upon but understood differently by Aliites. Moreover, while the vocabularies used by Aliites and state officials in courtroom encounters overlap, they often assign radically different meanings to the same words. With few common definitions or understandings between judges and Aliites, Aliite discourse has been described in legal rulings as a "senseless shuffling of legal terms" and a patchwork of "legally-senseless colloquial layperson's expressions."[31] Judges can become frustrated or confused, and can oscillate between attempting to instruct Aliites on proper procedure within the legal system and expressing outrage at the vernacular legal knowledge and practice being directed at them by Aliites.

One popular instance of such a sovereign state of performance of the law, posted online and viewed more than 1.5 million times, begins with a judge, surrounded by piles of *pro se* legal paperwork, admitting to being "discombobulated." Her confusion, however, quickly turns to anger. "You can read me this until the cows come home," she says to Amir KC El, in a black fez, who has been quoting from and citing legal decisions regarding jurisdiction as part of his rejection of her—and her court's—authority. "You can read it *ad nauseum* and *ad infinitum*. It doesn't change the fact that until the issue is brought appropriately before this court no ruling in regard to jurisdiction is ever going to be made." The Moorish defendant responds by declaring his intent to sue everyone in the courtroom.[32] In this video entitled "Moors in Court Got the Judge SHOOK!" the judge comes across, in fact, as calm, patient, instructing KC El in what she takes to be the proper, authoritative, and recognized legal procedure for raising questions of jurisdiction. KC El, however, is uninterested in the procedural details; he motions, ultimately, "that this court be dismissed." Yet evasion of a charge is only part of what is happening here. Rather than slipping out of the grasp of the law, KC El is performing his self-understood mastery of it, demonstrating his knowledge of the law and enacting his critique of the current corrupt state of the legal system.

Standing before the court—indeed, lecturing the judge on the law—KC El here is performing and experiencing sovereignty as a fleeting state of being. Such sovereignty is facilitated by the framework of the court, which requires a representative of the power of the state to give KC El's claims a hearing. It is the hearing that allows for the experience of sovereignty, a hearing read as recognition of one sovereign by another. Being heard is here an extension of the "equal hearing" principle, which Barry Sullivan has argued is "not simply a necessary structural element in a system of adjudication, but a normative requirement that constitutes part of the professional and moral obligation of judges."[33] Legal hearing is an ethical act, one recognized and valorized by citizens—such as Aliites—who understand the legal system to offer, in Sally Merry's words "the possibility of power."[34] In court, one's voice is heard, and one can appeal to the power of the system to address wrongs that one would otherwise be powerless to address. This access is understood, additionally, as a direct benefit of citizenship status, a characteristic of America's just design (even if the administration and enforcement of the legal system is often anything but just). "Recourse to court is rooted in such deep-seated cultural traditions of American society as individualism, equality, faith in the law, and the search for freedom from the control of neighbors and local leaders, traditions noted by Tocqueville early in the nineteenth century," Merry writes.[35] For Aliites, having one's voice heard also represents a chance to testify to the power of the true law in the hopes that the system, as represented by the judge or the police officer, will recognize its own errors of interpretation, be moved in heart and mind to correct such interpretations and align them with the true law spoken by Aliites.

Hence the climax of "Moors in Court Got the Judge SHOOK!" is not the announcement of the outcome of the proceeding, but the moment of most expertly exhibited skill—KC El's rapid-fire series of quotations and citations demonstrating his mastery of legal knowledge.[36] Rejecting the jurisdiction of the judge through reliance on previous legal cases and what he presents as accepted legal definitions, KC El uses U.S. law to contest this instantiation of the legal system. The judge is wrong because she does not know the true law; KC El is correct because he does. Richard Sherwin has noted the emotional power of litigants witnessing the state seeming to "cave" in response to skillful negotiation of legal protocol.[37] With Aliites, the state is often perceived as being chastised—or being guilty—in the face of statements of true law. Sherwin also notes that the rituals of the courts can be seen as having "become rigid, stale, deprived of the dynamism of symbolic drama . . . [and thus] perceived as sites for the exercise of naked power and illicit prejudice alone."[38] Aliite intervention in the courtroom turns this notion on its head: the courts are, in Aliite understanding, *revealed* to be corrupt sites of naked power and prejudice, and yet court representatives are shaken by their confrontation with truth. Such encounters are infused with symbolic drama. These dramatic performances, in turn, are distributed to potentially huge audiences, many members of which already share Aliite understandings of law and its relation to the legal, and thus have preconceptions about what they are watching. KC El's performance is understood by its intended audience, in accordance with the title this video has been given, as an instance of "shaking" the legal system. Regardless of the outcome declared by the judge, KC El has successfully "stood his square" and spoken truth, exemplified sovereignty, and offered a template for others to follow.

The sovereignty of the citizen experienced via practice of the law need not happen only in the courtroom, though it is almost guaranteed there, if Aliites operate within the basic framework of courtroom protocol. Such an experience can occur on the streets as well, though there it is more tenuous and, indeed, carries with it physical risks. Consider a confrontation between a young Moor and a police officer, recorded and posted on YouTube, which begins as a citizen's challenge to the agent of law enforcement for clarity regarding what law he, the citizen, has violated. "What law?" the Moor demands. "Recite it for me, sir." This exchange soon becomes an impromptu lecture, by the Moor, on the role of law in America as protecting rights, as siding for the oppressed. "I'm gonna show you what the Constitution of the United States says . . . the Supreme Court," the Moor begins. Rebuffed, he responds with another question: "Do you believe in the Supreme Court? Do you believe the Supreme Court is the law of the land?" The Moor's words, at the conclusion of the confrontation, express disbelief that there is such a divide between law, as understood in Aliite thought, and the legal, as understood and enforced by established institutions in society: "Wow. . . . And y'all supposed to be men of the law?"[39] The Moor's fate here remains unknown, and it is easy to imagine— even with the presence of the camera, recording the exchange—that it could end in violence, violence at the hand of an agent of the state. Yet in this precarious moment of encounter the Aliite enacts sovereignty and performs citizenship, receiving recognition for as long as the officer continues to listen to him, performing his knowledge of and appealing to true law in the hope of persuading this "man of the law" to come to the correct understanding.

The police officer is, of course, armed, and the Moor believes himself to be armed as well—armed with knowledge of the true law. The encounter could end violently, in catastrophe for the Moor. For those fleeting moments, however, the imbalance of power is potentially checked—at least called into question—by the Aliite insistence on a parallel imbalance of knowledge of true law. While the encounter could end badly for the Aliite, it could also end another way, with the officer accepting the teaching of true law, not only recognizing the Aliite as citizen but also being transformed by this work of citizenship, coming into consciousness of law in contrast to the fallible and unjust legal system the officer currently serves. Viewers are left in suspense—though, again, what matters most is the standing before the state, the squaring off, armed with truth, against the authority of the legal system. Such videos exhibit and thus offer evidence of Aliite sovereignty through true law, while also reiterating beliefs about an oppressive legal system.

Another popular online video—viewed more than 275,000 times— records a dramatic meltdown by a judge. After repeated objections and the recitation of legal citation after legal citation by the fez-wearing Aliite standing *pro se* before him, the judge slams his hand on his desk, yelling, "I'm tired of it!"

"We're done," he says, with "this mess," and he rises and walks out of chambers, even as the Aliite continues, right hand raised, to submit what he takes to be relevant facts "for the record."

"You can put whatever you want on the record, I'm done," the judge says, his back turned to the courtroom.[40]

This frustrated judge had decided, and was attempting to communicate, that the persistent paperwork and questions of jurisdiction raised by the

Moor, one Chancey El, had led him to rescind a previous ruling permitting *pro se* representation; the judge was now holding that only a *licensed* practitioner of the law for the state of New Jersey could serve as counsel. In the video, however, the judge's exasperation reads as surrender, a retreat before the barrage of true law performed by the Aliite. Chancey El repeatedly says, "for the record, on the record, and let the record show." He's speaking for posterity, into the chronicle of history, aware of multiple audiences in the present and future, including, surely, those Moors with him in the courtroom (one was ordered by the judge to move behind the barrier, back into the audience section, at the start of this clip), as well as those conscious and unconscious Aliites who might watch this video in its afterlife online. Richard Sherwin has argued that "law in our time has entered the age of images. Legal reality can no longer be properly understood, or assessed, apart from what appears on the screen," but the screens that are now ubiquitous are those used not merely for watching but also to facilitate engagement, dialogue, and debate, even the creation of communities of belief.[41]

The audience for Chancey El's performance, for instance, express their opinion through the interactive comments section on the webpage: they are overwhelmingly of the opinion that the Moor was in the right—"smart as hell," with accurate knowledge of the law, and courageous, "with the balls to stand up to the system"—while the judge was in the wrong. Indeed, the judge's emotional reaction offers evidence, to commentators, of his awareness that he was being called out for lack of knowledge of the law or outright corruption. "Look at the judge run . . . he couldn't handle it. They like it easy when people are ignorant of the law," one comment states, while another holds that the "sorry ass Judge got pissed because he got his ass handed to him on a Silver Platter"; one even says that "the judge deserves to be hung for treason, period." Chancey El's failure to preserve his ability to perform the law *pro se* is irrelevant to the success of this performance. The drama of the encounter serves to underline the power of such true law, to disrupt and disturb, to shake the legal system that refuses to recognize true law. "Go brother! What a rush! This man is a hero!" one commenter writes, while another expresses the expectation that this confrontation will eventually find its way before the Supreme Court. The video of the unnamed Moor expounding on true law to the police officer, posted with the title "POLICE VS MOOR—Who do you think is right? Plz share ur Opinon," also generates an active thread of commentary, primarily celebrating this Moor as an example for all citizens to learn and be able to cite the law, along with a lament that "as usual the Law Agents were not trained properly."[42] "Ignorance of the law is no excuse," the Moor in that video insists; Aliite viewers of such videos seem, overwhelmingly, to agree.

Aliite legal performance is a delicate balance between respect and argument, appeal and correction. Aliite religion, always aware that "the United States do wield the heaviest stick," as Robert Cover puts it (referencing the "superior brute force" of the state), seeks to be *jurigenerative* (law-making) through the courts, through the legal apparatuses of the state, urging not merely recognition of, but also compliance with, Aliite claims of true law through direct encounters with representatives of the state.[43] Aliites understand their claims of law, of course, as truth, and, as such, they understand their encounters with the legal system to have the power of that true law behind them. Aliites view their practice of the law—on all levels, from claiming and enacting identity to advancing arguments before the courts—to be "law-making" as T. R. S. Allan describes it: "a dialogue" over normative claims, but one that seeks to persuade those in positions of power that their interpretations represent a departure from true law.[44] Like Ali's prophetic mission, Aliite performance of law serves as a call for all human beings to *return* to the true law as laid out for all nations by Allah—true law, the knowledge of which is innate in human beings.

"PAPER TERRORISM": SOVEREIGNTY, CITIZENSHIP, LAW, LEGALITY, AND LABELS

Aliites are routinely accused of disregarding the law, even as representing, in one judge's words, "a notorious organization of scofflaws and ne'er-do-wells."[45] This criminalization happens explicitly in relation to Aliite practices of the law. Aliites are described as law-breakers due to those moments when they seek out representatives of the legal system and speak true law to them. By exercising their rights as citizens to be heard, by seeking recognition from state authorities through legal protocol, Aliites are labeled by law enforcement, the media, and members of the judiciary as "sovereign citizens." This distorting term, confusing on its face as it implies that the sovereignty of the citizen is not a tradition of American politics and law but rather an exercise of contempt of law, has come to be equated with, as one booklet on "sovereign citizen" thought and practice puts it, the "lawless."[46] While those who self-identify as "sovereign citizens" do so out of a stated devotion to law—understood, as in Aliite thought, to signify true, "natural law," usually also explicitly God's law—the term has become a way to dismiss and even criminalize vernacular legal theory and performance.

As an explicit, though diverse, ideology, "sovereign citizen" thought represents the development of theories of tax protest and limited jurisdiction, alongside idolization of the original U.S. Constitution as an exceptional representation of natural law. These theories were solidified by a range of thinkers in the 1980s, when such ideas held appeal to farmers across the American heartland who were facing foreclosure and economic hardships. Spread today through websites and publications, conventions and telephone conference calls, "sovereign citizen" thought and practice emphasizes that much of the current legal system is illegal. As part of this argument on the illegality of dominant legal interpretations, "sovereign citizen" thinkers turn to common law, the Uniform Commercial Code, rejection of the Fourteenth and Fifteenth Amendments as unratified, and various critiques and conspiracy theories about banking systems.

There are several unifying claims and practices across the diverse movement. First is the belief that certain taxes are illegitimate—an illegal overreach of governmental authority, in violation of the Constitution. Second is the belief that government overreach has occurred, too, in terms of regulatory and especially law enforcement agencies, which therefore do not have the legal jurisdiction they claim. This second facet of "sovereign citizen" ideology emphasizes the legal authority of the local sheriff and local citizenry—as posse and as jury—rejecting federal intrusion in local legal matters and therefore frequently rejecting the authority of the court system. Third is the claim to an authentic legal identity as "sovereign U.S. citizens," who engage in the practice of citizenship, from public protest and community organizing and education to legal practice, including "weaponized" legal filings, such as illegitimate real estate liens or tax forms, what law enforcement has termed acts of "paper terrorism." Fourth, related to this sense of claiming an authentic identity and the legal consequences thereof, "sovereign citizens" adopt new names to differentiate their living being from the legal fiction called a "person." These names can be unpronounceable or visually unique—with the inclusion of punctuation or special characters, for instance—as a way of linking the name to the irreproducible, distinct human form. Use of personal stamps and fingerprints, even signing a name in blood or, as a substitute, red ink, is part of this insistence on stopping the slippage from living being to legal fiction, from free individual to entity within a system outside one's control.[47]

The theories and practices of law within the "sovereign citizen" movement share some traits with Aliite thought and practice, and some Aliites are in dialogue with and even identify as "sovereign citizens." Still, the use of the label by law enforcement, the media, and the courts obfuscates Aliite logic and criminalizes Aliite existence, framing Aliites as dangerous, violent extremists and con artists operating in contempt of the law—criminals rejecting America and affiliation as Americans.

The watchdog organizations most dedicated to use of the term, and which are therefore responsible for its proliferation—the Southern Poverty Law Center (SPLC) foremost among them—perform two unjustified and irresponsible acts of elision, pushing the term "sovereign citizen" along a precipitous, slippery slope. In materials marketed for a popular audience, as well as those designed specifically for law enforcement, such as the twelve-minute "roll call" video for use by police departments, the SPLC presents the "sovereign citizen" movement as a potentially violent threat. The "roll call" video conflates the action of two men with all those who are categorized by the term "sovereign citizen."[48] A white Christian pastor and his son, who assassinated a police officer in West Memphis, Arkansas, and later engaged in a bloody shootout in a Walmart parking lot, are thus presented as paradigmatic of a broader movement.[49] All "sovereign citizens," this film argues, may be potential murderers.

The second move made consistently by the SPLC in its treatment of "sovereign citizens" is to link this term to the broader category of "anti-government extremists." By lumping the one category in with the second, larger category, the SPLC is able to ratchet up the sense of threat—claiming, for instance, that "at least 32 law enforcement officials . . . have been murdered by right-wing extremists since the 1995 Oklahoma City bombing."[50] Due to such elision, "sovereign citizen" becomes a catchall, both for categories of real action in the world and for vague fears of domestic revolt. This elision has led law enforcement officials to rank "sovereign citizens," in a 2014 survey, as "America's Top Terrorist Threat," "an ideological subculture of extreme opposition to the government."[51]

The SPLC links various marginal groups, on which it claims to offer "intelligence," to the white supremacists that were the organization's first target when it began as a project of lawyer Morris Dees, who used civil suits to litigate and bankrupt hate groups.[52] The problem is that "hate," "supremacy," "extremism," and an assortment of criminalizing terms are now used indiscriminately by the SPLC. The SPLC has published numerous articles on all three Aliite movements, describing them as "sovereigns in black" (the blackness in question referring not to garb but to skin color).[53] MSTA groups have been listed among "active antigovernment" groups, though the SPLC has noted that "there are numerous Moorish groups around the country" and that some "strenuously protest being lumped in with sovereign citizens, saying that they are, in fact, law-abiding citizens of the United States."[54] The Nuwaubian Yamassee have been described as "a cult that promotes a bizarre and complicated 'theology,' " and as "black supremacists."[55] The Washitaw have been called "antigovernment" as well as "sovereign citizen."[56] The persistent focus of the SPLC on Aliite religion has led to the Empire Washitaw's Dauphin Washington calling the organization out for "defamation and slander."[57]

The category "sovereign citizen" as it is popularly used implies a venal irrationality at the base of Aliite belief. In this way, the term reiterates racist tropes (Aliites as primitive, uneducated, or resistant to education) while characterizing Aliites as potentially violent and misrepresenting the nature of organization and authority in such communities.

The problems with "sovereign citizen" as a category play out especially in the judiciary, where the term shapes perceptions of the intent behind and risks of Aliite performance of law. In an especially striking case, largely due to the judge's reliance, for his judicial opinions, not only on his own research but also on internet research, former U.S. Appeals Court judge Richard Posner drew primarily on SPLC articles for a decision regarding the MSTA movement. Judge Posner wrote the decision with the stated "aim . . . to introduce readers who may not be familiar with the 'sovereign citizen' movement to its principal institutional establishment." In it, he manages both to insist that the MSTA is a monolithic organization with a clear central hierarchy ("The MSTA home office, located in Washington D.C., has issued a statement . . .") and to flatly refute the core Aliite claim as nonfactual, referring to "African Americans who belong to the Moorish Science Temple of America (MSTA) and claim to be descendants of the Moors of northern Africa, though they are not."[58] One article in a law journal, relying on such popular characterizations, goes so far as to declare claims of religious identity by "sovereign citizen" Moors to be "illegitimate"; rather than authentically religious, such individuals are, according to the article's author, "radicals stemming from the faith."[59] This sorting of legitimate (legal) religious claims from illegitimate (and thus illegal) claims disregards the reality of Aliite religion in terms of beliefs and practices as well as in terms of structure and organization. Aliite religion focuses on law, and these traditions are diverse, composed of myriad schismatic organizations with porous boundaries. There is no body of universally accepted authority over who is or is not a Moor, for instance, and, at the same time, the only universally accepted authority of all Aliites is, ironically, true law, which Aliite practices (whether or not they are deemed illegal) seek to emulate.

Posner's piece is an extreme example of judicial reliance on influence by watchdog activist groups and the sensational journalism they label as "intelligence," but it is a stark reminder of how accessible and compelling SPLC narratives are. That such narratives are aimed explicitly at law enforcement audiences raises real concerns about fair treatment of Aliites by police. Jeffrey Kaplan argued that watchdog groups impose an explicit or implicit normative frame on religious communities. Such a framework can range from an evangelical Christian worldview to a more general—and more common—conception that "real" religion must adhere to a Protestant model of private, rational faith.[60] Watchdog groups like the SPLC do a great deal of work popularizing a narrow understanding of what can and should count as religion in America, under U.S. law.

The SPLC itself has come under increasing criticism in recent years, both for its monetization of the threat of hate groups and for the validity of the data it offers and the categories it insists upon, yet my primary concern is with the damage done to minority religious communities when they find themselves subjected to such categorization.[61] The danger here is not limited to unjust police and judicial engagements; it includes internal obsession over the labels that have been applied to these communities.

"Sovereign citizen" and related terms have become obsessions for Aliite communities, which seek to distance themselves from the consequences of the label.[62] Other terms, such as "paper terrorism," are also much discussed, as in a recent public clarification by the Empire Washitaw that their letter-writing campaign to gain attention for their claims from elected officials was not an example of "paper terrorism."[63] That conversation, like so many of the Aliite discussions of the "sovereign citizen" category, reflected a deep anxiety about how Aliite communities are perceived by the media, law enforcement, and the courts. Applied to Aliites, the "sovereign citizen" category replicates a pervasive and longstanding racist assessment, a deeper trend of presenting black Americans as criminals, "ill-suited for American citizenship."[64]

"Sovereign citizen" is sufficiently expansive, as a term, to be used as a catchall for any form of criminal activity related, even tenuously, to Aliite religion. When, in July 2016, a military veteran and self-help guru named Cosmo Ausar Setepenra (Gavin Long) killed three police officers in Baton

Rouge, Louisiana, and was himself killed, police found on his body paper-work connected with the Unity Washitaw organization, prompting specu-lation that he represented a violent interpretation of "black supremacist," "sovereign citizen" logic.[65] The Washitaw, suddenly the object of national scrutiny, responded by giving interviews, seeking to distance "the real Washitaw" from Setepenra's claims. Umar Shabazz Bey opened his home museum to a reporter from the *Guardian*, but the resulting coverage none-theless represented his religion as "a branch of the so-called sovereign citi-zens movement," noting that "the FBI calls sovereign citizens 'a domestic terrorist movement' and according to a 2014 survey of law enforcement agencies, they pose a larger threat to America than jihadi militants." Sha-bazz Bey's claims of ancient history were noted, only to be followed by dis-missal of the factuality of those claims by "scientists, lawyers, the FBI and historians," as well as a quotation from a "researcher" at the SPLC, dismiss-ing Washitaw identity as "a fiction" and insisting that its goal was to escape American law.[66] Dauphin Washington had better luck with his hometown paper, the *Los Angeles Times*, which ran an article, based in part on an interview with Washington, sympathetic to the desire of the Washitaw to distance themselves from a murderer of whom they knew nothing. All the same, this article ends by quoting another watchdog expert insisting that "the Washitaw worldview" emphasizes racial purity and thus contains an inherent tendency toward violence.[67]

"Sovereign citizen," reframing their activities as criminal practices ranging from litigation to civil protest, becomes another restrictive "nick-name" Aliites must struggle to shake off. In Aliite understanding, the term is like "Negro," a misrecognition imposed by the state, denying Aliites the equal citizenship they seek. On the one hand, many Aliites communities respond internally by cautioning each other regarding *illegal* actions, of-fering cautionary tales and warnings of behaviors that, while marketed by some Aliites as expressions of fidelity to and use of the law, are viewed by other Aliites as scams, criminal plots, described in the same register used by watchdog groups. On the other hand, Aliites reach out externally, speak-ing to media, for instance, adopting the language of criminality to describe those practices and thinkers that are, thus, not really Aliite, lying outside the fold of the authentic religion. Finally, Aliites attempt—in speaking to the media and to each other, as well as to police and to judges, as in the videos mentioned above—to make clear their loyalty and devotion to law, true law, and thus explain why they are *not* "sovereign citizens," but "United States of America citizens."[68]

"RIGHTS THAT ARE ALREADY YOURS":
CITIZENSHIP AS THE PRACTICE OF LAW

The ability to speak law to power is a right under the American rule of the legal, a right open to all citizens. Aliites, proclaiming their nationality, insist upon citizenship and seek recognition of such status through their practice of law before representatives of the power of the state. As an idea, the state is an abstraction, but it is made of very real effects, effects that—especially to Aliites—are anything but abstract. Manifestations of the power of the state are everywhere, from the issuance of licenses and regulations to the police officer holding a gun pointed at your car window. This goes to the question political theorists have asked about the politics of recognition: namely, "by whom or how is recognition to be granted, indicated, or distributed?"[69] Aliites have multiple answers, from county clerks to police officers, judges to bureaucrats to politicians, all understood as instrumental in the process of the state and of its living representatives, wielding the state's power through their own hands and mouths, paperwork and guns. Realizing that such agents of the state are already everywhere and attentive to Aliite existence—through, for instance, processes of surveillance, as discussed in chapter 5—Aliites share the stance that engaging such agents is both a necessity and a responsibility. Indeed, Aliites frame their responsibility as an opportunity, not merely a task of citizenship but also a benefit that comes with the status—a status too long denied them. Having lived, for "generations," as El-Amin says, "in the state without being citizens . . . deprived of any civil rights," the exercise of the rights of citizenship is now all the more urgent—an attitude that prompts Aliites to take to the street and the courts to vocally perform citizenship through the practice of the law.[70]

America, Aliites believe, has an exceptional relation to true law not only through its democratic structure but also through its foundational texts, which Aliites frequently argue are, as they are written, already instantiations of true law. Legal interpretations of these texts have abandoned their original intent, Aliites believe. Aliite reference to the Constitution links to both a known and an imagined text, for Aliites understand the U.S. Constitution as a unique and authoritative phrasing of true law, citing that understanding of the text in their performances of law. The Nuwaubian Yamassee demonstrate this by carrying copies of the U.S. Constitution on their bodies as a reminder of their status as citizens and by making statements, as this one in their own, Nuwaubian Yamassee Constitution, revering the

American text, phrasing the political and legal demands of the community as "Simply That the Constitutional Laws of the U.S. and Its Amendments Be Respected . . . You Do Not Seek Rights That Are Already Yours."[71] This is a version of the Washitaw movement's "Are you going to obey your own laws?" and the kind of insistence on legal knowledge and accusation of ignorance of the law seen in the Moorish American video performances described above.

Seizing the power of the state to negotiate the power of the state is a common practice by minority religious communities, which turn to the legal system in order to find recognition and accommodation as well as to speak to their own higher law. As Hugh Urban has shown, the Church of Scientology's "war" with the Internal Revenue Service was, ultimately, a struggle for recognition from the IRS, which came not only with material rewards but with the authority of the U.S. government, used abroad by the church like the "Our Authority" document of the MSTA, as evidence of endorsement of the project and a legal judgment on the religion's validity.[72] Sarah Barringer Gordon has shown how marginalized religious communities, such as the Nation of Islam, have espoused a "popular constitutionalism" in order to claim rights not recognized under the current system of legal interpretation, as part of a struggle to reveal what these communities insist to be "the true meaning of the Constitution's religion clauses."[73] Akin to what Mari Matsuda calls "the victims' Constitution," the U.S. Constitution is idealized by such communities and claimed as their own.[74] These communities, while identifying America as a corrupt order, nonetheless have pursued rights through the state. For the Jehovah's Witnesses, this involved aggressive litigation and a "faith in the Bill of Rights" supported by offering legal training to missionaries. The Watchtower organization, the leadership for Jehovah's Witnesses, pursued a strategy of concentrating missionary activity in places identified as "localities ripe for litigation" and offering missionaries rehearsal experience at dealing with arrest by having community members dress in police uniforms and conduct mock raids on meetings.[75] Other religious groups, even more resistant to the authority of the state, have used legal proceedings as venues for protest and, thus, religious testimonial. Antinuclear Catholic Plowshares activists offer one example of this, defying the authority of the court in order to perform what they see as religious duties.[76] These activists—overwhelmingly white, usually priests and nuns, part of a mainstream religious tradition—exhibit a privilege that minority religious communities lack. Indeed, Plowshares activists seek to exclude themselves from the mainstream, pursuing criminality and protest, and taking dramatic steps, in the courtroom, to render themselves outside the confines of shared citizenship. Aliites, for whom the violent power of the state remains a constant threat, exhibit more pragmatism, investing hope in no power or order outside this earth *other* than the transcendent, metaphysical reality that is true law. God will not redeem this world through miracles; Allah's plan, rather, can only come to pass if citizens step up to their responsibility and seek to align the legal and political orders of this world with true law.

Unfortunately for their project, Aliites speak their claims of the true law in a way that is often incomprehensible to the representatives of the legal system to whom they are speaking. The legal practice carried out by Aliites is often at odds with accepted legal protocol, an inconsistent and idiosyncratic mix of references to existing legal protocols and precedents, a performance of desire more than one of authoritative knowledge expressed in terms the state could understand and would accept. As can be seen in the disjuncture between statements by judges in Aliite online legal performance videos and the celebratory comments attached to such videos, Aliite practice of the law can result in lack of communication, in a deepening of divisions between two conflicting *nomoi* of law. There are often real stakes involved in such exchanges—Aliites going to and remaining in prison, for instance.

Such miscommunication, even missed attempts at argumentation, carried out by *pro se* Aliite legal actors, calls to mind Alexandra Lahav's work championing litigation as an essential practice of democratic citizenship. Lahav characterizes litigation as a means of participating directly in the enforcement of law, a way of fostering transparency in regard to crucial policy-shaping information, even a form of "*participation* in self-government," which, moreover, "offers a form of *social equality* by giving litigants equal opportunities to speak and be heard."[77] While she expresses dismay at the limitations imposed on litigation, particularly the Prison Litigation Reform Act of 1996, which made it far more difficult for incarcerated citizens to file lawsuits, she gives special attention to the paradox of *pro se* legal practice, showing that this ability to represent oneself exists more on an ideal level than an actual practical, lived one. Instances of *pro se* legal performance reveal how much justice depends on resources, financial and educational (itself financially dependent). "Because litigation is an adversarial process, it depends on each side to present its arguments and proofs to best effect. In a society where income and educational inequality mean that people do not have equal capacities to hire lawyers and invest in litigation, the adversarial system cannot live up to its promise," Lahav writes.[78] The courts cannot usually provide aid for such individuals, with the result that "a self-represented plaintiff may get her day in court, but be unable to speak a language those in power can comprehend."[79] Despite a "well established" precedent "that the submissions of a *pro se* litigant must be construed liberally and interpreted to raise the strongest argument that they *suggest*," putting such ideals into practice requires patience, time, and a degree of sympathy with litigants who may present themselves as less than sympathetic to the court.[80] Former U.S. Court of Appeals judge Richard Posner self-published a book advancing a similar complaint, indicting the federal judiciary for its handling of *pro se* litigants.[81]

Procedural inequality, exacerbated by other forms of inequality (racial, for instance, but certainly economic and, linked to both, educational), raises real issues for the health and continued existence of democracy, a concern echoed throughout Aliite literature. Consider, for instance, Bandele El-Amin's thoughts on the lack of funding for public defenders (he contrasts public resources available for public defenders with that available for police officers) and his emphasis that the goal of understanding and legally fighting for one's civic rights is to escape the category of being "legally dead," a goal that is accomplished when one is truly "heard."[82] Within the Washitaw, too, emphasis is increasingly put—especially when framed in consideration of a Trump administration that many Washitaw believe to be opposed to actually returning the land—on the goal simply "to get a hearing" with the government regarding the land or Nuwaubian demands for a retrial for Malachi York.[83]

To be heard in court is read as being recognized by the state doing the hearing, proof of citizenship status. This is made visible in a Moorish adaptation of the Great Seal's eagle. Sheik Way-El's Moorish American Party has reimagined the seal, replacing the stars of sovereignty with the star and crescent of Ali's "Islamism" and the olive branch and arrows with the Moorish and American flags. The eagle, whose crest displays the cracked Liberty Bell on a solid red background, wears a red fez and has his head turned toward the American flag, symbolizing Ali's two-flagged illustration of how nationality guarantees citizenship.[84] Invoking the "Treaty of Peace and Friendship"—"a binding contract with the United States"—the Moorish American Party rehearses basic Aliite claims. Moors are a nation within a nation in the United States; Moorish "nationality is political unity" and offers political power through mobilization as a constituency. A Moorish American Party speaker defines politics, in an online video, as "the business of deal making," as negotiation, and he lays out the ultimate goal of Moorish participation in politics as "to run government," for the American eagle to become a Moorish American eagle. Insisting that Aliite ideals are and always have been American ideals, ideals that America has been reluctant and inconsistent in embodying, Aliites thus present themselves as exceptional Americans, exemplifications of what they, in turn, insist is America's exceptional promise. America, Aliites argue, has difficulty being true to its own best self. Thus, Aliites seek to help America *become* America. The opening soundtrack of the Moorish American Party video mentioned above lays out one means of doing so: speaking true law to representatives of the state. "I want to talk to the FBI, and the CIA, and the congressmen," a voice raps. "I want to talk to the man, you understand."[85] To speak the truth of law to power, this is the task of Aliite citizenship, performed not only in the courtroom or in explicit encounters with police but at all times, in everyday life, as Aliites understand themselves to be subjects of ubiquitous surveillance by the state. Just as the potential violence of the state is always hovering, so, too, the eyes of the state are always watching. As the next chapter argues, Aliites see opportunity as well as danger in these eyes.

5

THE ALL-SEEING EYE

Display and Surveillance

THE GAZE OF PROMISE AND THE
GAZE OF THREAT

AS AN ALIITE SYMBOL, THE EYE OF PROVIDENCE, sometimes called the Eye of Horus or the Eye of Allah, is said to be of ancient Moorish origin. Its presence on the Great Seal either acknowledges the debt America owes to the Moors or is evidence, concealed in plain sight, of a conspiracy to erase such history.[1] The all-seeing eye can be read as blessing or curse, a sign of God's beneficent presence or a sign of the police state's surveillance of minorities, ubiquitous and intrusive, "the fact of anti-blackness."[2] On the one hand, the providential gaze promises recognition of truth-claims, motivating proclamations of identity through visual displays and performances. Agents of the state, through their gaze, can encounter and recognize Aliites and their claims to identity and legal status. Yet ever-present surveillance brings with it different connotations and emotions, symbolizing the overseer state and its ability to manifest violent force in the service of its will. The Eye of Providence thus simultaneously represents both the most hoped-for and the most terrifying social realities for Aliite communities: the promise of recognition and the threat of armed police at the door. That salvation, through recognition of the status of citizen, and damnation—in the form of arrest, imprisonment, persecution, oppression, even execution—can come from the same source provides yet another structuring tension for the Aliite worldview. Hiding, however, is not possible. Imagining the eye as seeing all, Aliites actively court its gaze.

Visual presentation of identity is key to Ali's project. Nationality is expressed in clothes. The fez and turban, for instance, silently declare that one is Moorish and not Negro. Nationality, for the MSTA, found expression in "symbolic embodiment of amendment," to use Derek Hicks's terms. Hicks identified as characteristic of African American religion the dynamic of "recasting a new identity." Such a move "reminds wounded folks that they are in fact something else, something more," though Ali insisted that such "more" be understood always as also explicitly legal.[3] Display of distinctive garb was linked to citizenship from the beginning of the MSTA, with Ali's community staging public performances of identity. "The garment I have on represents power," Ali says in a quote attributed to him as a hadith.[4] This was true for all Moors, as clothes played an essential role in displaying Aliite claims to authentic national identity.

The first national convention, gathering Moors to Chicago in 1928, functioned in part as a media event, an opportunity for the creation of photographs of the nation that offered, in Aliite understanding, evidence of the truth of their claims. Aliites frequently reproduce two crowd shots from this event, images of men and women standing together, in an ordered crowd, dressed in national garb, looking both explicitly Moorish and like a local ethnic constituency rallied under the American flag.[5]

The parade the MSTA staged as part of this convention similarly displayed national identity as a way of demonstrating American citizenship. A visual spectacle of Moorish "regalia" that included the participation of a camel as a living symbol of the exotic cultural difference of Moorish heritage, this parade also served as a public performance of civic belonging.[6] The parade ended with a ritual echoing the famous portrait of Ali with two flags, in which the prophet "wrapped a little boy in the American, and a little girl in the Moorish flag," as a public representation—visual and embodied—of his movement's claims and goals.

That ethnic distinctiveness could be concurrent with incorporation within the American body politic was a popularly understood message conveyed by parades in Chicago.[7] The MSTA parade, however, also emerges from a distinct history of African American parades as opportunities "to enact and control public representations of themselves," as Susan Davis has shown.[8] African American parades, from the eighteenth century on, have facilitated the enaction of black agency and broadcast black claims to the rights of citizenship—for parade participants and black audiences, as well as for "skeptical and often hostile" whites.[9] The MSTA parade likewise performed authentic identity and its legal consequences not just for Moorish

Americans but also for those who could be converted to the movement, and for white witnesses, including those explicitly representing the authority of the state, such as the police officers serving as official escorts for the event.[10] A hadith cited by contemporary MSTA members quotes Ali as describing the importance of the event: "Our nationality in this government began with the parade."[11]

The flip side of this emphasis on visual display of identity is the suspicion or outright charge that the performance of identity is a masquerade. Accusations of masquerade have been leveled at Aliites from the 1920s to the present. Covering Ali's death in 1929, a *Chicago Tribune* article said of the founder of the MSTA, he "posed as Moor . . . [but] he was a Negro."[12] Likewise, contemporary judicial decisions, in which claims to nationality are dismissed as "nonsensical" or "frivolous," are an extension of this trend.[13]

The visual displays of identity so characteristic of Aliite religion—the acts of donning the fez or pharaonic headwear, parading through city streets or marching outside a courthouse chanting in an ancient language—are often read by critics of these movements (and also by the media and even by academics) as empty pomp, manipulative theatricality, or dissembling before the law. Aliite amendment of identity is thus seen not as authentic amendment but as merely a con.

This chapter first examines Aliite visual display of identity and Aliite claims to the authenticity of such identity in contrast to accusations of masquerade. I begin with Ali's role on stage as part of a theatrical spectacle aiming to differentiate himself and his community from those "false prophets" who worked as stage entertainers, fortunetellers, and magicians, tracing a path to the Nuwaubian Yamassee movement's public transition through fashions and symbols as part of a developmental trajectory and pedagogical tool. Turning to the stance taken by both the Nuwaubian Yamassee and the Washitaw Empress Goston that those who are really masquerading are the racist opponents of Aliite groups, I draw a parallel between Aliite visual display and the practice of "masking" engaged in by Mardi Gras Indians. This chapter then turns to Aliite understandings of and responses to surveillance. Like the rays that surround the Great Seal's all-seeing eye, radiating out in every direction, so too the state sends out agents, searching and scrutinizing and licensed to use violence. Aliites respond to surveillance with insistent faith—as citizens—in American ideals of justice and equality, while simultaneously interpreting the gaze of law enforcement as a means of acquiring recognition for claims related to their larger society-transforming work of citizenship. MSTA members, in the 1930s and 1940s, gazed *back* at the surveillance state and offered a subtle critique of the hypocrisy of a promise, unfulfilled, of "justice for all." The Yamassee, subjected to harsh scrutiny after the construction of Tama-Re, responded to surveillance first by rendering their movement more public, creating their own forms of media, and offering alternative narratives to those of their critics, grounded in Aliite faith in law and in the rights assumed to be granted to all Yamassee as equal citizens of the United States. Similarly, the largest faction within the Washitaw movement, fragmented by an FBI raid in 2000, views the FBI not in the role of enemy but in that of potential benefactor, interpreting the agency's constant surveillance presence as a possible means of recognition for Washitaw claims. Aliite faith in law, invested as it is in the power and legal institutions of the state as necessary for the transformation of society, thus emphasizes display before and openness to law enforcement surveillance, understood as intimate proximity to the power of the state and, thus, a source of recognition.

METAMORPHOSIS, NOT MASQUERADE:
MASKING TO SHOW A TRUE FACE

To distinguish himself from other self-proclaimed prophets and mystics from the east, Ali decided to take to the stage with a theatrical variety show called "The Great Moorish Drama." In 1927, as his movement was burgeoning nationwide, Ali contrasted the shtick of "false prophets whose mission is to fleece the people"[14] and stage mystics in exotic Eastern get-up with his own authentic "Asiatic" heritage and prophetic mission. Susan Nance has written of the numerous psychics, healers, numbers sellers, and grifters in Ali's Chicago, many of them exploiting orientalist tropes, even the title of "Muslim" or "Moslem," to bolster their claims.[15] In the month before Ali's death, the *Chicago Defender* carried a review of "Prince Ali, that mys-tee-rious master mind from the Orient," at the Regal.[16] Ali was later identified in that paper as "the world's greatest prophet."[17] The foreign name, the unusual headwear, the title of prophet: these were stock elements of kitsch entertainers and scam artists, routinely derided in the *Defender*'s muckracking.[18] Ali's "Great Moorish Drama" offered the allure of "feats" designed to attract and entertain a crowd while presenting the prophet's teachings about Moorish identity in the form of lecture and theater.[19]

The show climaxed with a double act: Ali demonstrating escape-artist legerdemain of the Harry Houdini or Black Herman sort, and Ali manifesting his divine potential by healing members of the audience.[20] All we know of this event is found in a promotional flier.[21] But the drama courted public attention and served as both entertainment and proselytization. It reiterated both metaphysical and political MSTA claims, "underscoring the prophet's divine authority" and serving "to embody and perform Moorish identity," as Judith Weisenfeld puts it.[22] "Look! Look!" the fliers advertising the event said, a repetition that can be read as gesturing toward the multivalence of this very visual display.

The "Great Moorish Drama" involved a theatrical reenactment of "events in the last days among the inhabitants of North America" (either a current apocalyptic scenario or a sacred historical retelling of a Moorish past), followed by "great lectures" from Ali and MSTA leaders on "the need of a nationality," then a Moorish musical performance. Finally, in the climactic act, Ali was "bound with several yards of rope, as Jesus was bound in the the [sic] Temple at Jerusalem and escaped before the authorities could take charge of Him; so will Prophet Drew Ali, perform the same act, after being bound by anyone in the audience and will escape in a few seconds."

The comparison of Ali to Jesus served to highlight the religiosity of his movement, distancing the MSTA from the suspicion raised by previous radical nationalist groups.[23] Simultaneously reminiscent of biblical narrative—the Samson story, even Jesus with the moneylenders—this scene is nonetheless novel, much like the treatment of Jesus in Ali's *Holy Koran of the Moorish Science Temple of America*. This text, which Ali claimed to have "compiled," was largely taken from a preexisting text, the New Thought *Aquarian Gospel of Jesus the Christ*, by Levi Dowling (though he himself claimed to have received it by transmission from the Akashic Records).[24] Jesus is the central character in Levi's *Gospel* and Ali's *Koran*, both of which chronicle the years between Jesus's youth and the start of his ministry, years of travel through Asia and encounters with various sages and adepts. In the pieces from Levi's book that Ali selects, moreover, Jesus is focused on uplifting and saving humanity, phrased explicitly as outreach "to the common people, to redeem them from under the great pressure of the hands of the unjust."[25] Like the singing of old church hymns with new lyrics—"Moslems That Old Time Religion," for instance—Ali's Jesus represents a deeper Aliite tradition of appropriation and revision of Christian symbolic vocabulary.[26]

Yet the comparison to Jesus functioned on other levels, as well, implying that Ali could work miracles and reminding the audience that a prophet is never respected in his own land. The final act of the show, when Ali "will heal many in the audience without touching them . . . manifesting his divine power,"[27] was likewise an exemplification of basic MSTA doctrine, the egalitarian New Thought notion that we are all "like Jesus" in the sense of divine potential. Jesus is the first "perfect man," united with the deity, but, as he says, "What I can do all men can do," according to his "Gospel of the Omnipotence of man."[28] As Ali's *Holy Koran* says, "Everyone on earth shall overcome and be like Him, a Son of Allah."[29]

But based on the stage performance, what does it mean to follow this Aliite Jesus? On the one hand, Ali is escaping from the bonds of the "lower self," rejecting the temptations of baser impulses as Jesus does in Ali's *Holy Koran*.[30] Yet Ali's escape act can also be read in relation to the racist oppression his movement aimed to circumvent. Indeed, Ali was slipping the bonds of racist categories by proclaiming his Moorish nationality and religion. "Look! Look!" This prophet is not like all the others; he is doing something real here, reiterating the arguments offered in his "great lectures" with this performance. Although to some eyes Ali's act would have amounted to nothing more than a commonplace demonstration of skill as an escape artist, it was nonetheless an illustration of his teaching, an enactment of the central promise of MSTA teachings: freedom from oppression via the example of Ali.

The movement currently known as the Nuwaubian Yamassee has been accused by its opponents—particularly the local media in Georgia, which sided with Sheriff Howard Sills in his feud against the community—of performing an elaborate masquerade. Linked specifically to the movement's practice of changing its style of dress, symbol system, and name with regularity, this charge finds an echo even in scholarship that generally takes seriously the movement's claims and practices. Scholarship has repeated tropes of masquerade, describing Nuwaubian Yamassee "shape-shifting strategies" as "theatrical"[31] displays of "bizarre costumes," and accusing the public of intentional and manipulative dissimulation, "assuming new titles and disguises like ritual masks."[32]

The changing styles of dress, as one of the most noticeable public facets of this movement, must be analyzed for the various functions such a commitment to continual "metamorphosis" fulfills.[33] Susan Palmer offers three suggestions. At one point she quotes a Nuwaubian Yamassee who explains the cowboy-hat-and-country-music phrase of the movement as "a test of loyalty" demonstrating that the community "truly followed the Lamb wherever he may lead them."[34] Elsewhere she suggests that by "deliberate distancing from racial stereotypes and ritual catharsis for racial rage," this pattern of changing fashions might fulfill a "therapeutic" purpose."[35] Finally, there is the "pedagogical" relation to York's mature thought, which allows for a rereading of the quotation about the loyalty test, for that Nuwaubian Yamassee says that clothes also helped "to get everybody away from doing their own thing."[36]

Disciplining the mind through dress to eliminate ego is York's most frequent explanation of the practice. "Ego," he teaches, is the cause of suffering in this life and a mentality of slavery, "the greatest obstacle" for Nuwaubian Yamassee.[37] He argues that his people are trapped in a "misconception of Reality," a mental confusion, limited by "lesser knowledge" and confusing fallible perceptions of truth.[38] Yet such "thought patterns" can be changed.[39] York aims to help his community eradicate "desire, pride, anger, delusion, greed, jealousy, lust, hatred, racism, and leadership," and to "control" or at least "subdue" the ego, "the greatest obstacle" to the Nuwaubian Yamassee project.[40] The changing array of fashion, symbols, and names assists this project. York has led his community "through all these phases in order to create an immunity from all the garbage that we've been taught all of our lives by the evil one. We had to live through it to make it."[41]

In the Aliite lineage, where clothing is a distinct mark of identity, what does it mean for York to insist that "it is useless to identify with clothing or hair style"?[42] The answer is in York's elaborate ontological claims. In *Man from the Planet Rizq*, York reveals his true identity, ontology, and origin. Ultimately, he claims, he is a being of green light, one of the alien others: "We are called Rizqiyian or Anunnagi or just the Aluhum. I am one of the teachers of the 19th galaxy."[43] He is not wearing disguises so much as garments that render him visible and comprehensible to his as-yet-unenlightened audience. Aliite thought holds that national dress allows one to be seen. York's ontological teachings take this literally: his true nature could not be physically perceived by humans.

Drawing on strands of the popular conspiracy theory narratives of David Icke, York reimagines the "Anunnaki," not as alien slavemasters discussed in ancient cuneiform texts, but as extraterrestrial beings mistaken, in the past, for gods, of which York himself is a messenger sent to teach and thus transform the Nuwaubian Yamassee. According to York, all Nuwaubian Yamassee are also extraterrestrials, ultimately beings of light only temporarily clothed in flesh, so on one level it is costumes all the way down. Costume

changes keep the community in touch with their authentic ontology, eschewing connection with the mere masks and false fronts of this reality.

York continues to draw on what scholars have called Icke's "Reptoid Hypothesis," "the idea that alien lizards conspiratorially control the Earth and
with it human destiny," only for York these reptilians are the ultimate enemies of the Nuwaubian Yamassee people, literal "shape-shifters" who keep
their reptilian nature concealed behind false (human) faces and elaborate
(human) masks.[44] Politicians and celebrities, even local police, can be, in
this worldview, nonhuman villains, part of an elaborate conspiracy to keep
the Nuwaubian Yamassee oppressed. Against these cunning opponents, de-
ceptively appearing as human beings, Nuwaubian Yamassee enact their true
identity; the enemies of the community hide their faces, while the members of the community change their clothes in order to dissociate from the
always-shifting and thus false reality of this world.

Changes in fashion are pedagogical, helping the Nuwaubian Yamassee
understand that their true selves are not synonymous with their bodies.
Shifting sartorial styles are an essential part of a process of unlearning, a
reversing of centuries of human brainwashing. Of all the lies and "garbage"
Nuwaubian Yamassee must unlearn, racism, attitudes of inferiority, and
even self-hatred of one's own blackness are at the fore. Simultaneous with
his more elaborate ontological teachings (about extraterrestrial origin and
identity), York has emphasized, always, that the blackness of the bodies the
Nuwaubian Yamassee inhabit in this world is authentic. While ultimately
beings of light, the community must always embrace the physical forms
they have been given as a means of rejecting the insidious damage to self-
worth that has been done through racism. York has urged the celebration of
black bodies and of blackness, phrasing his aim as one of "restoring racial
pride and self-respect."[45] All of the modes of fashion engaged by the Nuwaubian Yamassee frame this blackness.

Costumes function as a way of publicly displaying black bodies with
dignity, pride, and reference to nostalgic narratives of grand pasts and un-
limited potential. This influenced York's rejection of any philosophy that
would "demonize the *flesh*."[46] While he decried the world as illusory, as a
case of false perception confused with reality, York has never been willing
to accept that some notion of colorblindness could follow from such thinking. Racial categories and distinctions are lies, he teaches, following Ali's
example. But the color of Nuwaubian Yamassee skin is a natural, original,
beautiful, and powerful color, which needs to be recognized as such in order to counter the dehumanization, the mental slavery, foisted upon the

Nuwaubian Yamassee throughout history. In order to embrace your true nature as a being of light, you must first, York insists, take pride and find beauty in your (temporary) black skin.

This Aliite countercharge, that the *real* masquerade is perpetuated by those who doubt the authenticity of Aliites, is advanced in the Washitaw movement as well. A chapter in the Washitaw scripture, *Return of the Ancient Ones*, presents an autobiographical account of the infiltration of a Ku Klux Klan meeting by the movement's founder, Verdiacee Goston.[47] Using her characteristic research skills, she uncovered the details of a local KKK meeting, and, inspired by a white sheet hanging on her laundry line, she crafted a disguise in order to attend the event undercover. While her own makeshift mask provides invisibility for the Washitaw Empress within the crowd of anonymous racists, *their* masks allow their true nature to show. Indeed, in Goston's telling, Klan masks facilitate the expression of an overdetermined commitment to death—from murder, blood-drinking, and cannibalism to sodomy and sexual acts represented as perverse and parodic, fueled by indiscriminate lust, which ultimately does not care if the baby to be sacrificed is black or white.

Goston's chapter plays on the trope of reversal: masks reveal true faces, sexes are switched in Klansmen's fantasies, sex becomes death, newborns are killed, and the chapter begins and ends with bonfires in which Goston burns research notes she considers too dangerous to keep. In the dark smoke at the start of the chapter, Goston says she can see the ghosts of the white people who stole Washitaw land, dead white people rendered black just as white lies are described as black darkness earlier in her text.[48] Rather than constituting an erasure, however, these moments merely shed light on what she remembers and lays out here. The burned research notes are resurrected in the "Washitaw Files" that constitute *Return of the Ancient Ones*.

Embedded in a text largely given over to primary sources (historical and legal documents about Louisiana and the Louisiana Purchase), this chapter also functions as evidence, offering a firsthand account from Goston. Offering her testimony in plain, even crude, emotional language, she offers readers a visceral experience. She is shaken by what she sees, and she shakes her readers in turn. The Klansmen in Goston's text are "shits" spouting "shit"— their nature and their ideology pure filth, waste, corruption. Goston vomits inside her hood, "sick from [what she has witnessed], puking like a pregnant woman," her simile offering another reversal, a promise of life in the midst of all this death.[49]

Goston relays the words and deeds of the Klansmen, blending in with them but taking care not *actually* to participate in any of their actions. She describes herself as merely pantomiming clapping, for instance, "making no sound" as the crowd sets a rhythm, in unison, for singing. The songs that follow celebrate "Sweet nigger blood" and reminisce about raping black women and lynching black men. The crowd becomes frenzied, "humping" the air in a sexualized dance as they sing the praises of black women's behinds ("My old lady's butt ain't soft is [*sic*] yours") and celebrate sodomy even while presenting that desire as a form of suicide: "I found my waterloo at last / I want to die with my pecker in your black ass." Soon the song turns stranger, expressing sexual longing for black women as a longing for the male sex organ. Goston presents sodomy as a deadly parody of sex, but by having her Klansmen express their longing to "be tastin'" the penis of a black woman "till um' dead," the parodic element is amplified, and the men participate in another reversal, from rapist penetrators to those longing to be penetrated by their victims.[50] Goston's portrayal thus flips the Klansmen into a position of submission and debasement, begging to taste and be penetrated by the phallic equivalent of their own rage-for-death.

This theme continues after a brief interruption for the business part of the meeting, where the Grand Dragon lays out a plan to steal federal funds allocated for a new black public school and boasts of his control over local black teachers and preachers. Then Goston is mentioned as a powerful local political force. The crowd screams for her death, for a chance to eat her brain, even as the Grand Dragon insists that she is more useful alive. She brings economic development to the region, he argues, meaning money, which the Klansmen can then steal. Plus, he says, killing her would be too dangerous an act; the federal government as well as black protesters from around the nation would descend on Louisiana if she were killed. One Klansman declares that what he really wants is not Goston's brain: "I want her cock. I want to hand my tally-whacker in that nigger woman so bad til' every time her name is called, my tally-whacker gets on a hard!"[51]

This warped desire, simultaneously to penetrate and be penetrated by her, is met with approval by the crowd, who demand proof that this discussion has left him aroused. Goston cautions that she "could not see for the crowd," "could not make out for sure what they were doing," but the "moans and grunts" she hears make it clear that it is something sexual. Moreover, the Grand Dragon, lamenting that Goston will never allow herself to be raped alive and that sex with her is therefore impossible, offers himself as a compromise. All Kluxers, he says, should know that they can always penetrate "the grand dragon's ass." Sodomizing him would offer not merely sexual release, he argues, but also association with the "class and distinction" of another racist white man.[52] Goston's phrasing here reverses the nostalgic myth of Old South patriarchy, phrasing crudity with gentility, showing monstrousness framing itself in a rhetoric of chivalry. Carefully presented public appearances are masks, while the physical masks of the Klan rally liberate those racists who pose daily as masters of "class and distinction" to enact their true identities, their authentic natures.

Goston parodies a Klan rally—in keeping with her theory of "research" as unveiling truths hidden within texts—by showing what she insists the rally is *really* about, reading between the lines of such gatherings and offering, in her portrayal, a grotesque scene of abominable lust. While the Klan, historically, frames itself in a discourse of purity, Goston gives her readers a Klan obsessed with sex and death, wallowing in base scatology, irrationally driven by ultimately suicidal perversities of desire. While the Klan has a history of political power, of like-minded citizens gathering as a constituency, Goston presents the meeting as dominated by irrational impulses, more orgy than organizing.

Goston flees the ceremony, in her account, just as the group prepares to sacrifice a child and eat its brain along with black cats boiled in blood, a kind of white parody of hoodoo ritual, but she has seen enough.[53] Her disguise, assembled from pieces of laundry, granted her the fabled invisibility of the KKK, while Klan garb, in contrast, granted the Klansmen license to perform their most authentic behavior, thus revealing the true nature of the racist. Goston writes that the robes turned Klansmen into "ghosts" and "spooks," terms not only indicating proximity to and obsession with death but also, while reversing the racist valence on "spook," linking the Klan to the "spookism" or false religion frequently derided by Aliites.[54] In their costumes, Goston is able to see these racist men for what they are. Through their costumes, the abstractions of misogyny and racism are rendered scatologically real, as shit and puke, and given voice, in the frenzied perversity of song.

Goston occasionally wore a fez—labeled "Empress of the Washitaw"— and often appeared in what she identified as traditional, indigenous garb.[55] Although the use of clothing to proclaim nationality is less frequent among the Washitaw than among other Aliite branches, there are notable exceptions, like Crown Prince Bigbay Bagby Badger, whose use of Plains Indian regalia has helped him to receive "repatriated" Native American artifacts.[56]

Indeed, the excessive visibility of such displays is valorized, one reason Washitaw groups court affiliation with Mardi Gras Indians. Representatives of the Mardi Gras Indian tribes, particularly the aptly named, though unaffiliated Washitaw Nation of Mardi Gras Indians, have appeared at Washitaw celebrations. The performances of these Indians have been presented by the Washitaw as evidence of Washitaw claims, even though those claims are not shared by the Indians themselves.[57]

A distinctive tradition of African American New Orleans, Mardi Gras Indians "mask" by donning elaborate handmade outfits built in sections with panels of plumage that can be raised and moved to reveal more detail and handiwork, transforming the surface area and appearance of the outfit. In response to laws forbidding African Americans from wearing masks over their faces for Carnival, this distinct form of self-decoration and display developed as an alternate Mardi Gras and St. Joseph's Day practice. Various tribes of black Indians take to the streets of their neighborhoods, and, when two tribes meet, dueling via dance and song and display of garments commences. As George Lipsitz has argued, "Masking and marching manifests a strategic anti-essentialism wherein Blacks honor their own resistance to white rule by asserting affinities with Indigenous opposition to conquest and colonization," claiming a right to public space in the city.[58]

Nodding to a history of wise Indian voices emerging as authoritative if disembodied in New Orleans black spiritualist religion, and at once referencing and continuing as contemporary practice that maroonage of covert collaborative communities in defiance of the official state, Mardi Gras Indians offer vivid aesthetic display as political action. "Won't bow," one traditional song goes, "Don't know how."[59] The Big Chiefs and their tribes present themselves as an alternate sovereignty and a reversal of the grotesque excesses of the hegemony's Mardi Gras. In contrast to the white Kings and Queens feted at black-tie balls before donning masks and mounting elaborate floats in order to toss plastic trinkets—worthless beads and fraudulent coins—at intoxicated and adoring "subjects," Mardi Gras Indians subvert this carnival, taking it to *their* black backstreets, in costumes the resplendence of which bespeaks the careful labor invested in each stitch. Although the "official" parades are punctuated by street processions of (often black) teens performing brass band music and energetic dancing between floats, the Indians dance as part of elaborate rituals of hierarchy, of which their exclusive patois and forms of stylized confrontation are all part. George Lipsitz writes of "the emancipatory potential" of Mardi Gras Indian work,

by which he means that while "other revelers may use carnival masking
to escape the repressions of their everyday existence . . . the Indian tribes'
disguise brings out into the open dimensions of repression that the dominant culture generally tries to render invisible."[60] Quoting Big Chief of the
Guardians of the Flames Donald Harrison, Jr., Lipsitz also notes that among
Mardi Gras Indians, masking is sometimes understood as "a religious experience." As the Big Chief says, "It's something for your inner self, expressed
through your outer self."[61] This dynamic of masking is apparent in Aliite
practices as well. The Mardi Gras Indian tradition offers a tool for thinking about the subversive critique of society expressed by visible displays of
identity, and the alternative communalism enacted through such displays.
Masking does not conceal but rather reveals—calling attention to authenticity within a broader context of (and thus in contrast to) masquerade.
Instead of hiding, masking exaggerates visibility, framing and accentuating
black faces.

A newspaper article on the Moorish parade described how the "many
hued turbans of the women and children and the red fez and sashes worn
by the men attract much attention." Indeed, the "costumes" of the convention garnered more coverage in the media than the contents of the lectures.[62] Susan Palmer describes the costumes of the Nuwaubian Yamassee
at Tama-Re as "hokey, concocted," yet at the same time viscerally moving,
"very impressive," precisely because they were so theatrical in look and presentation.[63] Aliite understanding sees such theatrics as akin to Mardi Gras
Indian *masking*, a performance of claims of true identity. Further, Aliites
respond to claims of perpetuating a masquerade by charging that it is their
enemies who are really in disguise. Those who would deny Aliites, unjustly,
of their rights as citizens *wear* masks. Aliites, who know and enact their authentic national status as a means of ensuring their status as citizens, *mask*,
parading and displaying, slipping from the bonds of inaccurate and oppressive legal categories.

There is an epistemic authority to spectacle, an undeniable reality to
the materiality of costumes, which function as powerful visual evidence
for Aliite claims. Aliites, via this masking that eschews masks, perform the
authenticity of their identities. Aliites must be public in their identity—must
show themselves to be Aliites—because, otherwise, they could be mistaken
for that which they are not—namely, "negro, black, or colored" noncitizens.
Aliites' display of nationality is understood, as with the waving of the Moorish flag, to be necessary for, a requirement of, being American, as well as a
means by which one can receive recognition of one's claims by the state.

SURVEILLANCE, IDEALS, AND RECOGNITION:
THE MSTA AND THE JUSTICE DEPARTMENT

MSTA members, investigated by the Federal Bureau of Investigation in the 1930s and 1940s, met the gaze of the state, cast on them out of suspicion that they were not loyal American citizens, as an invitation to display their patriotism *as citizens* and to exercise the responsibilities *of citizenship*. The intimate, if intrusive, presence of the FBI allowed Moors to express characteristic Moorish optimism in law and the state, and to voice criticism with an eye toward building "a better America."[64] FBI files offer evidence of agents' bafflement at Moors who decorated their homes with American flags, spoke proudly of their sons' military service, and denied that they were "negro, colored, or black."[65]

The rhetoric deployed by Moorish Americans in response to the FBI gaze juxtaposed well-known American ideals with actual social realities. When, in 1944, a Grand Sheik (his name redacted) "drop[ped] by" FBI headquarters to "pay . . . respects" to FBI director J. Edgar Hoover, he delivered what an internal FBI memorandum described as "quite an impassioned spiel" about Moorish values to the FBI workers he met. The members of his movement, he said, "were not interested in subversive activity in the least but were wholly American and interested in the American way of life."[66] Like wearing or decorating with the American flag, like the declaration of citizenship printed in all-capital letters on MSTA nationality cards, the patriotism displayed by Aliites called attention to a disjunction, highlighting the less-than-full civil inclusion of Americans considered "black." In 1943, Grand Sheik Frederick Turner-El told FBI agents that "this is by no means a subversive organization, but one to make better American citizens . . . We pledge allegiance to the United States. We are going to fight to make America a better place."[67] In 1943, a Moor named Bey (the rest of his name redacted) sent a letter to President Franklin D. Roosevelt requesting a personal meeting to discuss "a proposal and plan for national recognition of 'The Brotherhood of Man.'" Such brotherhood was, Bey lamented, "at this time not a practice" in the United States, though he offered his help to resolve this problem. Bey noted that while he had received no response to his letter from the Office of the President, he "however received several visits from the 'Justice Dept' representative concerning our movement," in response to which he affixed a page featuring a photograph of himself and a complete set of his fingerprints "to be turned over to the Justice Dept."

Declaring his allegiance to "American Principle," to "justice and economic equality," this Moor readily offered evidence of his "true identity" in both biometrics and political truth-claims.[68]

Law, in Aliite understanding, represents a check on the power of the state, not merely in the practical sense of regulation and oversight but also according to Aliite faith in true law as a transcendent force, capable of exercising its influence over those—however corrupt or biased in the moment—who work within the fallible human legal system. With faith that even the agents of law enforcement ultimately desire true law, Aliites are able to respond to harassment by the so-called Justice Department in the hope that this department can come to discern and join in the struggle for true justice. FBI surveillance and infiltration of African American organizations under Director Hoover has been well documented, and the MSTA, with its vocal approach to citizenship and law, and its affiliation with both Islam and an "Asiatic" identity, raised concerns with the FBI.[69] From the 1930s on, the agency cultivated "colored informants" and placed them in MSTA branches as human monitors. The agency's files describe the use of "intermittent microphone surveillance" of MSTA meetings as well.[70] Yet MSTA members responded to the eyes of the state by calling on the state to examine itself. A Moor interviewed in 1943 insisted that he was "a loyal American citizen" and that he "want[ed] the United States to win the war . . . but only on condition that lynching and segregation are done away with and my people are given equal status." Until that happened, this Moorish American proclaimed, America would not be "a true democracy."[71]

"WE THE PEOPLE": NUWAUBIAN YAMASSEE RESPONSES TO SURVEILLANCE OF TAMA-RE

Nuwaubian Yamassee have likewise responded to the gaze of the state with a plea for the state to reform in recognition of its own ideals, particularly since the construction, in 1993, of the Tama-Re settlement in Georgia. Nuwaubian Yamassee turn to law as the means by which all wrongs—including those performed by law enforcement and the government—can and will be corrected, as well as the ideal to which all citizens are held. As one Nuwaubian Yamassee write puts it, "It is only fitting and proper that the true details of [York's] case be presented right at the doorstep of the Department of Justice in order to showcase this unlawful situation to the world."[72] Although dominant media and scholarly interpretations of the Nuwaubian Yamassee have ignored or misconstrued this impulse, the movement has consistently performed for legal, political, and law enforcement gazes, while simultaneously struggling to participate in these systems.

Construed as a "cult" by local media and law enforcement, the Nuwaubian Yamassee were subjected to further scrutiny following the 1997 group suicide of the California-based Heaven's Gate community, for their claims of extraterrestrial origin and speculation about intergalactic life.[73] Media and law enforcement have already linked the Nuwaubian Yamassee presence at Tama-Re to potential threat via parallels to other religiously linked social experiments that ended either in mass suicide (the People's Temple at Jonestown, Guyana) or mass death (the Branch Davidians at their Mount Carmel settlement in Waco, Texas, which was raided and burned to the ground by government agents).[74] In such narratives, either as agents of their own death or victims of death at the hands of law enforcement, the Nuwaubian Yamassee "cult" could only end badly. Sheriff Howard Sills, the figurehead of the movement against the Nuwaubian Yamassee who initiated the eventual raid of Tama-Re and then, later, personally destroyed the remaining buildings via bulldozer, said: "You can't have one of these cults and *not* have a problem."[75]

The "cult" claim hinged on suspicions of subterfuge, on the belief that the community was not what it seemed. Malachi York had to be up to something, because he could not be, as he presented himself, the religious leader of a peaceful community. Critics found evidence of masquerade even in the construction of Tama-Re, seeing the place as fake, a stage set, with a pasteboard, "mask" quality. Journalist Bill Osinski opens the first chapter of his anti–Nuwaubian Yamassee monograph with a description of drivit, that "cheap, plasticized form of stucco" that he calls "the basic construction material" at Tama-Re.[76] What the Nuwaubian Yamassee presented as "stone temples" were, as one picturesque travelogue treatment of this black "cult" puts it, merely façades put on trailer homes.[77] Assumptions about race and class reverberate through such critical treatments. Rather than a place of black pride, self-determination, and commitment to shared values, the settlement was merely a front, hiding the victimization of brainwashed followers, the covert assembly of a violent insurgency, or, as was ultimately decided by law enforcement, a scheme for stealing both sex and money.

In reaction to the rise in media attention and law enforcement around the Tama-Re complex, Nuwaubian Yamassee discourse from the Tama-Re period focused increasingly on the here and now, deemphasizing the extraterrestrial and reasserting their American citizenship. The community's rhetoric and actions focused on the need for a just, equal society in which the mental chrysalises of the Nuwaubian Yamassee could safely mature. According to this way of thinking, the path to such a society was through law, in keeping with ideals already enshrined in U.S. law. Assembled in their own constituency, the Nuwaubian Yamassee made a plea for equal rights within the American state. The movement issued press releases on letterhead marked "We the People" as a reminder to those fixated on the movement's teachings about being aliens in an ontological sense that they were still citizens in the political sense, with rights and responsibilities in the here and now.[78]

The Nuwaubian Yamassee further responded to surveillance by denying any secrecy on their own part and making their situation at least appear more public. Reacting in this way to a major allegation against them—that they were hiding behaviors, abuses, weapons, crimes—the Nuwaubian Yamassee turned to a rhetoric of equal justice under the law, emphasizing their American citizenship and their fealty to the legal. York warned his followers that their enemies aimed to "hoodwink" the world, spreading lies and hiding truth, slandering his name and the reputation of the community while seeking to obfuscate the legal possibilities available for the Nuwaubian Yamassee to seek redress and justice. Secrecy was the weapon of the enemy, Nuwaubian Yamassee statements and actions emphasized, while the community itself was made up of "public people." Taking advantage of new media, they were, York proclaimed, "gonna make sure everything we do goes up on the internet!"[79] Such publications often mimic the genre of the exposé, revealing the normalcy of life at Tama-Re and, in the wake of the raid, the abuses suffered at the hands of law enforcement. The community approached this commitment to transparency as double-edged, intending to match their own openness with revelations about their opponents. As journalist Bill Osinski writes, the community was so vigorous in filing Freedom of Information Act requests with the local clerk's office that "she increased the per-page charge from twenty-five cents to one dollar, as allowed by state law," citing the drain on her staff, but also making this process—an essential democratic citizen's right—more difficult for the Nuwaubian Yamassee.[80]

This public turn was understood and explicitly framed as the move of citizens calling attention to injustice and seeking recourse through the law. In their publications, including a newspaper, and in public statements, the Nuwaubian Yamassee represented their opponents—Sheriff Sills, whose surveillance ran the gamut from police work to vigilante activity, and the local "good ole boy" media—as "misusing the law to their advantage."[81] The communities called public attention to the abuses they were suffering and sought, beginning in 1999, to link themselves to mainstream political figures, such as Macon mayor Jack Ellis, national civil rights advocates Jesse Jackson and Al Sharpton, and state representative Tyrone Brooks, president of the Georgia Association of Black Elected Officials. Visits from these politicians provided visual proof of Nuwaubian Yamassee association with those in power, and these figures, in turn, voiced public advocacy of the community and its rights.[82] The Nuwaubian Yamassee also sought to increase their practical power as a constituency—and public knowledge of such power—as voters, running their own registration drives and putting up a slate of their own candidates for local political positions. That Nuwaubian Yamassee were serving as members of the local police and fire departments in and around Putnam County became another important public fact, cited as proof of the community's standing as good citizens, integrated into the larger social scene.

The problem the Nuwaubian Yamassee faced in Putnam County was not merely bad press or racism—ubiquitous facts of black life. Rather, according to the Nuwaubian Yamassee take on the situation, the problem was injustice within the system designed to guarantee, enforce, and communicate justice; threat and opposition arose from the system designated to protect and serve. "Terrorism" of the Nuwaubian Yamassee community by law enforcement, the sheriff's appearance in Tama-Re to investigate building and zoning code violations, the excessively and unnecessarily militarized 2002 raid, plus the shell game with charges and protocols in court designed to trick York and eliminate his chances of a fair trial: all these were "crimes" committed against a community that insisted on its own innocence (or, in the case of some zoning issues, admitted guilt but held that the response was radically disproportionate to the relatively minor, technical offense).[83]

Nuwaubian Yamassee use of legal means—public protests, lawsuits designed in part to make news and to focus attention and discussion on the activities of Sills and others—were ways that this "public" community responded to the mobilization of the legal, by others, against the community. "We're gonna hang signs, we're gonna be marching! . . . until we get a reaction on all these violations," York declared, insisting that true law—law as justice— was on the side of his people.[84] The Nuwaubian Yamassee practice of carrying copies of the U.S. Constitution at all times and the solicitation of displays of solidarity from politicians were touted as recognition of an injustice endured not merely by this community but by all "people of color in America."[85] In protest of the "lopsided justice system," Nuwaubian Yamassee turned to evidence from the Department of Justice ("or Injustice?" as one writer asked), citing official statistics that "admit that people of color in the United States are *not* treated equally by the federal, state, and local law enforcement agencies and the Penal systems throughout America."[86] Distributing fliers and staging public protests, Nuwaubian Yamassee organized in groups with names like "Concerned Citizens of Eatonton," emphasizing their rights as citizens and seeking to publicly air their complaints. When "700–800 Nuwaubians circled the courthouse in Eatonton chanting, 'Amun Ma-at'" [which they translated as "Hidden Justice"] during one of York's hearings, they sought to make the hidden visible and to make visible the act of hiding, to bring justice into existence by calling attention to its absence and inversion in the so-called justice system's treatment of York and the community.[87]

Ironically, the worry that the residents of Tama-Re were potentially dangerous and antisocial was only amplified by their public turn. Proactive use of the law and public mobilization of their status as citizens were cited by critics of the movement as evidence of the Nuwaubian Yamassee's criminality. It could also be that such confident, black engagement with the law further infuriated the community's opponents in law enforcement. "We started encountering Nuwaubians on traffic stops," recalls Lieutenant Tracey Bowen—as if such encounters were purely random, occurring without any agency on behalf of the police—"and they refused to roll down their windows." Bowen says the Nuwaubian Yamassee "would buck the system just anywhere they went," but the Nuwaubian view was that they were using the legal system to protect themselves, exercising their rights, demonstrating their knowledge of and skill at the law. Sheriff Sills told journalist Asher Elbein that, with fliers and lawsuits and the use of video cameras to record every interaction with law enforcement, the Nuwaubian Yamassee were doing "every fucking thing they could to start an altercation."[88]

Previous scholarship on the movement has characterized its legal tactics as fraudulent, in keeping with the rhetoric of masquerade or con, with Nuwaubian Yamassee voter registration an attempt to "stack the voters' rolls" and Nuwaubian Yamassee candidates for office part of an attempt to "take over" local politics. Whether cynical or sincere, such tactics are in keeping with Aliite faith that through civic participation one can achieve justice, bringing true law into actuality within the existing legal system. The theories of law engaged by the Nuwaubian Yamassee echo those used by white "sovereign

citizen" individuals and organizations. This causes further confusion for ob-
servers, academic and otherwise, though such confusion is predicated on a
lack of understanding of the centrality of the concept of rule of law and the
conception of law as a tool for the oppressed in what Palmer, for instance,
characterizes as "radical anti-government groups."[89] What such groups oppose, in fact, is perceived abuses of government power; they seek to mobilize
the power of the American citizenry to oppose such oppression. Mischarac-
terizations of this ideology, particularly as racialized, poses a false paradox, as
when Sheriff Sills expressed his incomprehension that "a Freeman . . . a *racist*,
a *white separatist*" would collaborate with "*black supremacists*," shock predicated on misrepresentation of the parties involved.[90] The Nuwaubian Yamassee have consistently argued that Sills himself is a racist; their collaboration
with the visiting Montana Freemen at Tama-Re, on theories and practices
of true law, looks from an Aliite perspective like the cooperation between
citizens seeking to restore justice through recourse to the legal system, not
separatism or supremacism of any sort.

Likewise, the Nuwaubian Yamassee community presented the resignation
of the seven police officers and one firefighter who, in the language of Nuwaubian Yamassee publications, "sacrificed their jobs" in a protest against unjust
treatment of the community, as a story about Nuwaubian Yamassee as fellow citizens. Important for this rhetoric was the fact that supervisors of these
officers spoke well of them in terms of character and professionalism, and
expressed related surprise that they were Nuwaubian Yamassee.[91] With their
resignation, these officers played a part in a broader push, by the Nuwaubian
Yamassee movement as a whole, to make itself and its situation public, to
perform to the eyes of the state, to "continue to put the facts out" in the hopes
that injustice would be recognized and made right.[92]

"YOU'RE TALKING TO THEM AS YOU SPEAK": WASHITAW AND LAW ENFORCEMENT SURVEILLANCE

In their response to state surveillance, the Washitaw have come to believe
in the possibility of recognition by those surveilling them. Such surveillance, as Dauphin Washington has told his Empire Washitaw community,
is "constant."[93] The same FBI that, in 2000, raided Goston's home in Winns-
boro, Louisiana, and acted as an agent of violence against the Washitaw

movement is now revered, within that movement, as a potential intercessor with the power to bring Washitaw claims before legal authorities.

As Goston recounts it, she had been eating breakfast when "the government of the United States" showed up at her door, seizing documents including license plates, driver's licenses, motor vehicle registration papers, passports, marriage certificates, and certificates of live birth produced by, and serving as proof of identity and membership within, the Washitaw de Dugdahmoundyah.[94] In the wake of "the raid," as it is remembered by the Washitaw, Goston's son Fredrix Joe Washington has emerged as a leader and has banned the production and use of what he calls "documents" or "paperwork" of Washitaw national identity, equating such documents with "fraud."[95] The Empire Washitaw will only issue paperwork when Washington can be sure that it will be respected as *real*, which means, primarily, that it will receive recognition from those in authority. "We want it recognized around the country," he has said, "around the world."[96]

Although Goston was never charged, the raid nonetheless disrupted the movement. A schism ensued—the result of ongoing debate over nationality practices—and Goston suffered a stroke and various other physical ailments widely blamed on the stress of the raid. She was placed in a nursing home and kept largely out of contact with the wider Washitaw community by Washington, who leads the group known as Empire Washitaw. His position has transformed, in recent years, from "Brother Joe" to "King Joe" or "Emperor Joe" to his current title of "Dauphin."[97] With a core constituency of a few dozen people but probably a few hundred affiliated in total, members of the Empire Washitaw are geographically dispersed across the United States, from Baltimore to California and Detroit to New Orleans, with vocal followers in rural parts of Georgia and the Carolinas. The Empire Washitaw communicate and conduct business over multiple weekly conference calls, the most important being the Sunday-night "State of the Empire" or nation-building call (described in the preface). This call, started by Washington seventeen years ago for the purpose of "getting the land back," has always been open to anyone, with callers able to publicly identify themselves or remain anonymous.[98] The calls offer opportunities for wide-ranging discussions of ways to advance Washitaw goals, and Washington insists he is open to all ideas, "unless they are illegal."[99]

Since the raid, Washington has been emphatic in reiterating that his community obeys and respects existing legal interpretations and seeks change through the legal system. In keeping with Aliite tradition, the members of this community seek to make public their desire for legal redress and to publicize what they take to be legal evidence in support of their claims. Thus, the Empire Washitaw run a letter-writing campaign to ask elected officials to "Give us our land" as the Supreme Court supposedly decided to do with the "Turner's Heirs" decision.[100] There has also been an online petition to elected officials on the same subject.[101] While Washington encouraged direct outreach to President Obama, he has urged all Washitaw to refrain from any contact with President Trump, calling Trump a "bigot" and expressing fear that "communication with him turns into a dialogue with evil," as he lies about and vilifies those with whom he corresponds, via his notorious use of the social media platform Twitter and other means.[102] Instead of seeking to persuade the current president, then, the Empire Washitaw now focus on the level of state governors, and they are preparing a new petition to be directed at all fifty governors, drawing on "the legal theory" laid out in *Return of the Ancient Ones*.[103] Quoting his mother, Washington says that the purpose of these actions is to ask those in official positions of power: "Are you going to abide by your own laws?"[104]

Washington's insistence on complying with existing interpretations of American law is coupled with Aliite emphasis on law enforcement agencies not only as agents of the legal system but also as individuals sworn to protect and serve the true law. While he repeatedly reminds his community of the ubiquitous presence of law enforcement surveillance, such presence represents an opportunity for advancing Washitaw claims. For a community that interacts primarily through public conference calls, the specter of surveillance places all Washitaw activity within a panopticon (at least imagined). "Authorities listen" to the Washitaw, Washington says.[105] "They are very interested in what we're doing."[106] When challenged by members of his community who contest his claims and his leadership, Washington shouts them down through recourse to the power of law enforcement: "You're talking to them as you speak, whether you realize it or not," he recently said to one persistent detractor.[107] Such assertions do not just come from Washington himself, nor are the law enforcement authorities referred to unnamed. A debate about documents was recently ended by a loyal defender of Washington who repeatedly declared, "The Emperor has the FBI on his side."[108]

Surveillance is invoked not only as a way to discipline behavior but also as a reward. On one occasion, the FBI was given honors and greetings at the beginning of the call, part of a ritual invocation of the ancestors, an acknowledgment of the lineage of prophets, and an honoring of present matriarchs within the community.[109] When the community remains polite, Washington congratulates them, telling them the authorities are "very proud of the ways you have conducted yourselves over the phone."[110] In statements that reiterate an implied connection between Washington, as leader of the community, and the authorities of the state, he speaks on behalf of various law enforcement agencies, reporting back their assessment of his community. "You are all being heard" is a statement of both threat and hope.[111] Indeed, this belief in the potential to transform society by being surveilled allows the Washitaw to invest hope in conversations that would otherwise seem inconsequential. Nothing is private; any comment is a comment made directly before representatives of the state. Since "authorities" must recognize Washitaw claims for their goals to come to pass, some Washitaw insist that they need go no further than their own conference call to voice their arguments to the state and thus be accorded "this recognition."[112]

On the Sunday following the bloody week of the killing of Alton Sterling by police officers in Baton Rouge, the killing of Philando Castile by police officers in Minnesota, and the killing of five police officers in Dallas during a Black Lives Matter protest over those deaths, a caller to the Washitaw nation-building call asked, distraught, what that community was doing and could do. Dauphin Washington's response was to remind his followers that "black people do matter . . . and blue-uniformed people matter, too." While avoiding suggesting any specific course of action, Washington reminded his nation to have faith in the state. Pressed by the caller about "those rogues" among the police who, in her imagery, wore the white robe and hood under their blue uniform, Washington had an immediate answer: due to FBI action, several officers with KKK affiliations have been fired in recent days. On the one hand, the systematic racism that Black Lives Matter seeks to call attention to is here reduced to explicit affiliation in a secret, conspiratorial group, the KKK. On the other hand, faith in the state, in the law—and, in this case, in a law enforcement that literally polices the police, as Washington insists the FBI does—dominates. This is framed explicitly in terms of surveillance. On the killing of Alton Sterling, Washington's response was, "Why would a person do such a dumb thing as take a gun out and shoot a man twice when he's already on the ground? . . . You got cameras everywhere."[113]

Under surveillance, communities in the Aliite tradition have responded by courting that surveillance, taking even hostile attention as desirable attention, and scrutiny by the state as official recognition. Surveillance, rather than being resented, is celebrated. This hinges, of course, on basic Aliite claims about law—an insistent faith that true law, that which equals justice and truth, can be actualized within and through the legal system. In such a system surveillance can only ever, ultimately, lead to a more just America, an America more in keeping with its own stated ideals.

"I just want to welcome them," a member of the Empire Washitaw proclaimed over that community's public conference call, speaking of the law enforcement and governmental agencies assumed to be listening in as these Aliites conduct their business and discuss their plans for getting their land back. "I just want to welcome them as lovers of truth."[114] The implication here is that through such listening, the listener can be changed and, in turn, can help change circumstances for the Washitaw. Such a hope is grounded in Aliite understanding of law as synonymous with truth and justice, and the related Aliite optimism, seen throughout the history of Aliite thought, that those who serve as representatives of institutions of (however failed, however incorrectly interpreted, even however corrupt) law and law enforcement in society can be convinced and compelled by such true law. Like those Moorish Americans who contacted employees of the Justice Department in the 1930s and 1940s, or the Yamassee who courted local law enforcement agencies during the Tama-Re period, the Empire Washitaw hold to a belief that those who say they are loyal to law are, ultimately, redeemable by and through their encounter with true law—true law spoken and exemplified by Aliites.

"YOU GOT CAMERAS EVERYWHERE"

"Love, truth, peace, freedom, and justice" chant the congregation of Chicago's MSTA Temple No. 1 as they parade down the streets of that city. Flagbearers carry the Moorish and the American flags, flanking a large framed photograph of Noble Drew Ali. The men wear fezzes, the women, turbans. Suits, dresses, and polo shirts alternate with African-inspired national garb. One man wears an American flag over his shoulders. Other Moors carry miniature flags, both U.S. and Moorish. "What is our nationality?" goes a shout. "Moorish American!" comes the response.

In the recording of this event, posted on YouTube, the camera keeps capturing images of community members who, in turn, are recording the parade with their cellphone cameras.[115] The ubiquity of the surveillance has led to an investment in self-surveillance. When Dauphin Washington spoke to his community in the wake of the killing of Alton Sterling, the only direct action he recommended was for his fellow Washitaw to "keep your camera with you, your telephone with you."[116] Participation in surveillance thus extends the panopticon. In line with seeking protection from the power of the state through affiliation with the state and its power, here, having a camera phone at the ready becomes a way of using surveillance to keep oneself safe from those forces of law enforcement so invested in surveilling the community they consider to be black. The cameras at the MSTA parade document Aliite embodiment of nationality and Aliite practice of citizenship, but, in this historical moment, they must be read also as a means of self-defense, an eye raised against the state. These handheld cameras mirror the eyes of the state, simultaneously serve as a way for Aliites to recognize and preserve—and publicize—Aliite performance of claims, but their presence also implies the threat inextricable from the history of state surveillance of African American communities.

For Aliites, the all-seeing gaze of the state is a source of both potential threat and potential grace. Like other aspects of state power, surveillance is seen as unavoidable, as ever-present, and while Aliites recognize the potential for catastrophic harm to themselves and their communities, they see no option but to negotiate with both the state's gaze and their ideas of that gaze. Aliite thought, here again, proves itself to be both practical and hopeful. Aliites equate the all-seeing eye of the state with justice because they insist that the legal systems of the state can and will ultimately be persuaded to align with true law. At the same time, Aliite silence or secrecy under the gaze of the state will only accentuate doubts, imply guilt, and lead to violent action by the state against Aliites. Aliites' embrace of surveillance thus reflects both the radical imbalance of power between Aliites and the state and the radical Aliite faith in the ability of true law to be communicated—communicated via an epistemology that is the subject of the next chapter.

6

THE UNFINISHED PYRAMID

Knowledge and the Legal

THE ANGLES OF THE PYRAMID

THE PYRAMID ON THE GREAT SEAL is a foundation unfinished. Half monument, half invitation, the structure is at once a product of the past and a process of practical labor in the present, uniting forebears and descendants in an ongoing, communal effort.

As an Aliite symbol, the pyramid has associations of confidence—in heritage as well as in contemporary progress along a trajectory arcing ever to justice and equality, through law—but the symbol also conveys associations of unease. Pyramids are seen in Aliite thought as declarations of African sovereignty, storehouses for and symbols of African learning and wisdom.[1] The iconic form signifying the grandeur of the Moorish past, pyramids are metonyms for Moorish industriousness, accomplishment, and potential.[2] Yet the pyramid's second association complicates this sense of nationalist pride, for pyramids, as symbols of pharaonic Egypt, always also recall the biblical narrative of slavery and escape. The Bible, though contested, is nonetheless central to Aliite thought, and the Exodus, as the West's dominant myth about slavery, thus casts the pyramid as a product of slave labor, a monument to an oppressive regime. The pyramid represents dichotomous views on history: a nostalgic imagining of ancient African civilization and a reminder of the reality of slavery and the attendant, transhistorical demand for liberation. Neither triumph nor oppression is complete. At once orienting and disorienting, the pyramid, as a key image in Aliite iconography, is a reminder of the tension at the heart of Ali's system of faith in law.

This chapter focuses on Aliite *knowledge practices*. In particular, Aliite communities valorize and engage in a process they call "research." This Aliite practice involves turning to sources widely acknowledged as authoritative within the broader society and producing from those sources pieces of "knowledge" that function as evidence in support of preconceived Aliite claims. This research process is one of creative resistance to the same sources of authority on which it depends, a kind of "signifyin(g)" with history, legal precedent, etymology, archaeology, and other disciplines, in which Aliite thinkers claim the ability to speak truth in the face of false interpretations, even as those false interpretations dominate popular understanding of those disciplines.[3] Such counterhegemonic knowledge practices mirror both the negotiations of relations with levels of sovereignty that characterize Aliite understandings of sovereignty and the equally characteristic Aliite emphasis on appealing for recognition and favor from existing authorities. Aliite knowledge practices negotiate recognized, authoritative sources of knowledge, claiming to uncover the truth hidden within them. Aliite research thus echoes Aliite understanding of true law's relation to the fallible human interpretations enforced as legal within society, insisting upon truth in contrast to the lies or misunderstandings that pass as "knowledge" within America.

The pyramid offers a useful metaphor for such practices, for MSTA legend offers another perspective on the symbol: as the site of an initiatory trial. Traveling the world as a circus magician or a merchant seaman, Drew Ali, in his teen years, visited Egypt, according to certain stories. At Giza, he was led, blindfolded, into the Pyramid of Cheops, and abandoned. Ali liberated himself and emerged as a prophet, given the title "Sharif" or "Noble."[4] Moorish accounts say that the mage or priest who led Ali into the pyramid and initiated him into an esoteric brotherhood taught him certain secrets. Ali's trial, his deciphering of the pyramid, offers a way to think about his ability to cope with the cognitive dissonance represented by the pyramid. Ali exemplifies this paradox, committing to the project of the Great Seal's unfinished pyramid (America), while aware of the suffering and blood on which this project was built. Dissonance over the civic goal—between the ideal of equal citizenship in a democracy and the actual lived experience of Aliites—echoes dissonance over the legal means of reaching that goal— between the ideal of justice as enshrined in and identified with true law and Aliite experience of injustice through legal history and the legal system. Aliites work with and within the state to reform the state. Aliite knowledge practices, in turn, appeal to accepted sources of authority to challenge how that authority has been used, simultaneously respecting and rebelling against, honoring and disrupting.

The knowledge practices considered fundamental to this work of contesting and correcting the law produce knowledge understood as *evidentiary*, that is, capable of functioning as compelling evidence within legal discourse.[5] "Evidentiary" in Aliite thought means having merit as evidence. I take it to imply, in addition to legal terms such as "admissible" or "relevant," that the objective, factual value of what is presented is beyond debate. A piece of evidence may be considered admissible in court and thus open for consideration and decision; Aliite knowledge is evidentiary and therefore bypasses the need for consideration by virtue of its indisputable nature. See, for instance, pieces of knowledge said to "stand on their own evidentiary merit" in the anonymous MSTA text, *Moorish Science of Salvation True*. Evidentiary knowledge is understood as objective, empirical, and "undisputable"—contributing to the legal work of *proving* Aliite claims.[6] Consisting of knowledge in a recognizable form, suitable for the presumably universal mode of communication that is legal discourse, such knowledge "uncovers" truth from the midst of lies. Evidence is mined from the very sources seen as key to the erasure of Aliite claims and the oppression of Aliites.

Three ramifications follow from this mining of evidence, this "uncovering" of truth from the midst of lies. First, Aliite thinkers must negotiate the cognitive dissonance generated by their simultaneous contestation and cooptation of authoritative sources. Sources condemned for their role in maintaining ignorance and oppression are simultaneously privileged for the hidden truths attributed to them. The realities of oppression and the mechanisms of its maintenance are constantly engaged, even canonized, in Aliite texts.

Second, in part as a means of resolving the related dissonance between truth-claims and social reality, Aliite thinkers do not merely "uncover" knowledge, they also safeguard both pieces and practices of knowledge. A dynamic of decryption and encryption of knowledge—rendering knowledge public yet also securing it as the exclusive property of a given thinker—responds to and reflects this tension. At the same time, this dynamic also reflects and addresses tensions in Aliite communities over individual authority and contested leadership roles, the dissonance between selfless commitment to communal uplift and the entrepreneurial spirit of individuals marketing their own thought, charisma, and authority. In a competitive marketplace of ideas, individual Aliite thinkers engage in practices of encryption concomitant with their rhetorical emphasis on decryption. By keeping knowledge in between public access and private authority, thinkers allow themselves to bolster their own positions within Aliite circles. Even as they espouse populist values regarding the liberation of secret knowledge, Aliite thinkers also grant themselves elite status as researchers. Demonstrations of supposedly objective facts are thus often contests of charisma and performative skill, "battles" to determine the more persuasive thinkers.

Third, Aliite emphasis on fact over belief, and truth over superstition, leads to reconceptualizing and, in some cases, rejecting the term "religion"— with preference given to "science" or "factology," for instance, as terms to describe the Aliite worldview. Yet, at the same time, "religion," understood to be a privileged and particularly efficacious legal category, is mobilized by Aliites, who engage in a discourse of "religious freedom" to achieve rights and accommodations within the legal system.

"THERE IS CONVINCING EVIDENCE": CONTESTATION AND COOPTATION OF SOURCES OF KNOWLEDGE

Aliites widely consider the characteristic Aliite knowledge practice called *research* to be a definitive trait of national identity.[7] In order to be a Moor, Nuwaubian Yamassee, or Washitaw, many Aliite thinkers insist, "you got to research."[8] Empire Washitaw chief spiritual minister OukhaRa has explained that his name means "one who studies" in the indigenous Washitaw language, "because I am a researcher."[9] R. A. Umar Shabazz Bey declares, "I am a researcher," and states that "the most important reason for writing this book is to spark a new wave of research," which he presents as an ongoing and necessarily communal project.[10] "We are commanded to 'Know thyself' and this is achieved in numerous ways such as 'study' in the history of your ancestors, the geography, the language etc," writes MSTA thinker B. Denham El.[11] Taj Tarik Bey insists that "in Moorish culture, you are encouraged to read, research and study as a normal state of custom, duty and general affairs."[12] The MSTA activist group Ali's Men is self-described as "a group of researchers."[13] "DO YOUR OWN RESEARCH" is a prominent admonition on the major Nuwaubian Yamassee website, and Nuwaubian Yamassee thinker Phil Valentine describes his central task as "research . . . to find out the information no matter where it may lie," and notes that knowledge is usually "buried deep, purposefully."[14]

This Aliite method of research does not use data to determine an argument; rather, it assembles as data only that which can be made to support a preexisting argument. The truth is already *known*; it must now be publicly proven. Aliites "compile" texts and lectures, films and websites, anthologizing historical texts that ignore or counter Aliite claims. With the end goal (the truth-claim) in mind, readers will thus see these sources as evidence marshaled in support of that claim. Aliites emphasize the importance of such research and its centrality to Aliite identity, teaching each other that, for instance, "all Moors must have libraries in their house," that both proximity to and mastery of intellectual resources are essential.[15]

Aliite research requires a particular sort of reading, and sources assembled by Aliite thinkers are to be approached, a priori, as evidence in favor of the major truth-claims of those thinkers. Readers of such texts—textbooks, really, manuals for research—feel that they learn research skills, which is accurate within this particular Aliite sense. Readers of such texts learn the process of producing evidence from sources in support of a predetermined "truth"—eisegesis rather than exegesis, an act of construction called "uncovering" or "decoding."[16] Goston's *Return of the Ancient Ones* is a prime example, collecting "authentic copies of the treaties, maps, conventions, Supreme Court cases and other legal documents," the relation of which to Goston's project can ultimately be traced back only to her decision to include them in her book.[17] As one Washitaw puts it, Goston "was an archivist . . . [who] found the truth."[18] The material she includes in her book is there because it proves her case. Goston's readers, in turn, are to study the sources she has assembled with her movement's broader truth-claims in mind. Sources are thus read as evidence in hindsight; the conclusion precedes the work of research.

The goal of research is the production of evidentiary knowledge, understood as knowledge that can be recognized as evidentiary by non-Aliites. To be evidentiary is to be legally efficacious—able to be communicated and compelling in legal encounters. Such evidentiary knowledge needs to be derived from a source that is likewise widely recognized as authoritative. Aliites rely on a broadly shared American legal consciousness to determine those sources of knowledge recognized as authoritative and potentially evidentiary. Historical, archaeological, and etymological knowledge, for instance, are frequently employed as evidence in legal discourse in America, as are certain sorts of images, such as photographs and maps. Presumed to be objective and empirical, these are sources and conveyers of facts. A photograph documents what it captures; etymology determines the meaning of a word; archaeology establishes a date and location for a given artifact. This approach to knowledge, following from the centrality of law and legal discourse in Aliite tradition, leads to the general rejection of certain forms of knowledge practice—like the "mathematical theology" or numerological interpretations popular among Nation of Islam and Five Percent Nation thinkers—at the same time that it encourages, even forces, Aliite thinkers to engage with oppressive sources, to confront ways by which oppression is maintained.[19]

The dominant, accepted narrative of history is viewed simultaneously as a lie and as the documentation of that lie. Washitaw Empress Goston, for example, uses the word "his-story" to flag the biases (patriarchal and classist as well as racist) at play in that narrative, yet she insists that both primary historical documents and secondary scholarship also serve as "his lie documented," offering the researcher access to hidden truth. Sources are simultaneously coopted (as containing true testimony to the past) and contested (as part of a system of lies designed to keep dark-skinned people, in particular, ignorant of their past and their rights). As a researcher, Goston turns to the letters of Thomas Jefferson or pages from the journals of the explorers Meriwether Lewis and William Clark in order to pull "the lying cover . . . off the past and present,"[20] revealing the "documented truth" that was always already present in the text.[21] Some sources are assumed to have a recognized, mainstream authority, while others accrue credibility by association with prestigious institutions or thinkers assumed to have mainstream respect. UNESCO's designation of Poverty Point as a World Heritage site, for instance, was cited by the Washitaw as recognition of their own claims. The UNESCO declaration was read aloud over the weekly nation-building conference call, as evidence that "the world is recognizing" Washitaw claims, that "the UN is recognizing" Washitaw.[22]

Photographs are employed under the assumption of incontestability. Offering objective proof of that which is captured in the image, photographs are assumed to be evidentiary. Their rhetorical force is presumed to be such that often images are presented without commentary in Aliite texts. As with historical sources, readers must construct their own connections to the argument in play. Giant, carved-stone Olmec heads offer a frequently cited piece of archaeological knowledge across all Aliite communities, the supposedly "Negroid" facial features of these heads offering uncontestable proof that this element of accepted ancient American history is, in fact, Moorish.[23] Such images are often presented with no context or identification beyond proclamations of the truth viewers are supposed to take from them. For example, when Najee-Ullah El and Taylor El offer a pair of "Original paintings of Black Mohawk Indians in Moorish garb," they make no mention of the painter, provenance, or story behind these works. The images serve, instead, as evidence for diverse arguments about the connections between Moorish and indigenous identity that readers may bring to those images.[24]

Maps are assumed to function in a similar manner, requiring little or no commentary. Goston devotes an entire, entirely wordless, chapter to maps in *Return of the Ancient Ones*.[25] MSTA thinker Timothy Myers-El, in his *The Huevolution of Sacred Muur Science Past and Present*, includes a map of North Africa and the Middle East, and a modern highway map of New Jersey, centered on Newark, the first serving as evidence of Moorish origins, the second referencing the life of Noble Drew Ali.[26] Maps, like other images, can thus be offered as evidence of otherwise outlandish claims, presented as objective and factual proof of these claims. Among the Washitaw, one of the most frequent uses of maps is to show images of the supercontinent of Pangea or diagrams of the current continents in the process of splitting off from this unified land mass. With such images, according to Washitaw thinkers, an entire historical narrative is proven true: the story that, as Goston said, "the whole world was Africa," with the northern half of what would become the continent of Africa tucked against and thus connected to the Gulf of Mexico and what would become the coast of Louisiana.[27]

Similarly, other Aliite thinkers link photographs as evidence to their own claims, as with the Moorish insistence, voiced by Najee-Ullah El and Taylor El as well as others, that the American holiday of Thanksgiving was initiated to celebrate the slaughter not of turkeys but of "Turks," meaning indigenous Moors/Moslems. As evidence, the authors merely write: "Case in point, the massacre of Wounded Knee," and then include the famous 1890 photograph of federal troops surrounding the mass grave. A caption, cut and pasted from some other source, describes the image but the connection between that description and the specific argument about the "slaughtering of thousands of turkeys/Turks" is one the reader must make for him- or herself, one that precedes examination of the (horrific) image.[28]

A striking Nuwaubian Yamassee example of this use of images can be found in an online video purporting to offer objective proof of the close genetic relation between canines and Caucasians. To establish that whites are more like animals than humans, a montage of photographs from a website called www.marrymypet.com is offered. These images of white people sprawling in beds, clutching and kissing their pets, needs, within the context of the film, no interpretation. While this is certainly not a source with mainstream authority, the medium of photograph does have such authority: these images are evidentiary, proof positive of a claim the Yamassee audience already know well and to which they assent. Reiterating the role of evidentiary knowledge, after flashing through several such photographs, a basic Yamassee credo is repeated in this video: "We deal with facts!"[29] As one contemporary Nuwaubian thinker insists, "Everything can be researched." Indeed, this is offered as the central teaching, by this thinker, of "Pop" (Malachi York). The Master Teacher's message was not to believe him, but to research it yourself. "If You Can't Prove It, We Don't Want to Hear It," states the UNNM Constitution, declaring the Nuwaubian Yamassee a people who "Deal with Just the Facts."[30]

Research must be done by the individual in order to truly count as Aliite research. "Perform your own due diligence," write Kudjo Adwo El and Rami A. Salaam El toward the end of their *77 Amazing Facts about the Moors: With Complete Proof.* Admitting that, in fact, they have not offered "complete proof" in their book, they argue that this decision to neglect such proof is the key to their book's pedagogical purpose. The volume is less concerned with teaching "facts" than with inspiring research: "This text could have matched every fact with a source so it would be easy for the readers to confirm its contents, but that would be a disservice. The mission of this book is not to work your journey for you." Readers are urged, "Pick up these books and go study. Go to the websites and study. . . . Study! It is insufficient to simply believe what one tells you, even if they are recognized scholars. . . . You can believe us, or believe others, but if you do so, you will never know. You must seek the truth for yourself."[31]

Aliite knowledge practices, drawing on sources and/or media the epistemic authority of which is recognizable and shared throughout broader American culture, respond to the cognitive dissonance of a reality that does not match Aliite claims. In contesting and coopting these existing authorities, and insisting on the objective, factual, evidentiary nature of the knowledge produced by such engagement, the Aliite practice of research quells disorientation by emphasizing the preexisting orientation of truth-claims. With the end of research always known in advance, Aliites can read and raid widely, always emerging from their encounters in sources of knowledge with more evidence and, thus, more of a sense that they deal with facts rather than beliefs, that they are engaging in practices of proof rather than mere speculation.

"MANY DEFINITIONS WERE ALTERED":
ETYMOLOGY, EPISTEMOLOGY, AND AUTHORITY

Truth-claims predicate knowledge practices. Aliite research is the accumulation of evidence to prove that which is already known and accepted. Evidentiary knowledge, as objective fact, is not debatable; however, it is often accompanied by the challenge to those who doubt: "Do your own research like we did."[32] This is the challenge accompanying Aliite anthologies of primary sources, but the rhetoric here does not match with an Aliite reality in which competing charismatic thinkers need to differentiate and maintain possession of their own arguments. The emphasis on individual research gives way, for many Aliite thinkers, to a need to follow a particular thinker's arguments and interpretations. With the schismatic and splintered nature of Aliite movements, this is as true within individual communities as between them.

One means by which the authority of Aliite thinkers is exerted and contested is through the Aliite knowledge practices categorized as "etymology." "Etymology is the origin and history of words," as Abdullah El Talib Mosi Bey explains it. For a researcher, however, to enter into such questions of origin, such study of the accretions of history, is to reveal the layers of "distorted" meanings that have been intentionally added to or otherwise have come to displace the authentic, true signification of words. "Etymology opens up a new whole world of thinking for you," says MSTA thinker Abdullah El Talib Mosi Bey, allowing the thinker to get "in the right track of thought and understanding," while also revealing the oppressive history of "how words are suppressed" and "true meaning" is concealed.[33] Such "meaning" can have legal consequence. "When we voluntarily identify ourselves" with false labels, with the wrong words, "legally, we are subjecting ourselves to slavery," G. S. Kudjo Adwo El and G. S. Rami A. Salaam El insist.[34] The archaeological work of returning to the authentic meaning of the historical roots of words is thus essential for the practice of citizenship, for throwing off cognitive, spiritual, legal, and political shackles imposed by the unconscious use of words.

While the evidentiary status of etymological knowledge is universally recognized in Aliite communities, there is debate about the means of acquiring such knowledge and, thus, about specific etymological claims. Etymological discourse—engagement with words and an excavation of their true and thus legally valid meanings—offers Aliite thinkers an astounding degree of interpretive freedom, allowing for the creative linkage of ideas. Amid a chaos of contested stances, Aliite etymological arguments are opportunities for individual thinkers to show their acumen—their charisma, their quick wits, their performative skill.

Words are mobilized rhetorically as evidence for Aliite claims in four ways. First, following patterns similar to those of Aliite mathematical discourse, in what some thinkers call the "science of letters & numerology," words can be networked with other words, starting with the letters that compose that word.[35] This sort of "letter by letter" work allows for the linkage of "science," for instance, with "sacred," "secret," "shield," "sword," "sex," and "scribe," as well as "shit" (fertilizer), "ski," and "sail."[36] Allowing for a reasonably free association, such technique can advance an argument via accumulation (science is linked to lots of knowledge words) but is, obviously, somewhat scattershot. The second way of engaging words is by associative linkage between sounds. This can be done by splitting a word at the syllables ("lie-bury," for instance, or "his-story," in which case the rhetorical power resides in the new pronunciation functioning as a pun for a broader argument) or by linking the sounds of syllables to other words, in English or other languages (this is often presented as etymological work, as when, for instance, "black" is explained as sharing the same "root" as Kabbalah, via its syllables, "ba, la, and ka."[37] Describing such linkage of terms via the sounds of syllables is frequently described as—and justified on the authority of—Kabbalah. For instance, when Kudja Adwo El discusses the "spiritual energy" of the word "Nationality," he explicitly cites "the teachings of the Kabballah" [sic] for his claim that the "N-A" sound signifies "stability, the first principle and the double virtue of recoiling on itself and spreading out," offering related words that, as an associative constellation, deepen understanding of what "nationality" truly *means*, even how it *functions*, on a "spiritual" level linked to the linguistic and intellectual, and yet always transcending these levels.[38]

Another means of engaging words is to offer direct definitions of one's own, often in the form of a glossary. Eric Mungin Bey has produced a whole book using this technique, glossing key words in the writings of Drew Ali.[39] The final technique used in Aliite circles is that most recognizable as etymology, recourse to recognized and cited dictionaries for the definition and historical usage and roots of a given word. Knowledge of the precise meaning of words is a requirement for effective communication in legal discourse presumed by general American legal consciousness, yet for Aliites, such knowledge, like all knowledge, takes effort to excavate from under the cover of lies.

Dictionaries are treated like historical sources, like scripture, as authoritative containers of truth that simultaneously bear the marks of corruption over time, either by accident or with the express purpose of oppressing Moors. An introductory page on many of the books published by the MSTA-affiliated Califa Media urges readers to keep on hand a "good standard dictionary of the English language, preferably one printed before 1965," in order to "make the most effective use" of the text. Voicing a popular argument in Aliite communities, the text explains:

> The reason[s] for this suggestion are two-fold: First, the book you hold is revised from a text originally published in 1928. Some of the words contained herein may no longer be in common use and/or may have a different definition in modern dictionaries. Second, I suggest using a dictionary of this sort as many definitions—especially those pertaining to our people—were altered after the Civil Rights Movement in the United States. An example would be comparing the definitions of "American" in a pre-1965 dictionary versus one printed more recently.[40]

Aliite thinkers must, then, be selective in their use of dictionaries; a dictionary useful for producing a reliable definition of one word may not be reliable for another. This stance allows for the freedom to selectively link the authority of a given dictionary with a particular argument about a given word.[41] Such excessive creativity, unchecked by shared rules, leads to the multiplicity of conflicting approaches and claims lamented by many Aliite thinkers. Taj Tarik Bey, one of the most vocal theorists on the importance of etymology, frequently expresses frustration that the Aliite project is being held back by lack of universal "knowledge of the etymon," without which, he insists, there can be no communication. His solution is to insist that all thinkers use the same dictionary, the *Oxford English Dictionary*, choice of "all scholars around the world . . . because Oxford is always going to the etymon."[42]

As fervently as Tarik Bey appeals to his fellow Aliites for a shared first principle in etymology, he also benefits from the situation as it is, gaining credibility—and fame—within Aliite circles through his display of charisma, speed at argumentation, and persuasive power, frequently featured in online videos showing him contesting knowledge with other Aliites, "on the battlefield" of the streets. The tension here, between a desire for unity as essential for communal uplift and the benefits of individual entrepreneurialism, exists throughout the Aliite tradition. The project of uplift—selfless, a matter of sacrifice for others—becomes, also, a business opportunity.

Knowledge is not only functional, it can also serve as a product and marker of a distinct thinker's celebrity. Since Aliite history is always also about practical political, historical-material concerns, it is essential to note here that Aliite thinkers make their livings from their own, unique presentations of knowledge. Writings, lectures, and seminars exist in a competitive marketplace, and the distinguishing traits of charisma, argumentative dexterity, and rhetorical strength make the difference between a known and valuable name and those anonymous Moors that a thinker like Tarik Bey "destroys" with demonstrations of knowledge in the street battles that constitute a special genre of Aliite media.[43]

The lack of shared rules or definitive sources, the arbitrary nature of etymological knowledge practices, facilitate one means of battle, allowing for contestation between thinkers. One thinker can undermine the credibility of another by delegitimizing what, for that thinker, passes as etymology. This is often the case in Taj Tarik Bey's attempts to school other Aliites on real etymology—he dismisses, for instance, lesser approaches, such as phonetics and connotative definitions. It is also the case in *Return of the Ancient Ones*, where a "last minute entry," an afterword, by MSTA thinker C. Nelson Bey attempts, via etymology, to make claims about Washitaw origins. Nelson Bey argues for the "celestial heritage" of all Moors, tracing them back to the Planet X through etymological reading of words like "Louisiana." Breaking the word down into syllables and bouncing between Sumerian and Hebrew, Kemetic and Hieroglyphics, he holds that "Louisiana = The great dark warriors in the city of Ta'Moori who came down from heaven or Planet X."[44] Goston, in an afterword to his afterword, asserts her authority and trumps both his story and his approach, drawing associative connections between his arguments and words from her life. Nelson Bey mentions the Sea of Reeds and mulberry as a name for morusberry or Moor's berry; Goston writes, "My cousin is named Washington Reed," and all the Washitaw are "born on the lake or near water"; further, "We were a people whose parents planted a mulberry tree at the kitchen window where the birds played and sang." Likewise, "Louis and Lewis are family so is Annie my mother's name. Anna, my great grandmother's name." Such "signifyin(g)" at once unearths real significance, constructing and calling attention to patterns, and also, as Goston admits, reads like random coincidence, deflating the force of Bey's performance and calling into question the entire enterprise of producing knowledge in this way.[45]

Etymology here demonstrates a larger dynamic within Aliite epistemology in general. While decrypting truth, Aliite thinkers simultaneously render the knowledge thus liberated as a unique possession, encrypting it as the exclusive property of individual communities and thinkers, and thus as to some extent still secretive. Etymological claims proliferate, and terms universally respected as having real consequence in American legal discourse—"indigenous," for instance—are glossed in scores of different ways by different thinkers, leading to conflict over the applicability of the term. Often this is framed in terms of contesting histories: is the term merely designed to oppress, a "nickname" of the sort eschewed by Ali, or is there a counterhistory hidden in the term? Disagreements over whether "indigenous," "aboriginal," or "Indian" are accurate descriptions of Aliite identity are always explicitly legal disagreements with practical, real-world ramifications. Notably, etymological knowledge is the most frequently cited type of knowledge in debates within Aliite communities over whether or not to apply for federal recognition with the Bureau of Indian Affairs. That words matter—carrying legal consequence—is universally accepted. What they mean and how that meaning might be determined becomes a subjective, individual affair.

"JUST THE FACTS, MA'AM": SUPERSEDING RELIGION

Within the American legal system, religious claims are not generally considered admissible as evidence. At the same time, however, religion does have a well-recognized role in legal discourse, denoting a special, protected category of rights. Aliite thinkers respond to both of these attitudes toward religion. On the one hand, Aliites reject the term "religion," dismissing it as an oppressive fallacy, a superstitious means of social control. On the other hand, and simultaneously, Aliites mobilize the term "religion" as a legal category, reclaiming the term to denote objective knowledge and uniquely Aliite truth.

The Aliite objection to the category of religion is rooted in Aliite devotion to knowledge practices. Any model of religion rooted in belief must be rejected, Aliites thinkers argue, in favor of objective facts. As a Nuwaubian Yamassee told Susan Palmer, "we're not a religion, we study factology . . . we don't *believe* in anything—we just study the facts, ma'am."[46] York emphasized to his community that they were to follow his example, not his teachings: "Don't believe me. Look it up! Ain't no more time for beliefs," he said, offering a vernacular etymological breakdown of "belief" as "be" and "lie."[47] This stance facilitates, and stands as a criticism of, the history of American Christianity in relation to African American citizens—as a means of placation and oppression, a tool of the slaveowner, a means of making Aliites into Negroes and keeping them in that mindset. Yet this insistence on facts over belief also allows for supersessionist claims about religious thought and traditions, claiming Aliite interpretations thereof as objective, a matter of fact rather than faith. Thus, Aliite thinkers advance arguments about Christianity, Islam, ancient Mesopotamian traditions, and religion in general, presenting such arguments as statements of fact. There are Washitaw readings of Exodus as evidence for their own histori- cal claims, Aliite retellings of biblical stories and Sumerian epics, as well as reinterpretations of Buddhism and Hinduism, and claims to "restore Islaam to its pristine purity" (including rereadings of the Qur'an via the Dead Sea Scrolls).[48] Connected to this is the general sense that Aliite religion super- sedes all previous religions, because Aliite thought replaces belief with facts and corrects the facts. This is the meaning of the Yamassee line, "We over- stand *all* the world religions."[49]

Rather than religion, Aliites pursue "factology," "overstanding," or what they broadly call "science" (a term for truth). Such not-religion approaches depend on research; Aliites hold that traditional religious sources, like any other historical sources, conceal the truth amid lies. "The bible is a book tampered with," for instance, but as with other historical sources, it cannot be discredited but must be read properly.[50] Aliites offer corrective readings of religious texts from the Vedas to the Qur'an. Such readings are held to be objective and empirical, such that York, when reading a pro-matriarchal, pro-sex message from the Bible and the Qur'an, can hastens to tell doubters "Don't take my word for it, ask the anthropologists and the learned histo- rians" to which he adds a scriptural citation much quoted in Aliite circles: "John 8:32—'And ye shall know the truth, and the truth shall make you free.'"[51]

Aliites cite the fact that religion has been used historically to bring about consequences such as injustice and inequality, to justify their wari- ness about this category. Ali himself wrote that the history of religions is one of "unscrupulous" use of "religious influence" and that such traditions have both "hindered . . . the nations" by "keeping [them] ignorant," though he also argued that religions have helped with uplift throughout history.[52] Likewise, Aliite critiques are followed by reclamations. York calls for reli- gion to be "dismantled," and describes it as a "crutch" used by those who are "failure[s]": "You need religion because, you were ruled by beings. And on your own you don't function well."[53] Goston identifies religion as a tool used by Satan as she offers up a renovation of original Christianity.[54] In this regard, Aliites are part of a deep American tradition, from early Jehovah's Witnesses, who argued, in the words of the movement's second president Joseph Rutherford, that religion was "a snare and a racket," to contemporary Evangelical Christians who argue that Jesus came to destroy religion.[55]

Eschewing the term religion in favor of other terms, notably "science," also serves to remind Aliites of their investment in the here and now, the historical-material goals of the divine and national Aliite project. "Moorish Science," after all, is the science of New Thought, the science of human perfectibility. Yet the associations of this term go beyond its meaning for Aliites. The rhetoric of science plays an essential role in emphasizing the supposedly objective nature of Aliite truth-claims, mobilizing what Jenna Reinbold calls "the tremendous empirical authority wielded by the natural sciences within our society."[56] Through the frame of science, Aliite claims are presented as the true products of empirical research, the product of engaged citizenship. Yet "science" is not only the "Science of Learning" or "the Law of learning," an explicit gift from God and responsibility of the fully human citizen; "science" is also understood to have different valences in the world, the most important of which is "the science that treats positive law," the science of "jurisprudence" and "civics." As one Moorish thinker argues in an online lecture, while physics, for instance, is a kind of science, the science that matters most to Aliites is "the perspective of civics and law . . . [the] law perspective"—that is, science the claims of which have immediate social consequences.[57]

Aliites, as I have argued throughout this book, locate law as the primary concern of their own religious worldviews, and they are explicit not only in describing law using the vocabulary of religion—Allah as All-Law, prayers for justice compacted to the recitation "Droit Droit"—but also in claiming that law, as divine truth, predates the concept of "religion," just as Aliite claims of Allah's universal design exist before and above the diversity of national revelations and particular religions.[58] As such, it is under the sign of law that Aliites return to religion, or to the explicit use of the term "religion," for Aliites recognize that the term is a privileged legal category and thus represents a means of having their legal claims recognized, heard, and accommodated.

MSTA thinker A. Hopkins-Bey turns to Drew Ali's writings for a concept of "religious freedom" that frames opposition to the MSTA as illegal, for "the legal right to oppose citizens, individuals and organizations alike for their religious beliefs does not exist in the United States."[59] The MSTA's status as "religion" is thus protected and its activities "secured and safe-guarded" by the Constitution.[60] The Nuwaubian Yamassee, despite frequent rejection of the term "religion," nonetheless mobilize arguments for "freedom of religion" as a means of showing how illegal the persecution of their movement has been. York has suffered, says the movement's main website, "a violation of his constitutional rights (freedom of religion, freedom of speech)" and his attackers, modern-day "Confederates," are, like their ancestors, waging "illegal wars" against the Yamassee and other "indigenous people."[61] Recourse to indigeneity—as discussed in the previous chapter—is common in Yamassee discourse and offers a far better known (real-life) model for the sort of "nation within a nation" model of sovereignty and rights the Washitaw are fighting for, as well.[62] Dauphin Washington of the Empire Washitaw has gone further than most Aliite thinkers in rejecting any specific religious identity as a part of Aliite identity. He applies Ali's system of religious secularism and democratic theology to the Empire Washitaw community, insisting that Washitaw "have different spiritual beliefs" and that his role as "government" is to "stand for everybody's beliefs," to guarantee religious freedom within his own community.[63] Washington urges his community members to keep their religion "private," to "agree to disagree" with each other but always be "considerate" and civil.[64] In an attempt to maintain cohesion within a community of multiple and conflicting religious commitments, Washington echoes Marcus Garvey, embracing pluralism in order to avoid "inciting schism."[65] Yet as vehemently as he insists that "Washitaw is not a religion," he is equally vehement that "freedom of religious belief" is one legal principle that will allow the Washitaw to operate with a degree of sovereign autonomy from the government of the United States. As he sees it, "dual citizenship status" has not just been accorded (other) Native American communities, it has also resulted from successful legal struggles on "religious freedom" grounds by communities such as the Latter Day Saints in Utah, Quaker settlements in Pennsylvania, and even unidentified Catholic communities, all of which stand as practical examples for the Washitaw to follow.[66]

Aliite history offers examples of the use of religion as a legal category, described by Tisa Wenger as "a valuable tool for resistance, a meaningful way to claim protection," and by Isaac Weiner, who suggests that religious claims are also generated in response to, and as a part of, a process of negotiating the accommodations offered for them under the law.[67] Washitaw leader Washington aptly invokes Jehovah's Witnesses, Baptists, Mormons, Catholics, Jews, Mennonites, and Amish as examples of minority religions that have, while maintaining their distinctiveness and some degree of autonomy, nonetheless been accepted into a broader understanding of Americanness, such that they are no longer widely seen as threats to the diverse fabric of this country, but as part of it. Such citations represent an attempt to grasp parallels for how Aliite religion, too, through display of authentic identity and public practice of "law-abiding" behavior, might be accepted into the fold of American religious life—accepted into Americanness via the label and model of religion.[68] Religion, in such an understanding, offers a path to acceptance of diversity. While Ali considered religion to be merely one aspect of a requisite American diversity, contemporary Aliites realize that the promise of *e pluribus unum* is not available, equally, to all. Mobilizing discourse of religious identity and making claims to "religious freedom" offer a privileged path to equal status as Americans.

As Aliites reconceptualize religion to emphasize knowledge rather than superstition, truth rather than belief, they likewise reconceptualize the way in which religion has a privileged status in American legal discourse, rejecting the term "religion" as an oppressive label but embracing "religious freedom" as a means of achieving the legal recognition they desire. In his writings on "religious freedom"—most notably a short text rebuking Christian ministers for expressing reservations about his organization—Drew Ali similarly reinterpreted the term, linking it, moreover, to the quest for truth. Just as he cited registration with county authorities as proof of his own prophetic authority, here he cited the Constitution as protection for his organization: "Without religious freedom, no search for truth would be possible," he wrote.[69]

THE CAPSTONE

The fez worn by Ali and most Moors—as well as by York and certain Nuwaubian Yamassee, and by Goston and certain Washitaw—represents the unfinished pyramid, a house of wisdom still under construction. Aliite knowledge practices are an ongoing process.[70] The cap on the head thus indicates the lack of conclusion to the ever-ongoing process of citizenship, while at the same time symbolizing that the work of the head—knowledge and the uses thereof—is the capstone of the Aliite project.

Aliite knowledge practices recode claims as facts and desires as reality. While Aliites present such practices as objective, they are, in reality, subjective. Presented as resisting the politics involved in concealing knowledge, Aliite knowledge practices, likewise, advance Aliite political claims. Framed as the excavation of concealed truths, Aliite knowledge practices are, in fact, a means of rhetorically reiterating already held beliefs, while at the same time adamantly denying that such claims are beliefs. Moreover, the act of rendering public heretofore hidden knowledge, for the purpose of communal uplift, is counterbalanced by the act of individual thinkers encrypting knowledge as their own exclusive possession, for the purposes of individual advancement.

Aliite knowledge practices have an underlying metaphysics to them, as well. Thought manifests in reality, in the identity of the thinker. Put plainly, as Eric Mungin Bey says, "you become what you think about most of the time."[71] Education becomes essential to uplift, but there is more than a practical social function at play here. In this Aliite understanding, research deepens not only one's sense of identity but also one's actual, ontological identity, making a person more of a Moor the more they know. The inverse is true, too—hence the threat of "Negro" as an ontology that can be instantiated, understood here as a kind of mental trap. If you think too much on the wrong things, in the wrong ways, identifying with the wrong labels, putting faith in the wrong (inaccurate) categorical frameworks and explanatory systems, you will become—and become more and more, descending down a trajectory of devolution—"Negro." This is understood as akin to brainwashing, but the responsibility is put firmly on the individual. Azeem Hopkins-Bey quotes Jose Pimiento-Bey (whose Ph.D. from Temple University provides him with a particular authority as an Aliite thinker): "A person calling themselves black trying to make it positive is like pushing a elephant uphill on roller-skates."[72] Knowledge of truth is essential, and, thus, knowledge practices that discover, discern, and defend such truth are essential for Aliite existence and productive, positive, function in the world. Those who do not research are mental slaves, noncitizens, less than human, Negroes, and lost. Aliite knowledge practices and epistemology produce their own jarring juxtapositions as imagined past clashes with the undeniable present, as the oppressive reality of society contrasts with the profound hope in the ideal of justice for all. Like Ali emerging from the pyramid with a new perspective on the problems of the world, so, too, Aliite thinkers, through the push and pull of their knowledge practices, employ a vision that is not merely predetermined by desire but also recognizes the perniciousness of the problem—the reality of Aliite existence in a society still far from that promised in Ali's teachings. The problems—of status unrecognized, rights not granted, recognition not given, land not returned, freedom forcefully and violently taken away—are emphasized, even through the articulation of the potential solution. York, when he describes his *Holy Tablets* as "The Problem Book," may be flagging how the text offers a "last chance of salvation," but he also reiterates the relentless return, in Aliite thought, to problems, to the historical-material conditions in which Aliites find themselves, an unacceptable reality.[73] America at present is an unfinished pyramid, the foundation built on slavery and oppression, but Aliites move toward, with faith in All-Law, confident that the pyramid of justice and equality can be perfected—that *America* can be perfected.

7

NOVUS ORDO SECLORUM

Experiments in Reordering Society

CITIZENSHIP AS
IMAGINING AN ALTERNATIVE STATE

THE FINAL PHRASE ON THE GREAT SEAL, *novus ordo seclorum*, "a new order for the ages," commemorates the founding of America as the beginning of a new era in world history, while simultaneously gesturing toward an ever-new beginning of and for America. The phrase *novus ordo seclorum* references the founders' belief in the American experiment as a promise and model for transformed social and moral orders through democracy and rule of law, but it also speaks to the founders' concept of perennial revolution, history as a human struggle of resistance against tyranny, a process, generation by generation, of perfecting society into a new order.

Aliite declarations of citizenship, Aliite investment in the ideals and cosmic stakes of "the sacred obligations of American citizenship," have always involved a parallel and audacious insistence on a reimagining of America. Aliites are citizens not merely in the present order of the American state but also always in a future America aligned with Allah's plan, a society of true law. Hence, citizenship is struggle, it is the project for which prophet Ali was sent and the "divine and national movement" founded on his teachings begun.

Aliite declarations of citizenship are statements not merely of identity but also of faith in *novus ordo seclorum*. Aliites imagine a future in which the ideal of true law will be made manifest in society, an America where freedom and equality become actualities for all. Like *novus ordo seclorum*,

"I AM A CITIZEN OF THE USA" calls attention to what George Steiner has termed "alternity," "the 'other than the case,' the counterfactual propositions . . . with which we charge our mental being and by means of which we build the changing, largely fictive milieu for our somatic and our social existence."[1] Robert Cover turned to this theory of "alternity" to describe the space opened between ideal law and the legal as interpreted and enforced.[2] The tension between justice and reality serves, for Aliites, as an engine for action, for struggle through the work of citizenship.

This chapter examines three Aliite social experiments: utopias real, imagined, and hoped for, embarked upon as part of the project of larger social renovation understood by Aliites as the work of citizenship. All of the three experiments under consideration are Aliite-only enclaves, removed from the emphasis on recognition, at a remove from the white world yet never entirely divorced from it. The three experiments are, first, the Moorish National Home run by Charles Kirkman Bey's MSTA organization in the decades after Ali's death (with particular attention to the 1940s); second, the Nuwaubian Yamassee Georgian settlement and Afro-futurist tourist attraction of Tama-Re (1993–2002); and third, the dream among present members of the Washitaw de Dugdahmoundyah for a reservation with a casino patterned on real and imagined Native American examples. These are all examples of Aliite self-determination, though all also involve necessary negotiation with the state in which they exist.

On the one hand, these experiments are part of a deep tradition of black utopianism, territorial and otherwise, from the social experiments written about by William and Jane Pease to the imaginative visions of new alternatives celebrated by Robin Kelley.[3] Yet while these Aliite projects instantiated the radical self-determination of a communal *home* not determined by white conceptions or white society, such spaces were never fully autonomous.[4] Not merely located within, but always engaging in relations with, the power of the American state—from the collaborative (R. Nelson Bey turning over a parolee, living at the Moorish Home, to local law enforcement for a violation of that parole) to the destructive (the state wiping Tama-Re off the map)—these social experiments represent Aliite attempts at negotiating both survival and self-determination through the grace of recognition.[5] As the Washitaw phrase their dream, the goal is to be citizens of America but owners of their own land and their own institutions, to be a "nation within a nation" under their own "vine and fig tree," in control of their own vital interests. These utopian experiments, then, speak to a possibility for American society in general, a democracy as envisioned by

Ali, composed of nationalities under their own flags, living harmoniously together in a society aligned with ideal law.

Existing in the present, in an interactive memory of the past, and as a focus for future expectations, these social experiments were imagined by Aliites, many of whom never visited them in a geographic sense but only came to know them as utopian ideas, represented and remembered, anticipated and described. To study them is to study, primarily, communication through media, ranging from texts to films, from drawings to conversations, from letters to interactive websites. Testified to, memorialized, and anticipated, these three social experiments model the benefits of nationality adhered to and authentically manifest in community. Emphasizing laughter, celebration, feasting, dancing, commerce, and feelings, these are visions of pleasure, pride, and emotional connection to, as well as evidence of, Aliite truth-claims. Aliite engagement with the idea of these social experiments helps keep alive the hope of Aliite eschatology—of a world transformed through the struggle of citizenship.

While the power of the state can neither be denied nor escaped, these social experiments, as imagined by Aliites, serve as examples of success under and despite that power, as proof of the truth of Ali's teachings and as proof of the possibility of an alternative America. As brutal as life in America may be, as difficult as it may be to be recognized and accepted as citizens, these moments of Aliite community exemplify a possibility of *novus ordo seclorum*, a society reordered, through Aliite effort, in accord with Allah's true law.

THE MOORISH NATIONAL HOME: THE ABUNDANT PLEASURES OF COMMUNITY

In the 1940s, the "National Home" in Prince George, Virginia, united a community scattered across the country and shocked by schism within the broader Moorish Science Temple of America movement. This was the symbolic home of the Chicago-centered MSTA community led by C. Kirkman Bey, which emerged from and was marked by the violence and internecine drama that followed Ali's death. Moors had long discussed the possibility of forming "their own town . . . in connection with a large farm,"[6] and in the years after Drew Ali's death in 1929 several such farms were started by Moorish groups.[7] The primary source for information about this community is articles published in this branch of the MSTA's national newsletter, the *Moor-ish Voice*, issues of which were preserved in the MSTA file of the Federal Bureau of Investigation, in the MSTA archives at the Schomburg Center for Research in Black Culture, and in Aliite archives, one of which is available online.[8]

For the MSTA branch associated with it, a community scattered across the United States, the National Home became a symbol of Moorish indus-triousness and community, offering evidence of a degree of political au-tonomy as well as material self-sufficiency. Produce grown at the home was transported by at least one Moorish national truck to Moorish communi-ties across the United States, where it was eaten as a means of connection with the home. The home also became a symbol of the immediate, visceral, emotional rewards of Moorish identity and Moorish community, repre-sented via testimonies and anecdotes, in terms of experiences of pleasure, abundance, and laughter.

The Moorish National Home began with the purchase of 200 acres of Virginia woodland that F. and R. Nelson Bey, husband and wife, cleared and began construction on in 1939. With first a "clayhouse," then a house of stone, the settlement grew to include twenty-eight buildings housing at least twenty-five families in residence. Lettuce, carrots, corn, cabbage, beets, col-lard greens, radishes, peas, beans, and sweet potatoes were among the crops grown "for table use and for canning purposes." Cows, horses, goats, geese, turkeys, and chickens were all kept at the home. By July 1942 several houses, a communal dining building (of white sand blocks decorated with the star and crescent and the circle seven), a garage, a store, and a temple were stand-ing on the Virginia property, while a structure called "the big house" was nearing completion. By the next year there was a barn, featured in a draw-ing on the cover of the May 1943 *Moorish Voice*; the barn was "trimmed in the Moorish colors of red and green" and equipped with "a look-out tower." The barn, according to one *Voice* article, was a local attraction: "From the Main Highway, passersby stop to take a good view of it and declare it to be anything but a barn." Ruth Howell Bey wrote that she had "never seen such beautiful buildings designed with our Moorish Emblems," and that the barn looked "more like a castle at a distance than a shelter for animals."[9]

Since so many Moors had left behind life in the South, moving north to the cities where they would encounter Ali's teachings, the home gave Moors a chance to *re*-experience rural life, only at a remove from the wider soci-ety and its racism. The home, described in terms of purity, with its "natu-ral environs" seen as safe and bountiful, serene and spiritually refreshing, represented a renovated rural experience, one by and for Moors. The home was described by Moors who saw it as safe and celebratory, a place of laughter and the joy of work, a manifestation of Moorish industriousness, self-determination, and collective uplift, with everyone sharing and sharing alike. Moors in this state of nature were also Moors in a *natural* state of Moorishness, unfettered ("unmolested," in Ali's terminology) by any powers or authority other than their own.

This is not to say that the need for recognition was entirely removed. The *Voice* mentioned audiences of outsiders on occasion, from "passersby" who marveled at the home's architecture from the highway to "both Europeans and Asiatics" who encountered groups of Moors, in full national regalia, as they made their pilgrimage across the country and toward the home.[10] Such "civilians . . . gazed in admiring wonder at the definitely proud and happy Moors in their beautiful headdress of turbans and fezes," displaying their identity and the emotional consequences of accepting it as truth.[11]

The major yearly event at the Moorish National Home was the "mass celebration" of the Fourth of July holiday, when Moorish Americans from around the country would travel to Virginia "to dine and make merry on their Home Land," to enjoy what various Moorish writers called, in the pages of the *Voice*, "that land of wonder," "a Moorish Heaven," and like "another world; a fairyland; it's really a Mecca for the Moors."[12] "I'm simply delirious with gaiety and feel like singing and dancing," writes Ruth Howell Bey, in a typical expression of sentiment about time at the home.[13] Yet even while removed from the wider society, the emphasis on America and American citizenship remained, as witness that this celebration was arranged around and focused on the American Independence Day, a festival of patriotism and time for reflecting on the meaning and possibilities of the American state. The "national inconsistencies" Frederick Douglass described, in his own essay on the Fourth of July, here served to generate a sense of "alternity."[14] The paradox of American ideals, the ideals of true law, held against American history and the American legal system is not denied by Aliite thinkers, but, rather, serves as a prompt for engaged citizenship. Indeed, the story of Aliite religion in relation to race, law, and citizenship is a story of the theological interpretations, legal theories, and range of actions taken in response to tensions between an imagined ideal of justice and the lived injustices of this society. Aliite salvation, understood as salvation for both the Aliite community and America, is itself a project of *alternity*, a commitment to a new order.

Moors shared their experience of the home with their own community through the national newspaper of the Kirkman Bey MSTA, the *Moorish*

Voice, a publication that served to stitch together a geographically dispersed organization. With its sick lists and surgery reports, birth and death announcements, and news of family celebrations from congregations across the United States, this monthly newspaper facilitated intimate connection between readers and the broader Moorish nation. Just as the Moorish national truck, Big Bertha, transported food from the home to communities in the Midwest, at a far remove from the home, so, too, the *Voice,* by publishing testimonies and anecdotes about the experience of visiting the home, spread that experience to those Moors who might never see the place in person. These testimonials emphasized unity and equality, the pleasures of shared community, and located such community not merely in the actual location of the home but also in ways that transcended geographic location and were conveyed through the texts in the *Moorish Voice,* particularly in terms of shared laughter and shared labor.

Experience of the home, conveyed by sensually descriptive, emotional, and humorous testimonials, emphasized Moorish time at this place as eliciting "a deep thrill in [the] heart," as making "the heart . . . really contented."[15] Writers repeated that "words are inadequate to describe" such experience, but the *Voice* was devoted to collecting and publishing such words, all the same.[16] These words served to collapse the distance between firsthand experience of those who visited the home and the broader experience of all Moors reading about the home, for they, too, were part of the project of the home and the possible Moorish future the home exemplified.

The home rendered Moorish values concrete, and, thus, "Home-coming" offered Moors a chance to exemplify, in turn, the unity of their nation, to demonstrate what each individual meant to the community as a whole. This was performed most strikingly through the "all night vigil . . . by the light of the camp-fire around the Barbeque pit," as Moors stayed up late drinking coffee and waiting for the next group of visitors to arrive for the Fourth of July celebration. Whether they shuttled from the bus and train stations or pulled up in their own vehicles, the arrival of these new Moors was the source of "much joy and happiness and a gay spirit [that] prevailed everywhere." Indeed, the "old homesteaders [who] had been working steadily in preparation for this great homecoming," found themselves caught up in a contagious spirit of merriment and glee. "Some of them laughed to themselves, because it seemed that the more Moors came, the nuttier the others became as things certainly piled up on top of themselves."[17]

Accounts of community at the home are characterized by joy and pleasure. Kirkman Bey sits beside his fellow Moors, "laughing and telling jokes."

When the barbeque pit was used for cooking, Kirkman Bey tied on a "white chef's apron" and "played the role of High Chef and personally directed the Barb-e-que routine." Moors gathered together at "long tables of plenty . . . laid out in the open [under]neath the pines," feasting on the "Barbeque Goat and other meats, slaw, beans, brown bread, cake, lemonade, wine, beer, etc.," or, later, "fresh corn on the cobb [*sic*], specially prepared lamb chops, relish dish of sliced tomatoes, onions, whole cucumber, pickles, lemonade."[18] This catalog of excess is characteristic of testimonials' attention to both the productivity of the home as an agricultural site and the material pleasures in which the Moorish community here partook. The *Voice* was a publication attentive to food, regaling readers with accounts of shared Moorish meals, offering Moorish recipes, and celebrating the pleasures of the abundant table. Accounts within the *Voice* characterized the community in terms of abundance. In the wake of the Great Depression and in the midst of the deprivations of World War II, members of this community, according to articles published in its newspaper, ate to the point of satiation—with Kirkman Bey even popping the buttons "from behind and in front of his pants releasing his suspenders" due to his enjoyment of a fish fry, according to one account—"and it took all the Sisters' Crack Squad to hold them up until he could reach shelter."[19] Such abundance was tied to community, to the Moorish characteristics, emphasized in these articles, of industriousness, labor, and commitment to unity—a unity that bore fruit, which was then shared at the communal feast table and bonfire. It is notable that, in contrast to Arthur Huff Fauset's early ethnographic work in Philadelphia, this community had no dietary taboos or restrictions on alcohol or on practices like mixed dancing or card games. The Kirkman Bey MSTA took pleasure in all manner of foods—chitterlings and fried possum, sweet potatoes and spinach, sherbet and blackberry pie and doughnut holes—as well as wine, motion pictures, theatrical skits, music, and dancing. One *Voice* article describes the piano at the home being moved outdoors to better facilitate Moorish merriment; accompanied by "a guitar player in our midst," this performance "kept all with their feet tapping."[20] One memorable account of dancing at the home involves one sister abandoning herself so much to "the excitement of the dance" that she "came out of her shoes! But she was most unconcerned," readers are told, "and laughingly finished the dance in her bare feet."[21]

"Such a happy time for all," that anecdote concludes, bringing the joy of that event into the moment, sharing the contagious sense of happiness and laughter. Laughter is a particularly privileged mode of communicating the experience of the home, generally through slapstick humor, often playing on the fish-out-of-water element of "city Moors" in the country—as when visiting Moors "take a fancy to spills in the spring" and have to be "fished out." One article recounts how sister Paige El fell into her vegetable-picking basket, from which several other Moors had trouble extracting her ("It was a tight fit"). Another notes that some visiting Moors accidentally riled up the home's billy goat, named Billie, such that he butted down part of the gate. All such tales are lighthearted and reiterate the central theme of the pleasures of community: "In the midst of all the confusion, which was a happy one, each one realized what a wonderful thing it was to get together in this fashion."

One A. Malono Bey reportedly "strayed a little away from the group following turkey and deer track" while out hunting and soon found himself "'Babes in the Woods' lost," as the *Voice* writer puts it. Yet here, too, the story is devoid of danger, emphasizing, instead, reliance on community. Bey "gave the 'Old-time Whoop' which echoed through the woods and reached the ears of those sitting around the log-fire, and the worst part about it night was coming on and it was getting darker and darker. The brothers soon were on the job and went in search for him and he was soon located and brought back to the Moorish Fold, unharmed."[22] Pieces on the home contrast the creature-filled woods with city life, but they give no sense of threat, just the promise of pleasure from the humorous tales to come as city Moors experience the world of nature at the home. Readers, likewise, left city life behind, briefly, as they experienced the home through words, a utopian alternative and thus an emotionally charged example of a possibility for a Moorish society.

Testimonials and anecdotes about the home conveyed—and canonized—a sense of the atmosphere, and stitched readers, even if they had never visited the place, into the unique type of community that characterized it. Testimonials offered detailed descriptions of the physical attributes of the natural setting, the impressive quality of the architecture and agricultural project there. Readers of the monthly Moorish newsletter were also given a play-by-play of always respectful and good-natured gossip, let in on in-jokes, and given an intimate sense of what it was like to sit around the bonfire at the home, drinking coffee or wine, waiting for the next batch of Moors to arrive and be welcomed. Participation in community was conveyed textually, through the mail, uniting Moors around the country and offering them a model of what a new order of Moorish American unity could—and should—look like. The home, as represented in these testimonies and thus experienced by a far-flung community through these texts, was an alternative society but also a preview of what society could be if

Moorish truths and values were to permeate it. By offering an experience, to readers, of what was presented as the nature of Moorish community, testimonials of time at the home served as guideposts for the struggle to transform the world.

"A PLACE FOR OUR CHILDREN":
THE AFTERLIFE OF TAMA-RE

The Nuwaubian Yamassee community (then called the United Nuwaubian Nation of Moors) purchased 476 acres of land in Putnam County, Georgia, in 1993, with members of the community moving to this "Holy Land" and constructing the first buildings of what would become a settlement offering an Afro-futurist take on ancient Egypt. Brightly colored buildings and statues of Egyptian deities were arranged around expansive grounds. The decorations featured obelisks, a black-faced sphinx, pillars covered in hieroglyphics (or approximations thereof), a giant freestanding ankh, and a monolithic head resembling those iconic artifacts of Olmec culture, mentioned earlier. A large, arched gateway marked the entrance into the settlement—and the departure from the outside world. While grand and striking, the settlement also, as one outside observer noted with surprise, "felt like a place built for humans," intimately accessible.[23] Tama-Re was an alternate reality, a new order concretized and territorialized, populated both by residents invested in the meaning and power of the symbols around them and by visitors who came to marvel at the grandeur of this display of nationality. Two massive pyramids towered over the place, one of them broadcasting recitation of the mystical syllable "AUM," as Nuwaubian Yamassee residents, pilgrims, and assorted African American tourists conducted business, performed cultural shows, paraded across the grounds, shopped for Africana, or posed for photos next to these re-creations of an idea of Africa, a romanticized past made concrete.

Sometimes called, respectfully as well as critically, a "theme park," Tama-Re was, from the beginning, a popular tourist attraction for African Americans. For the Savior's Day holiday commemorating York's birthday, on June 26, five thousand visitors came to Tama-Re in 1998.[24] Susan Palmer writes of her ethnographic visit to the site at another time: "my impression was that most of the 1000-odd folks attending this festival were just plain, middle-class African-Americans with a general interest in Black Identity, who wanted to show their kids the Black History museum."[25] The place functioned not only as a venue for Aliite display, courting recognition, but also as a model of an alternative, perfected, society. As such, it spoke to both Nuwaubian Yamassee and outsiders.

Tama-Re, in keeping with Aliite tradition and its emphasis on the public display of identity, was a profoundly *visual* place, referencing the grandeurs of an African past for the purposes of instilling pride in the present and confidence in the future. Displaying an excess of what Geoff Manaugh, in an architectural analysis of the settlement, called *functional ornament*, Tama-Re looked resolutely *black*, a manifestation of a nostalgic repertoire of black nationalist consciousness in America.[26]

In addition to the spectacle of black-skinned residents, often in dramatic costumes mimicking ancient Egyptian frescoes, organizing parades and rituals and public performances in a milieu designed to *look* like a black utopia, there was also an obvious emphasis on (black) economic self-determination. Tama-Re was a place of multiple businesses, and its own financial function as part of the uplift of its community extended to the requirement that guests purchase a "passport" at the gate and exchange American currency for local currency.

The resolute blackness of the place—from black aesthetic to black entrepreneurship to black political control—was read by some non–Nuwaubian Yamassee as a promise, by others as a threat. This divide was racialized. Activist, civil rights elder, and former presidential candidate Jesse Jackson, visiting in 2001, described the settlement as a manifestation of "the American Dream."[27] Local white critics described Tama-Re as a "compound" of "black supremacists," dismissing the religion as a "cult" with presumed apocalyptic leanings.[28] White fears won out over black pride, and in 2002, the power of the state descended on the Nuwaubian Yamassee utopia of Tama-Re. As Wright and Palmer describe it, the raid

> was planned and executed as a spectacular show of force. Three armored vehicles accompanied by over 300 agents from the FBI, ATF, and the local county sheriff's office burst past the armed guards and rammed through the flimsy painted obelisks that formed the front gate of Tama-Re. The FBI's SWAT team, comprised of 80 agents, leapt out of trucks to make a "dynamic entry," armed with machine guns, semi-automatic Glocks, hand grenades, head masks, body shields, and tear gas. They were followed by a force of deputy sheriffs, snipers, and a rifle team. Two helicopters hovered over the theme park as armored trucks breached the front entrance to Tama-Re.[29]

The destruction of Tama-Re followed the script of hyperbolic symbolism associated with the destruction of Carthage. The state—and particular the lead anti–Nuwaubian Yamassee official, local sheriff Howard Sills—proceeded to wipe the settlement off the map. Sills proudly drove one of the bulldozers that, in 2005, smashed through and scraped away the structures of the Golden City.

Although physically erased, however, Tama-Re has been kept alive through memory practices, most particularly online memorializations, usually in video form complete with a platform for interactive commentary from, and discussion among, viewers. Memorialization extends the settlement, as a utopian experiment, into the future, educating and incorporating into it others—Nuwaubian Yamassee and not—many of whom never visited the site when it existed geographically. These videos function similarly to testimonials about the Moorish National Home published in the *Moorish Voice*, offering an intimate and idealized experience of community even for those far away, in space and time, from the event itself.

Crafted by members of the community, who select music to accompany images and add voiceover or narration via caption, these homemade films continue the project of "Home" that was the settlement—acts of creativity and industriousness in keeping with the place itself. Internet technology allows for widespread sharing of images, making traditional photo albums now globally accessible, as, for example on websites devoted to "beautiful pictures" of the settlement or "Old Photos" of Nuwaubian times there. Technology also allows for community formation through discussion and exchange, and for presentation of the community as an experiment in time—with, for instance, pictures of pregnancy and ultrasounds of fetuses being paired with pictures of the Nuwaubian Yamassee children that resulted.[30]

Memorialization thrives as a way to remember, to teach, and to reexperience the glory that was the Golden City. Memorial videos serve to reproduce the spectacular visual elements that visitors to Tama-Re once saw, allowing a virtual experience of the place, focusing on statuary and architecture, for instance, or collecting images of rituals, dances, and parades.[31] A repeated set of aerial shots establishes the scope and visual complexity of the site, from the vibrant yellow circle surrounding the black pyramid to the distinction between the simple line of residences and the more elaborate common grounds.[32] There are memorials, even, of the raid. One video opens with news footage and then cuts to testimonials from various community members about the project and promise of Tama-Re, the violence and trauma of the raid. An artist describes a "temple" he was in the process of constructing; an office worker describes the screams and terror of children in reaction to the invasion.[33]

Most videos focus on the settlement as a social movement, assembling images of residents and visitors. One video includes, in a series of family photographs, an ultrasound of an unborn child, a future Nuwaubian Yamassee, included as part of the ongoing story of Tama-Re.[34] These memorial videos offer viewers an experience curated to convey the nature of Tama-Re, the nature of Nuwaubian Yamassee community and, thus, the Nuwaubian Yamassee project.

Such memorials respond directly to the main charges the community's critics leveled against it: that the movement was a cult devoted to the criminal mastermind, that the settlement was a place of abuse of children, and (the standard criticism) that the Nuwaubian Yamassee were engaged in a kind of sham. Critics of the community focused on York as a pathological sex criminal, further viewing the residents of Tama-Re as victims of his charismatic control, who, once this leader was removed, would abandon this elaborate charade and go back to being *blacks*.

At times the assessment of critics seems to counter this fantasy of the leader holding his victims in thrall—as when Sheriff Sills, the chief of the anti–Tama-Re campaign, describes the only time he heard York preach in public, saying, "I thought I was gonna see some Adolf Hitler shit, somebody who mesmerized people to the fact that they would follow him," but insisting that what he saw, in his opinion, was "pitiful"[35]—but the fantasy is too compelling, too resonant with a history of thinking about "cults," to be abandoned. This notion of a corrupt but commanding leader is also satisfying in terms of law enforcement policy. If removal of York was understood as liberating innocent victims (community members) from his power, the violence done to them through the raid could be justified as an act of compassion, a rough rescue. This stance, of course, strips the Nuwaubian Yamassee of self-determination, rendering them passive and childlike, another reiterated racist trope—with child abuse a metaphor for the entire community.

Yet one characteristic of the Nuwaubian Yamassee community after the destruction of Tama-Re and, thus, of the rhetoric around Tama-Re after its destruction, is the view of York as an ancillary to the central focus on the Nuwaubian Yamassee people. While the movement remains focused today on legal struggle to obtain his release, videos made as memorials to the settlement focus almost exclusively on the Nuwaubian Yamassee people and what they built as a community. York's voice is rarely heard, and while he is sometimes pictured, it is almost always in the presence of other members of the community. Such images, moreover, are only ever shown as part of larger slide shows or montages of the community as a whole and its many individual faces. Even when videos are framed explicitly as evidence in York's defense, the focus is always elsewhere—on the grassroots community rather than the leader. This rhetorical move counters the idea of York as controller of the community and portrays the settlement as a place of happy, peaceful coexistence. One video ends with an image of the Master Teacher flanked by smiling young Nuwaubian men, but the camera pans out, and that image, in turn, is shown as a framed photograph on a wall, exemplifying both the afterlife of this community and the related role of the video, which itself functions like the photo hung on the wall, alongside images of an ever-broadening, Nuwaubian Yamassee family for which York plays, increasingly, the role of an ancestor, a figure of memory, rather than a real presence.[36]

Nuwaubian Yamassee memorial videos focus particularly on children, offering rebuttals of charges that Tama-Re was a place of predation on children and insisting instead that the settlement was "a place for our children," "a place where there is no crime," "a city of brotherly love," and a social experiment dedicated to, steeped in, and always educating "our culture." One such video contrasts paradisiacal images of the settlement with the campaign to destroy it. "What kind of a person would want to attack this?" a caption asks, superimposed over and after images of smiling, joking, celebrating community members, displaying their culture, posing in front of the art and architecture of the place.[37] Another video shows children bouncing on a trampoline or playing with giant basketballs and inflatable goals. There are even shots of a petting zoo brought in for the amusement and edification of the youth, featuring that most Aliite of animals, a camel.[38]

The homepage of the primary official Nuwaubian Yamassee website, "Nuwaubian Facts," features images of smiling Nuwaubian Yamassee children paired with a journalistic account of how a doctor examined such children and found them "the healthiest children she has ever had the pleasure too [sic] examine." Allegations of abuse are mentioned, but are dismissed as false.[39] "Our Children" are described by a lingering caption as "Our Future" in another film, which likewise features image after image of young people, from toddlers to young adults, in various moments of play or formal performance, happy and dignified and demonstrating their national identity.

This video includes an image of York, in a fez, holding a toddler. The image is captioned: "The Man and His Dream," while the film repeats the claim that the project—of Nuwaubian Yamassee community—is not finished. York's vision, like Ali's, extends beyond his own career and will extend even beyond his life. Indeed, his teachings must unfold into the future through these children living authentic, Aliite lives and working to instantiate the social order achieved but briefly at Tama-Re.[40]

Memorial videos present Tama-Re as a place of authenticity, a place that facilitated the experience of authentic identity for the Nuwaubian Yamassee. Here Nuwaubian Yamassee could best experience their own true *nature*, an identity that is both informal and formal, embodied on the basketball court or in the act of jokingly attempting to catch fish, as well as in the ordered procession of a parade or the choreographed public dance. At Tama-Re, Nuwaubian Yamassee were finally able to be *citizens* in the sense of being just part of the society, unstigmatized and, within the confines of Tama-Re, unremarkable. These videos preserve and publicize this natural state of being one's authentic self.

In light of this, it is worth noting that there are, within the Nuwaubian Yamassee community, concrete plans to "rebuild" Kodesh, the Holy Land, in another place. In one video posted online, for instance, two Nuwaubian Yamassee take the viewer on a tour of land they have purchased in Temple, Georgia, with plans to develop, to build residences for families and a recreation of some of the structures that characterized Tama-Re. The purpose of the video, often repeated by the female guide, is to show the land and its beauty and potential. "This is just an amazing, amazing place, and it has so much potential for families," she says. "You gotta see how beautiful this land is. . . . I just want everybody to just really see how beautiful this land is. This is the holy land." The two guides talk about the bounty (in terms of edible plants and livestock) of the place, assuring the audience that there is potential here to grow enough food "to take care of our nation." At one point the female cameraperson chimes in, breaking the fourth wall with her voice, with her thoughts on how they plan to stock the pond with freshwater fish.[41] The project of a new Holy Land will be a communal project, requiring participation by all Nuwaubian Yamassee, physically for some, in terms of support and belief from many others. Should such a social experiment come to be, it would be following in the possibility laid out both by Tama-Re as a site and by the virtual Tama-Re remembered and imagined and engaged by the broader Nuwaubian Yamassee community via online memorials.

"A PLACE TO PLANT OUR FLAG":
WASHITAW DREAMS OF A RESERVATION

Washitaw desires revolve around territory, the return of and return to Washitaw land. As part of this desire, the Washitaw imagine the possibility of owning their own reservation on some portion of their ancestral land, where they will be able to establish their own police force; a self-sustaining economy, in the sense of both bringing income to the Washitaw and allowing Washitaw to work at and patronize their own businesses; and, most important, an educational system in which Washitaw children can be taught the truth of their history and heritage. This dream of sovereignty is one of semiautonomy, Washitaw political authority existing within and under the overarching governance of the United States. The Washitaw desire for "a place to plant our flag" thus depends upon a powerful government, seen as once as adversary and illegal occupier as well as the necessary authority for any future existence.[42] The Empire Washitaw's Dauphin Washington says that his community is "trying to . . . pattern ourselves off of" Native Americans who have successfully been recognized and granted reservations by the federal government.[43] He describes a sovereignty with "dual citizenship status" as a "nation within a nation" model that simultaneously accounts for the radical asymmetry of power between the United States and this minority group but also promises a special path to a set of privileges and accommodations. Claiming to be indigenous to America themselves, the Washitaw express the desire to open a casino on their reservation, employing a model understood to be both financially and politically successful for Native Americans.

"We have the *right*," insists Dauphin Washington, "to be recognized as a sovereign Indian nation, as indigenous," and thus to their own territory.[44] Indigeneity is understood to have particular legal consequences, as a claim; as Washington says, "when you say indigenous people of the United States, that's what gets recognized."[45] The Native American parallel functions for the Washitaw not only as an imagined model of what their reservation might be like—and how it might manifest sovereignty, help the Washitaw economically, and help perpetuate Washitaw culture and heritage—but also as a legal model, one of those examples of "your own laws" of the American state to which the Washitaw appeal. Dauphin Washington can thus ask the U.S. government: "Why have you given other Indians their reservations and marked it off" but not done so for the Washitaw?[46]

The indigenous Ancient Ones from whom the Washitaw trace their descent already marked off the land by building mounds and earthworks. "They was proclaiming their sovereignty and their rights a long time ago," Washington says. The community's concern now, however, is proving ownership of land as a legal claim. To do this they must "make sure the paperwork is right," and "get the Turners' land" through state recognition of previous legal decisions by that state.[47] The Washitaw describe Goston's discovery of the "Turner's Heirs" case and acquisition of copies of the land grant discussed in that case as her fulfillment of her mission of "getting the land marked off" for the community—but this is, on its own, insufficient.[48] America must recognize these claims and allow the Washitaw to "put a flag on that land" and "build a nation" as settlers on their own territory.[49]

The reservation imagined by the Washitaw depends upon state recognition, permission, and support, including financial assistance and tax exemption—while simultaneously allowing for some self-determination and distance from government interference. The Washitaw anticipate a degree of political sovereignty similar to that of Native Americans on reservations, existing under the sovereignty of the United States and under the rule of the American legal system, but allowing for Washitaw control of aspects of society they take to be crucial to Washitaw uplift. These aspects include law enforcement, reflecting a desire for freedom from a hostile law enforcement system that has long harassed and surveilled the Washitaw. Likewise, the Washitaw speak of control of economic opportunities on the reservation, a corrective to a current condition of widespread financial need. Finally, the Washitaw express a desire to be able to inculcate their children with Washitaw culture. This would involve teaching both *truth* and the Washitaw method of *research*, in contrast to the brainwashing perpetuated by what T. Matheno Matthews-El calls "the public fool system" and R. A. Umar Shabazz Bey called "mis-education."[50] The need to "educate our young and steer them toward self-employment" is foremost in discussions of a future reservation, prompting Dauphin Washington to frame Washitaw desires in a tripartite form: "our land, our flag, our educational system."[51]

In the meantime, the Washitaw are able to engage in the sacred land directly and thus experience something of what the future might feel like. Washitaw hopes for a reservation draw from and allow for expression of a distinct bond to the land, a connection understood as characteristic of Washitaw identity and as providing visceral evidence of the truth of Washitaw claims. In much Washitaw rhetoric, a "charged" connection to the land, particularly to that land marked out by ancient mounds, is central. The

Washitaw speak of mounds not merely as offering legal evidence for historical claim but also as emotional experiences, a way of connecting present and future generations with the Ancient Ones. As in both the Moorish and Nuwaubian Yamassee examples, Washitaw imaginings of an alternate society are inextricable from feelings understood as evidence of authentic identity—the truth of Washitaw identity, for instance, is revealed in the experiences Washitaw have at mound sites. Visits to such sites—many of them currently government-administered parks with accompanying museums—also provide the Washitaw with opportunities to seek recognition and display their identity and knowledge. One caller to the Empire Washitaw Sunday-night conference call spoke excitedly about a family visit to the Ocmulgee National Monument and encouraged other Washitaw to go and, in particular, to "watch the film on the Mississippians," an ancient word that translated, he held, as Washitaw. "We got to sit down with some people at the museum," he went on. "We gave them some correct information . . . openly exposing them to the truth."[52] Such museums are often attentive, these days, to contemporary indigenous voices, a likely factor in the respectful hearings the Washitaw claim to have received from curators and museum workers at mound sites.

Mounds are central to the Washitaw religion, with Goston speaking of them as one and the same: "Our religion, the sacred MOUNDS and the SACRED LAND."[53] In *Return of the Ancient Ones*, Goston relays a story about her family, specifically an old relative she remembers from her childhood, a man called Grant who "made [a] circuit every month up to the Mound to pray."[54] This Grant, whose name, Goston says, was given to him so that he might serve as a living reminder of the Spanish land grant that handed the Turner heirs' property to her family, exemplifies a pattern of Washitaw practice in relation to the land. While the legal claim to the land is always foregrounded, engagement with and experience of the land offers a connection both with the past (and glorious accomplishments of the empire of the Ancient Ones) and with the future (a future of Washitaw ownership, again, of the land, where mounds will not merely be visited but will be the core of a Washitaw state). Grant engaged in pilgrimage to and prayer at these sites.[55] Likewise, contemporary Washitaw are "constantly visiting these mounds," as one Washitaw puts it. "Every time we visit these mounds we get new experiences," experiences on the "spiritual side to things."[56] The Washitaw describe mounds in terms of "ley lines" and manifestations of natural power as well as through their own direct experience of supernatural "presence" on visits to mound sites.[57] Washitaw descriptions of these experiences address the ubiquitous Washitaw concern with power imbalance by reimagining power itself, from the physical power of the state to a "spiritual" power, a "feeling" interpreted as evidence of Washitaw claims, true law manifesting as an emotion, in the heart. The felt power of mounds offers irrefutable evidence in favor of Washitaw claims of history and connection to the land.

The Washitaw tell each other (and the state authorities and law enforcement agents they believe to be listening in) of their experiences at the mounds, on the public Sunday Empire Washitaw conference call. Often, Washitaw otherwise unaffiliated with this particular community call in to testify to their own deeply felt Washitaw identity and to the role that visits to "the land" played in their conversion to this truth. Or the Washitaw tell of inviting friends—even, in a recent case, a reluctant friend, who, as a Christian, was "afraid" of Washitaw "spirituality"—to the mounds so that they may experience the visceral revelation of truth (in this case the friend dropped to her knees in prayer, overcome by a feeling of peace at the site).[58] Two recent callers to the Empire Washitaw conference call, led to embrace Washitaw teaching after their own study of Drew Ali's writings, testified to a trip they made to mounds in Georgia, the two men, who are brothers, and the young son of one of them. Their accounts center on a sense of awe and visceral evidence that they had, in embracing Washitaw beliefs, "come back home." Felt connection to the land was offered as proof of the truth of Washitaw identity. One of these brothers, who worked in construction, marveled at Washitaw engineering, expressing disbelief at the "little huts and houses that were still standing" on the site (a confusion of reconstruction with remains that is common), responding both to curatorial decisions at such sites and to a Washitaw desire for continuity between past and present.[59]

The older man also framed his experience in terms of what Dauphin Washington called the "very unusual," the nature of Washitaw claims manifesting in near supernatural occurrence. On top of all of his admiration, pride, and sense of connection, this Washitaw had a further feeling from his visit to the mounds. In the site's museum, he had been struck by representations showing mound-builders with butterfly tattoos on their hands. The butterfly has no symbolic currency in Washitaw thought, but for this man it seemed more than coincidence that, having noticed the butterfly as a marker of identity in these artifacts he took to be Washitaw, he then "had these experiences with these butterflies" himself. On the ground of two separate mound sites, in a part of the country where he had previously noticed no butterflies, he saw numerous "like a brown little butterfly," which other Washitaw on the conference call were quick to identify as "monarch butterflies," in keeping with Washitaw themes of royalty. He offered no explanation of the event, but cited it as part of his encouragement of anyone interested in Washitaw teachings to personally visit a mound.

Corrine Dempsey has written on "events that cooperate with the natural, everyday order" that are "understood by believers as part of divine providence," as *miracles*. Analyzing a famous instance of bees appearing to a community of Krishna devotees, Dempsey stresses the importance of contextual desire for meaning over interpretation of such events as "insignificant or plain good luck." In the Washitaw case, the physical context of mound sites is so charged, generally, so emotionally fraught and weighty with significance, that experiencing the miraculous in the commonplace seems quite likely. The Washitaw case also highlights conscious or unconscious desire: more than merely a "frame of reference," there is a need for the ultimate function Dempsey attributes to the miraculous, which is as "an important means for sustaining a reassuring sense" of the validity of beliefs.[60] Trained in "research" that finds evidence hidden in plain sight, the Washitaw likewise find evidence in these public mound sites, with emotional experience serving as palpable proof of their connection with and claims to the land.

The younger of the two men, who had brought his two-year-old, spoke first of the overwhelming sensations he experienced at the site, a sense of unity with the Ancient Ones, a felt knowledge of authentic identity. Then, on the verge of tears, he told a story about his son. The child had asked to plant a flower that his father had dug up and given to him, which the caller read as a precocious, even intuitive understanding of the sacrality of Washitaw land. The child began to dig a hole, with his hands. His father, using his keys, helped widen the hole. In this way the two participated symbolically in rebuilding their nation, in returning to their land, experiencing the ancient order as a once and future order. Opening up the earth, planting a living emblem of nationality within it, the two contributed to and gestured toward a broader resurrection of the Washitaw empire. Dauphin Washington expressed amazement, telling the man that he would remember this special moment for the rest of his life. The man agreed that it was an "awesome experience," to feel a connection of generations—from the Ancient Ones to the present and, through this child, to the future—together on the sacred land.[61]

CITIZENSHIP IN THE ORDER YET TO COME

Citizenship, for Aliites, is a process of transforming the world through knowledge and practice of true law. Aliite faith believes in the possibility, even the eventuality, of a new world order for the ages. The process of salvation laid out by Ali begins with recognition by the state of claims to identity and the legal status they confer, but extends through the work of such "sacred obligations" as campaigning and voting and organizing and protesting, displaying authentic nationality and proof of recognition, practicing law before representatives of the state, and, finally, instantiating an ideal social order under one's own "vine and fig tree." Aliite utopian experiments are not a departure from the Aliite religion's investment in citizenship, but, rather, an essential component of it. Never divorcing themselves from America or from engagement in American identity—from MSTA Fourth of July celebrations to the Nuwaubian Yamassee carrying copies of the U.S. Constitution with them at Tama-Re to Washitaw understanding of their reservation as always under a level of federal U.S. jurisdiction—Aliites organize by nationality in enclaves not unlike the ethnic neighborhoods Ali encountered in 1920s Chicago. These social experiments represent Aliites rallying under their own national flag in keeping with Allah's democratic distribution of religion and culture, a self-ordered and self-determining example of one of the many diverse peoples of which the United States is constituted. American citizenship begins, always, Ali taught, with nationality. Authentic and effective national communities thus model a possibility for the country, the United States.

Aliite understanding of identity—of nationality as necessary for citizenship—represents one example, as mentioned before, of the "amendment" of self that Derek Hicks identifies as characteristic of the broad spectrum of African American religions. Such amendment serves as "metaphoric symbol and physical manifestation perpetually encouraging [further] amendment in black life," exemplifying "possible reality" or what Ashon Crawley has described as "the irreducibility of otherwise possibilities," an effervescent effect of black experience itself.[62] As an example of testifying to such possibility, Hicks cites David Walker's radical 1829 *An Appeal to the Coloured Citizens of the World*, with its insistent reference to the founding documents of America: "See your Declaration Americans!!! Do you understand your own language? . . . ALL MEN ARE CREATED EQUAL!!"[63] The disjuncture—the gaping, violent chasm—between stated ideal and lived reality serves not as cause for rejection of the ideal but as prophetic protest, an insistence on *alternity*. Walker's cry finds echo, generations later, in Aliites who similarly cite the ideals of founding legal and political texts, insisting upon the possibility of instantiation thereof. Such a cry finds expression in Aliite declarations of citizenship, verbally and across a spectrum of legal and political practices, but it is expressed, too, through the communal projects of possibility, the creation of "home" as a state of as-yet-unrealizable self-determination. In keeping with the etymology of "utopia" as "nowhere," the experiments imagined by Aliites imagine, in turn, an America that does not yet exist—a *novus ordo seclorum* possible only through the work of citizenship. Aliite claims of citizenship in the United States are claims to a vision of an "otherwise possibility" for the United States, a radically *other* reality defiantly imagined as possible. Aliite utopian experiments instantiate such a more perfect society, synonymous with Aliite ideals, even as the broader struggle of Aliite religion, "the sacred obligations of American citizenship," is undertaken in order to enact such a social order within the United States as a whole.

The Aliite vision of and for American democracy is, itself, utopian. The divine design of nationalities living in harmony, with some degree of autonomy and self-determination, while part of a broader body politic, each with equal access to justice—this was far from even the most optimistic early MSTA interpretations of their proximity to power through Mayor Thompson's Republican machine in 1920s Chicago, and that now-legendary era remains, in Aliite understanding, the closest any Aliite community has ever come to being citizens of the United States in the full sense imagined in Ali's writing.

The utopian experiments described in this chapter are, at best, possible, temporary, and, at worst, they remind Aliites (and the world) of the power, the violence, of the American state. How long the Moorish National Home project continued is unknown. Tama-Re was destroyed, utterly erased, its population dispersed and traumatized, York convicted and imprisoned for what will surely be the rest of his life. The Washitaw remain scattered across the country, and while they can visit select mounds individually or in groups, they remain far away from owning and establishing a community on even a remnant of their ancient ancestral land.

Yet utopian desires continue to motivate Aliites. Nostalgic representation, romantic reframing, and idealistic interpretation of select, Aliite-centric social experiments as utopian play an essential function for Aliite communities by maintaining their hope in the long arc of America toward justice. While most of the Aliite historical narratives lauded as sources of Aliite pride involve civilizations that predate the United States—the grandeur of Moorish Africa and Spain, York's space-opera origin stories, Washitaw musing about the lost continent of Mu—these more recent historical social experiments have happened (or can happen) here in America. With little evidence that in their struggle to align America with true law Aliites are achieving much success, these rare instances, so freighted with emotion, are important instances of proof that the Aliite project can work, evidence of the possibility of a *novus ordo seclorum*, a transformed America. This utopian dream is of a society in which the Aliite declaration "I AM A CITIZEN OF THE USA" becomes not a provocation, prospect, or even prophecy, but a declaration of plain and universally accepted fact.

CONCLUSION

Aliite Faith in American Citizenship

"I AM A CITIZEN OF THE USA"

IN WHAT IS DESCRIBED as the largest such ceremony ever filmed, seven people—two women and five men, one with a toddler in tow—proclaim their Moorish identity and the legal consequences thereof. "Under the divine law of love, truth, peace, freedom and justice," the leader says, before nudging the crowd to recite along with him the words printed on their newly acquired nationality cards: "I AM A CITIZEN OF THE USA."[1]

This nationalization ceremony—patterned on the naturalization ceremony that incorporates immigrants as new citizens of the United States—is understood as legally marking one's reclamation of Moorish nationality and, thus, transforming participants from outsiders, excluded from the American political process, into citizens, Moorish Americans.

The Moor who is filming—and whose reactions offer running commentary throughout the video, posted online—is rapturous at this ritual's conclusion, commenting that the long bus trip he endured to get there "was worth it, man." This is a special, powerful, event to have witnessed: emancipation into full humanity, salvation via legal status.

The ceremony also serves as an induction into citizenship as a process, a practice. With two flags—Moorish and American—hanging on the wall behind them, with a portrait of Ali in between as a guiding figure, these Moorish Americans are vested not merely with rights but also with responsibilities, "sacred obligations," as Ali put it. Having come into consciousness of their Moorish identity, they must now join the struggle, as citizens, to transform society. "[T]here is work enough for all to do in helping to build a better world," taught Drew Ali.[2]

Here, however, the new Moorish Americans are recognized only by their fellow Moors. Their real task awaits outside this room, in encounters with representatives of the sovereign state, politicians and police officers, judges and clerks. This ritual is initiation into and blessing on their mission, as Aliites, and their new lives as American citizens. "I want to thank you all for making history on the planet," the cameraman says. He references the ceremony's size, though the comment speaks, too, to Aliite eschatology. Aliite religion is not reducible to legal or political action, though Ali's "divine and national" refused to recognize these as separate spheres, insisting, instead, that ethics and spirituality, theology and metaphysics are inextricable from civics and from political organizing, from legal knowledge and the practice of law. Aliite religion frames *citizenship* as the ultimate purpose of life, the means of serving, living in accord with, and enacting Allah's plan for humanity. To be a citizen is to be a world-changer, to work for the salvation of the world, the instantiation of true law here on earth.

I began the research for this book when Chicago police officers, students in courses I was teaching, urged me to investigate Aliite practices and claims— practices and claims that were recognizably "law-stuff," but of the legality of which officers were, at best, suspicious.[3] I am finishing this book in a moment characterized, around the globe, by the rise of ethnonationalism and ethnonationalist regimes, a time not only of closing borders, but of internal exclusion and denationalization, from Hungary to India, Turkey to Russia, Israel to the United States. Citizenship, as a status, has come into question. Citizens march, here in America, under the Nazi swastika paired with the Stars and Stripes, declaring their refusal to be "replaced" as authentic citizens by those whom they consider to be unworthy of such standing—religious and racial others.[4] In both popular discourse and official U.S. government rhetoric, the divide between citizen and noncitizen involves a move from criminalization to blatant dehumanization. "Illegality," no longer merely a description of actions, is recast as an ontological category for migrants and asylum seekers. The president of the United States, warning of "invasion" by "aliens," "illegals" who will "infest" the country, states plainly: "These aren't people. These are animals."[5] Citizenship is simultaneously reimagined as linked to ancestry, as a mark of essential difference, and, in practical terms, prioritized as necessary for survival, with documentation thereof, evidence of recognition by the authority of the state, granting life rather than deportation and death. Law enforcement agencies, reinterpreting the borders of the country to be ubiquitous, board buses and make random raids and traffic stops, employing an array of surveillance technologies, from military drones to cellphone tracking—and even hacking—devices.

Aliite religion speaks to this moment, echoing and amplifying its anxieties and emphases, contesting and rejecting its visions of American society and democracy, offering examples of creative negotiations and surprising tactics in response to law enforcement suspicion and surveillance.

Aliite faith exists not despite but because of constant awareness of the dangers of the state and the stakes of citizenship—as status and as practice. One reason why Aliite ceremonies like the one just described can be so moving is the understanding that such events are life-changing; the participants know what there is to gain and what it means to lose. America always represents both palpable threat and possible empowerment, a sovereign power with the ability to crush and destroy, yet simultaneously a political system offering sovereignty to its citizens. A state—in theory—composed of and guided by "We the People," America also always interrupts Aliite life in the form of individuals in positions of power with their own interpretations and agendas giving orders to armed agents who enact their will. There is no avoiding this reality; survival, in Aliite tradition, is never merely endurance, but participation in an ongoing struggle to transform social reality. "The only way out of the fire is through the fire," Ali said. Aliite faith offers incitement for the fulfillment of America's long-state ideals through, in part, indictment of the nation for failing to live up to those ideals—what Matthews-El calls the nation's "fundamental doctrine."[6]

Aliite religion responds to the unjust, even unbearable social reality of America by insisting on America's promise, America's intended exceptional, divinely designed possibility. Matthews-El writes: "Millions of people continue to sit on the sidelines of life, hopeless, in the very land of opportunity, marginalized, living an American nightmare, while praying for the American dream."[7] This dream is offered as a counter to the nightmare, an *alternity*, an *otherwise possibility*, an achievable project evidenced on the authority of the state itself. Aliite religion pits a vision of America as it should be against America as it is. Aliite thought contrasts love, truth, peace, freedom, and justice with the absence and opposite of such ideals. Aliite practices hold the unlawful legal up against the eternal and transcendent All-Law. Aliite citizens ask America—the sovereign state through its official representatives but also their fellow and likewise sovereign American citizens— *Are you going to obey your own true law?*

ACKNOWLEDGMENTS

THIS BOOK OWES ITS EXISTENCE to three factors.

My six summers as an instructor for Saint Xavier University's Chicago Police Department B.A. program taught me to think about the entanglements of religion with race and law and state power. The CPD officers who were my students urged me to research this topic, generously shared stories of their professional encounters with Aliites, and engaged in my developing theories about Aliite thought and practice. I am grateful for their role in initiating this project.

A 2011 summer fellowship grant with the Black Metropolis Research Consortium of Chicago bought me the time to begin researching Aliite history and helped me situate Aliite religion in a broader context of both African American political thought and Chicago political history. The financial and collegial support of the BMRC was invaluable. Such organizations are essential for the advancement of scholarship.

Winni Sullivan encouraged my investigations into Aliite relations with law and the legal, challenging me to push past easy assumptions and immerse myself in the logic and the stakes of Aliite thought. For years, she offered commentary on my work, provided me with reading recommendations, and, most important, expressed unwavering enthusiasm for and genuine excitement about the *questions* at the heart of this book. I am thankful for her support, and I am inspired by her example of what it means to be a thinker.

Numerous other friends, colleagues, and institutions have played important roles in this project. Religion faculty at the University of Wisconsin–Stevens Point came in on a holiday to give feedback on an early lecture about Ali and his two flags. A summer research grant from the Wabash Center facilitated the drafting of the first chapters. Audiences at public presentations at Centenary College, Monmouth College, University of Pittsburgh,

Indiana University, and the Disciples Divinity House of the University of Chicago offered valuable feedback, as did panel members, moderators, and audiences at meetings of the American Academy of Religion, the Law & Society Association, the Society for Utopian Studies, the Memory Studies Association, and the Midwest Regional AAR, as well as participants in a Princeton University workshop on religion and book history and my fellow members of the Taking Exception: Queering American Religion group, led by Cooper Harriss and Sarah Imhoff. I am indebted to the patient help of librarians at the Chicago Historical Society; the Chicago Public Library (especially at the Vivian G. Harsh Research Collection of the Carter G. Woodson Regional branch); the Regenstein Library of the University of Chicago; the Schomburg Center for Research in Black Culture of the New York Public Library; and the Kislak Center for Special Collections, Rare Books, and Manuscripts at the University of Pennsylvania. The staff of the University of Wisconsin–Stevens Point Library were exceptionally helpful in this project's earliest days, and in my time in Louisiana I depended on Sharon Chevalier at Centenary College's Magale Library for interlibrary loan services.

Countless students of mine—in the CPD program, at Iowa State University, University of Wisconsin–Stevens Point, and Centenary College—helped me think through my arguments here, as did students in courses for which I guest-lectured at Franklin & Marshall (via Skype) and the Ohio State University (in person). At Centenary College, three provosts provided research funding, and a sabbatical leave from Centenary allowed me to complete this book. Colleagues who read drafts of this project include Jenna Gray-Hildenbrand, Rhiannon Graybill, Jeremy Biles, Isaac Weiner, Stephen Selka, and Caleb Elfenbein. Jamie Michelle Wright, as a student research assistant, proved an invaluable dialogue partner. Other important interlocutors, on issues large and small, include Noah Salomon, Seth Perry, Cooper Harriss, SherAli Tareen, Judith Weisenfeld, J. Kameron Carter, Robert Yelle, Joseph Tucker Edmonds, Edward Ragan, Lloyd Sullivan, Lerone Martin, Mike Hogue, and Kellan Klaus. I am thankful to Alan Thomas and Kyle Wagner for their support for this project and to the two anonymous readers for the University of Chicago Press, whose detailed feedback and enthusiasm shaped the final version of this book. I am grateful, too, to Kathryn Lofton and John Modern for seeing fit to include this book in their excellent series.

Above all else, the continual support of Cristina Caldari-Torres has been vital to this project and to my life. Words will never approach adequate expression of my love for you, which is utter, wild, and greater every day.

My remarkable good fortune in finding a partner is matched only by my simultaneous good fortune in finding a stepson, Nico Farren, whose relentless and energizing interrogations deserve a final mention in relation to this project. Nico, your sensibility cuts to the heart of many issues, perhaps never more so than when pairing the declaration, "I am a sovereign!" with the query, "But are we sovereigns really?" May you always retain that emphatic belief *and* that wary suspicion. My prayer for you is Fanon's prayer, that life make you "a man who questions."

NOTES

PREFACE

1. Empire Washitaw Sunday-night conference call (hereafter EWCC), October 8, 2017.

INTRODUCTION

1. Ali, *Holy Koran of the Moorish Science Temple of America*, 48:1–3. First published in 1927, also called the *Circle Seven Koran* after a symbol on its cover, this text is available in various editions, including *The Foundations of a Nation, Volume One: The Circle 7 Holy Koran: Noble Drew Ali & The Moorish Science Temple of America* (CreateSpace, 2009), https://hermetic.com/moorish/7koran. For a biography of Drew Ali, see Judith Weisenfeld, *New World A-Coming: Black Religion and Racial Identity during the Great Migration* (New York: New York University Press, 2016), 46–48; and Fathie Ali Abdat, "Before the Fez: The Life and Times of Drew Ali, 1886–1924," *Journal of Race, Ethnicity, and Religion* 5, no 8 (August 2014), available at http://raceandreligion.com/JRER /Volume_5_(2014)_files/Abdat%205%208.pdf; and Azeem Hopkins-Bey, *Prophet Noble Drew Ali: Saviour of Humanity* (Ali's Men Publishing, 2014).

2. Ali, "Prophet Warns All Moslems," January 15, 1929, collected in the *Moorish Literature* (hereafter *ML*). There are multiple versions of the *Moorish Literature*, and many communities produce their own version. See, for instance, Drew Ali, *The Moorish Literature* (Lulu, 2014); and Sheik Way-El, *The Moorish Literature by Prophet Noble Drew Ali* (Lulu, 2015). The Schomburg Center's MSTA archive contains a copy dated 1928 but containing a letter from one of the "reincarnated" prophets dated 1935. As this example shows, versions differ in their inclusion of texts by later MSTA leaders or in their inclusion of sayings attributed to Ali, called by the Arabic term "hadiths." Allah's Temple online version, called "The New Moorish Literature," includes the announcement for the Great Moorish Drama, http://moorishkingdom.tripod.com/id56.html. Salaam El

of the International Asiatic Moorish Hiphop Temple MSTA community explains, in a YouTube video, how the compilation functions as the authentic and authoritative voice of Ali. Reading aloud from the *Moorish Literature*, Salaam El argues that study of the text is an opportunity to "talk to Noble Drew Ali" in the sense of understanding the ideas and intentions of the prophet. "The Moorish Science Temple of America: Moorish Literature," IAMHH Temple, February 9, 2016, https://www.youtube.com /watch?v=zrnWz8pi-24.

3. Ali, *Holy Koran*, 13:6.

4. Ali, *Holy Koran*, 47:13. In a brief statement on theology, "What Is Islam?" Ali writes: "We believe in one God. Allah who is All God, All Mercy and All Power. He is perfect and holy. All Wisdom, All Knowledge, and All Truth. These are some of His great attributes so far as we can understand. He is free from all defects, holy and transcendent. He is personal to us in so far as we can see His attributes working for us; but He is, nevertheless, impersonal. Because He is infinite, perfect, and Holy, we do not believe that death, decay, or sleep overtake Him, neither do we believe that He is a helplessly inactive and inert force. Nothing happens without his knowledge and will. He neither begets nor is He begotten, because these are the traits of frail and weak humanity" (*ML*).

5. Ali, "Plea to Nation," in *ML*.

6. Ali, *Holy Koran*, 47:17.

7. Ali, "Prophet Makes a Plea to Nation," in *ML*.

8. Ali, *Holy Koran* 47:15 and 46:8; Ali, "Warning from the Prophet," in *ML*. The reference to a "vine and fig tree" is from the biblical book of Micah 4:4; Ali frequently revisits the imagery of the Bible, images that were presumably well known to those who joined his movement. "We honor all divine prophets" was printed on the original MSTA nationality cards. "Jesus, Mohamed, Buddha and Confucius" are those usually mentioned.

9. Ali, "Moorish Leader's Historical Message to America," in *ML*; Kevin K. Gaines, *Uplifting the Race: Black Leadership, Politics, and Culture in the Twentieth Century* (Chapel Hill: University of North Carolina Press, 1996), 3.

10. Ali, "Moorish Head Makes Plan for Conclave," in *ML*.

11. Ali, "To Be Proclaimed at Every Meeting," in *ML*.

12. Bandele El-Amin, *Moors, Moabite, and Man: Reflection and Redemption* (Indigenous Peoples, Inc., 2011), 55; and Bandele El Amin, *Wake Up I Free Ka* (Moorish Republic Press, 2009), 19.

13. Ali, "Moorish Leader's Historical Message to America," in *ML*; Gaines, *Uplifting the Race*, 99.

14. *Califa Uhuru: A Compilation of Literature from the Moorish Science Temple of America*, ed. Tauheedah Najee-Ullah El and Rami Abdullah Salaam El (Califa Media, 2014), 169.

15. Ali, "Saviour of Humanity," in *ML*.

16. This formulation, used throughout Aliite communities, was repeated by Ali in many of his writings, such as "Moorish Leader's Historical Message to America," "Prophet Makes a Plea to the Nation," and "Caveat Emptor," all in *ML*.

17. Ali, *Holy Koran*, 48:6–8.

18. Ali, "A Divine Warning," in *ML*. This text, a jeremiad—as implied by its title—couples this potential for providential blessing with another alternative: "if the above principles are not carried out by the citizens and my people in the government, the worst is yet to come, because the Great God of the Universe is not pleased with the works that are being performed in North America by my people and this great sin must be removed from the land to save it from enormous earthquakes, diseases, etc."

19. Consider contemporary MSTA thinker Eric Mungin Bey's statement that "religion means governmental principles, law and order," in *Discover the Key to the Moorish Questionary: A Study Guide for All Moorish Americans* (Xlibris, 2009), 23.

20. The dispersed nature of the MSTA movement makes accurate estimation of participants impossible. Yvonne Yazbeck Haddad and Jane Idleman Smith estimate that there were around a hundred thousand members in the movement in the 1930s, in their *Mission to America: Five Islamic Sectarian Communities in North America* (Tallahassee: University Press of Florida, 1993).

21. T. Matheno Matthews-El, *Moorish America's Archival Palladium: An Exposition of Alternative Moorish-American Philosophical Thought* (CreateSpace, 2010), 27.

22. Ali, "Nick Named," in *ML*.

23. "Mike Brown, Ferguson, Talib Kweli, Dred Scott, and Nationality," *Moorish Oakland Star*, August 26, 2014, https://moorishoaklandstar.wordpress.com/tag/dred-scott/.

24. For the usage of "Ultimate Law," see Bandele El Amin, *Nationality, Birthrights and Jurisprudence: New Social and Cultural Blueprint for Melaninated Indigenous People* (San Bernardino, CA: self-published, 2014), 42. "All-Law" is a name taught by Valahra Renita El Harre Bey, popularly known as Queen V, in lectures like "Queen Valahra Renita El Harre Bey: 'MOORISH LAW,'" Asaru Alim El-Bey, January 2, 2017, https://www.youtube.com/watch?v=wA0yoWRW5-M&spfreload=10. One source for identifying the five values with names of Allah is B. Denham El, *The Divine Creed of the Moorish Scientist: An Interpretation* (CreateSpace, 2015).

25. This phrase was not without precedent. The Chicago Urban League furnished new migrants with a flier that included the phrase, similarly in all capital letters: "I AM AN AMERICAN CITIZEN." Farah Jasmine Griffin, *"Who Set You Flowin'?" The African-American Migration Narrative* (New York: Oxford University Press, 1995), 104.

26. Academic work on the MSTA remains largely indebted to Arthur Huff Fauset's 1944 *Black Gods of the Metropolis: Negro Religious Cults of the Urban North* (Philadelphia: University of Pennsylvania Press, 2002), which focused on a particularly secretive and taboo-conscious community in Philadelphia. Fauset treated the MSTA as a monolithic organization rather than the extremely varied movement that, by the 1940s, it already was. This variety has only increased with time, while the tendency to speak of a single MSTA remains. Harder to understand is the inability to note the central emphasis given to law in MSTA thought and practice. Richard Brent Turner, who called attention to Ali's insistence that "the name means everything," describes the change from "Negro" to "Moor" as merely "erasing the stigma of slavery and distancing them from ordinary Negroes who were not respected as Americans" without noting how these names are understood as legal terms, as markers of status under the law. See his *Islam in the African American Experience*, 2nd ed. (Bloomington: Indiana

University Press, 2003), 96. Edward Curtis, in his repeated treatments of the MSTA, likewise ignores the focus on law and the emphasis on citizenship, going so far as to drop the "A" from MSTA when he abbreviates it. Edward E. Curtis IV, *Islam in Black America: Identity, Liberation and Difference in African American Islamic Thought* (Albany: State University of New York Press, 2002); Curtis, "Debating the Origins of the Moorish Science Temple," in Edward E. Curtis IV and Danielle Brune Sigler, eds., *The New Black Gods: Arthur Huff Fauset and the Study of African American Religions* (Bloomington: Indiana University Press, 2009); and Curtis, *Muslims in America: A Short History* (Oxford: Oxford University Press, 2009). Contextualizing the MSTA alongside other "religio-racial" movements, Judith Weisenfeld, while also using the abbreviation "MST," is attentive to Ali's claims about American identity and the role of citizenship for later MSTA members in the Kirkman Bey branch of the movement. She also offers useful engagement with Moorish American litigation for accommodation in public schools. See Weisenfeld, *New World*, 201. Robert Dannin is attentive to Ali's ideas about citizenship but approaches them outside the framing logic of law and thus dismisses the MSTA as a "crisis cult." See his *Black Pilgrimage to Islam* (Oxford: Oxford University Press, 2002). Sylvester Johnson coined the notion of an "ethnic turn," in an important article addressing the MSTA, "The Rise of Black Ethnics: The Ethnic Turn in African American Religions, 1916–1945," *Religion and American Culture: A Journal of Interpretation* 20, no. 2 (Summer 2010): 125–63. He considered the MSTA within his *African American Religions, 1500–2000: Colonialism, Democracy, and Freedom* (Cambridge: Cambridge University Press, 2015), attentive particularly to the rhetorical uses of Ali's universalism and to later MSTA negotiations of FBI surveillance. The contemporary MSTA has been subject to little scholarly attention, one exception being Spencer Dew, " 'Moors Know the Law': Sovereign Legal Discourse in Moorish Science Religious Communities and the Hermeneutics of Supersession," *Journal of Law and Religion* 31, no. 1 (March 2016): 70–91. On the Nuwaubian Yamassee, Susan Palmer has contributed several works, most notably *The Nuwaubian Nation: Black Spirituality and State Control* (Farnham, UK: Ashgate, 2010). Julius Bailey addressed issues of privacy and publicity around Tama-Re in his "The Final Frontier: Secrecy, Identity, and the Media in the Rise and Fall of the United Nuwaubian Nation of Moors," *Journal of the American Academy of Religion* 74, no. 2 (June 2006): 302–23. The Washitaw de Dugdahmoundyah have received no academic attention except for one article on the centrality of Washitaw claims about "United States v. Henry Turner's Heirs": Spencer Dew, "Washitaw de Dugdahmoundyah: Counterfactual Religious Readings of the Law," *Nova Religio: The Journal of Alternative and Emergent Religions* 19, no. 2 (November 2015): 65–82.

27. Ian Haney Lopez, *White by Law: The Legal Construction of Race*, 10th Anniversary Edition (New York: New York University Press, 2006), 79.

28. Derek Hicks, *Reclaiming Spirit in the Black Faith Tradition* (New York: Palgrave Macmillan, 2012), 90.

29. Ibram X. Kendi, *Stamped from the Beginning: A Definitive History of Racist Ideas in America* (New York: Nation Books, 2016), 124. On slavery as self-caused, see Ali, *Holy Koran*, 47:9.

30. Gaines, *Uplifting the Race*, 3. Ali, *Holy Koran*, 47:16: "Through sin and disobedience every nation has suffered slavery, due to the fact that they honored not the creed and principles of their forefathers."

31. "What to the Slave Is the Fourth of July?" July 5, 1852, available at https://www.the nation.com/article/what-slave-fourth-july-frederick-douglass/.

32. Sally Merry, *Getting Justice and Getting Even: Legal Consciousness among Working-Class Americans* (Chicago: University of Chicago Press, 1990), 8.

33. See Theophus Harold Smith, *Conjuring Culture: Biblical Formations of Black America* (Oxford: Oxford University Press, 1994); and Mari J. Matsuda, "Looking to the Bottom: Critical Legal Studies and Reparations," *Harvard Civil Rights–Civil Liberties Law Review* 323 (1987): 22.

34. Winnifred Fallers Sullivan, "Religion, Law, and the Construction of Identities. Introduction," *Numen: Religion, Law, and the Construction of Identities* 43, no. 2 (May 1996): 128–38, especially 132.

35. Catherine Albanese, *America: Religions and Religion* (Boston: Wadsworth, 2013), 276; Janet Jakobsen and Ann Pellegrini, *Love the Sin: Sexual Regulations and the Limits of Religious Tolerance* (Boston: Beacon Press, 2004); Robert Orsi, *Between Heaven and Earth: The Religious Worlds People Make and the Scholars Who Study Them* (Princeton, NJ: Princeton University Press, 2005).

36. See Winnifred Sullivan's discussion of "legal religion" in *The Impossibility of Religious Freedom*, new ed. (Princeton, NJ: Princeton University Press, 2018), 8.

37. R. Laurence Moore, *Religious Outsiders and the Making of Americans* (Oxford: Oxford University Press, 1997).

38. Eric Michael Mazur, *The Americanization of Religious Minorities: Confronting the Constitutional Order* (Baltimore: Johns Hopkins University Press, 1999), 133.

39. Sally Engle Merry, "Culture, Power, and the Discourse of Law," *New York Law School Law Review* 209 (1992): 37.

40. Susan S. Sibley, "After Legal Consciousness," *Annual Review of Law and Social Science* 1 (December 2005): 323–67, 334.

41. Audra Simpson, *Mohawk Interruptus: Political Life Across the Borders of Settler States* (Durham, NC: Duke University Press, 2006).

42. Giorgio Agamben, *Homo Sacer: Sovereign Power and Bare Life* (Stanford: Stanford University Press, 1998), 65, 170.

43. Paul Kahn, *The Cultural Study of Law: Reconstructing Legal Scholarship* (Chicago: University of Chicago Press, 1999), 2.

44. Kahn, *Cultural Study*, 36; Robert M. Cover, "The Supreme Court, 1982 Term—Foreword: *Nomos* and Narrative," Faculty Scholarship Series, Paper 2705, 1983, http://digitalcommons.law.yale.edu/fss_papers/2705, 4.

45. Cover, "*Nomos*," 8.

46. Cover, "*Nomos*," 34, 39.

47. Like other hadiths attributed to Ali, this saying is widely published. See, for instance, "Noble Drew Ali, Canons Prophecies," Moorish Science Temple of America, Subordinate Temple Mir No. 9, January 28, 2014, http://mstofamir9.blogspot.com/2014/01/prophet-noble-drew-ali-canons-prophecies.html.

48. Susan F. Hirsch and Mindie Lazarus-Black, "Introduction/Performance and Paradox: Exploring Law's Role in Hegemony and Resistance," in Mindie Lazarus-Black and Susan F. Hirsch, eds., *Contested States: Law, Hegemony and Resistance* (New York: Routledge, 1994), 1–31.

49. Vincent Lloyd, *Black Natural Law* (Oxford: Oxford University Press, 2016), 5.

50. Ali, "Divine Warning," in *ML*.

51. Arna Bontemps and Jack Conroy, *Anyplace But Here* (New York: Hill & Wang, 1945, 1966), 206–7.

52. Acts 4 and 5 of the "Divine Constitution and By-laws." This text, instituted during Ali's leadership of the MSTA, consists of seven "Acts," establishing rules for temple meetings and governance as well as emphasizing basic ethical requirements for all MSTA members. This document was hung in all MSTA meeting spaces and continues to be so displayed, often with an image of Noble Drew Ali surrounded by the text of the Acts. (For an example of this, see https://moorishsociety.wordpress.com/tag/divine -constitution-and-by-laws/.) The text of the "Divine Constitution" is also reprinted in many MSTA and Aliite publications, whether books (such as *Califa Uhuru*) or videos (such as "The Divine Constitution and By-laws," posted by Damorrious Fuller, January 13, 2016, https://www.youtube.com/watch?v=szo1rW5hbeI).

53. Ali, "Organization's Growth Enormous Temples in All Principal Cities," *Moorish Guide*, August 19, 1928.

54. Carl Schmitt, *The Crisis of Parliamentary Democracy* (Cambridge: MIT Press, 1988), 9.

55. Seyla Benhabib, *The Rights of Others: Aliens, Residents and Citizens* (Cambridge: Cambridge University Press, 2004), 145.

56. See Nira Yuval-Davis, *The Politics of Belonging: Intersectional Contestations* (Los Angeles: Sage, 2011).

57. *Moorish Voice*, May 1943, 15.

58. On "mis-education," see R. A. Umar Shabazz Bey, *We Are the Washitaw: The Indigenous Black Inhabitants of North America* (Washitaw Proper: Washitaw International Human Rights Network, 1996), 5.

59. C. Eric Lincoln, "The Muslim Mission in the Context of American Social History," in Gayraud S. Wilmore, ed., *African American Religious Studies: An Interdisciplinary Anthology* (Durham, NC: Duke University Press, 1989), 345.

60. My approach here follows the example of scholars such as Kahn, *Cultural Study*, 39; and Cover, "*Nomos*," 4.

61. The term "cult" constructs and polices the concept of religion. The implication is that the "cult" is irrational and primitive, expressive and emotional in ways that clash with implicit Protestant assumptions about religion as private and rational. "Cults" are threateningly strange, too, in that they blend boundaries, mixing "religion" and "politics," for instance. As David Chidester writes, "The term 'cult' has come to represent a deviant social organization masquerading as religion . . . the opposite of legitimate religion—evil, dangerous, mind controlling, brainwashing, financially exploitative, and politically subversive." David Chidester, *Salvation and Suicide: An Interpretation of Jim Jones, the Peoples Temple, and Jonestown*, rev. ed. (Bloomington: Indiana University Press, 2003), xix.

62. *Chicago Tribune*, September 29, 1929; Bill Osinski, *Ungodly: A True Story of Unprecedented Evil* (Indigo Publishing, 2007), 268.

63. Lloyd, *Black Natural Law*, xiii.

64. "The Divine Warning pt 4" begins with this anecdote, posted by brothahaneed, July 12, 2007, https://www.youtube.com/watch?v=oHMsG5EO9u4&list=PL37C53AC08376445 C&index=4. This Hakim Bey is a distinct person from the pseudonym Hakim Bey used by Peter Lamborn Wilson, a member of the multiracial Aliite organization the Moorish Orthodox Church and author of an important early treatment of MSTA history in his book *Sacred Drift: Essays on the Margins of Islam* (San Francisco: City Lights Books, 1993).

CHAPTER ONE

1. Ali, "Moorish Head Makes Plan for Conclate," in *ML*. For a contemporary take, see Shem El, "Is American Citizenship Important," *Moorish American News*, April 16, 2016, http://moorishamericannews.com/is-american-citizenship-important.

2. Ali, "A Divine Warning," in *ML*.

3. Ali, *Holy Koran*, 46:9. The phrase "true and divine prophets," like "all divine prophets," is common in MSTA usage, as, for instance, in this contemporary MSTA manual: https://www.bop.gov/foia/docs/moorishsciencetemplemanual.pdf. For discussion of the concept of "Universal Prophet," see http://rvbeypublications.com/id76.html.

4. Johnson, *African American Religions*, 303.

5. Wilson, *Sacred Drift*, 29.

6. Ali, *Holy Koran*, 48:7, 10–11.

7. The MSTA catechism, called Koran Questions for Moorish Americans or sometimes the Moorish Questionary, describes Islamism as Moors' "old time religion." See "Koran Questions for Moorish Americans–101," *Moorish Oakland Star*, n.d., https://mooris hoaklandstar.wordpress.com/koran-questions-for-moorish-americans-101/. Copies of this catechism are widely available in print and online; archival versions from Ali's time are included in the FBI's MSTA file and in the MSTA archive at the Schomburg Center for Research in Black Culture. "Islamism" is used to differentiate Aliite Islam from what Aliites sometimes call "Arab Islam." For a detailed contemporary description of Ali's Islamism, see Lasana Tunica El's contemporary poem, "Islamism is . . . ," *Moorish American News*, February 25, 2015, http://moorishamericannews.com/islamism.

8. Ali, "So This Is Chicago," in *ML*.

9. Ali, "So This Is Chicago," in *ML*.

10. See Hopkins-Bey, *Prophet Noble Drew Ali*, 57; and Kudjo Adwo El and Rami A. Salaam El, *77 Amazing Facts about the Moors with Complete Proof: Black & White Student Edition Paperback*, ed. Tauheedah S. Najee-Ullah El (CreateSpace: 2015), 10.

11. *Moorish Guide* article quoted in Hopkins-Bey, *Prophet Noble Drew Ali*, 62.

12. Ali, *Holy Koran*, 48:3. The *Holy Koran* describes Garvey in relation to Ali as John the Baptist was in relation to Jesus. Contemporary Moors continue this emphasis, often

referring to Garvey as Ali's "harbinger." See, for instance, Sheik Way-El (Lord Abba), *Noble Drew Ali and the Moorish Science Temple of America: The Foundation of Consciousness, and Light in America* (Self-published, 2011), 31.

13. Aliite texts often reproduce, as evidence, a postcard supposedly sent from Atlanta, the site of the prison, in 1927. See Hopkins-Bey, *Prophet Noble Drew Ali*, 39. On Ali's presentation of "'America' as a redeemable sovereign entity," in contrast to Garveyite separatism, see Scott J. Varda, "Drew Ali and the Moorish Science Temple of America: A Minor Rhetoric of Black Nationalism," *Rhetoric and Public Affairs* 16, no. 4 (Winter 2013): 685–717.

14. See Darnise C. Martin, *Beyond Christianity: African Americans in a New Thought Church* (New York: NYU Press, 2005); and Johnson, *African American Religion*, 290.

15. Douglas Bukowski, *Big Bill Thompson, Chicago, and the Politics of Image* (Urbana: University of Illinois Press, 1998), 82

16. Bukowski, *Big Bill Thompson*, 182. "In 1920 Chicago counted 884,000 registered voters. By 1924 the figure had grown to 1,065,000 before reaching 1,314,000 in 1928; the ethnic ghettoes were coming of age" (123). Political scientist Harold Gosnell has argued that "the ballot box" (access to suffrage) marked the major social "transformation" of the Great Migration. Harold F. Gosnell, *Negro Politicians: The Rise of Negro Politics in Chicago* (Chicago: University of Chicago Press, 1969), 18–19.

17. Bukowski, *Big Bill Thompson*, 49.

18. Gosnell, *Machine Politics*, 74.

19. Evelyn Brooks Higgenbotham, *Righteous Discontent: The Women's Movement in the Black Baptist Church, 1880–1920* (Cambridge, MA: Harvard University Press, 1993), 187.

20. Higgenbotham, *Righteous Discontent*, 189.

21. Adam Cohen and Elizabeth Taylor, *American Pharaoh: Mayor Richard J. Daley: His Battle for Chicago and the Nation* (Boston: Little, Brown, 2000), 48. The popularity of ethnic political organizations in Chicago should not be underestimated; there were more than a thousand such groups active by 1919.

22. Gosnell, *Machine Politics*, 74, 84.

23. Gosnell, *Machine Politics*, 82. On such negotiation as a central social process, see Lawrence Rosen, *Bargaining for Reality: The Construction of Social Relations in a Muslim Community* (Chicago: University of Chicago Press, 1984).

24. Ali, "Our Dollars and Sense," in *ML*.

25. Hadith quoted in Azeem Hopkins-Bey, *What Your History Books Failed to Tell You* (Bloomington, IN: Author House, 2004),45; emphasis in original.

26. *Moorish Voice*, November 1942, 6.

27. See Emily Suzanne Clark, "Noble Drew Ali's 'Clean and Pure Nation': The Moorish Science Temple, Identity, and Healing," *Nova Religio: The Journal of Alternative and Emergent Religions* 16, no. 3 (2013): 31–51. See also Weisenfeld, *New World*, 222.

28. Bukowski, *Big Bill Thompson*, 6. "Precinct captains are the backbone of any metropolitan political organization," as they "maintain face-to-face contacts with individual citizens" on behalf of the machine. Gosnell, *Machine Politics*, 51.

29. Ali, "All Registering," in *ML*.

30. Ali, "The Voice of the Prophet," in *ML*.

31. Sheldon S. Wolin, "Fugitive Democracy," *Constellations* 1, no. 1 (December 1994): 11–25, quotation on 11.

32. Sheldon S. Wolin, *Politics and Vision: Continuity and Innovation in Western Political Thought*, expanded ed. (Princeton, NJ: Princeton University Press, 2004), 602.

33. See Susan Nance, "Mystery of the Moorish Science Temple: Southern Blacks and American Alternative Spirituality in 1920s Chicago," *Religion and American Culture: A Journal of Interpretation* 12, no. 2 (Summer 2002):123–66; and Nance, "Respectability and Representation: The Moorish Science Temple, Morocco, and Black Public Culture in 1920s Chicago," *American Quarterly* 54, no. 4 (December 2002): 623–59, especially 626. Jacob Dorman has argued that "'black orientalism' was generative of many African American new religious movements and must be recognized as an important part of the black cultural imagination in the late nineteenth and early twentieth centuries." Jacob Dorman, "'A True Moslem is a True Spiritualist': Black Orientalism and *Black Gods*," in Edward E. Curtis IV and Danielle Brune Sigler, eds., *The New Black Gods: Arthur Huff Fauset and the Study of African American Religions* 117. As for the fez's role in mainstream American political culture, Warren G. Harding, as president of the United States, wore a red fez for at least two White House receptions for Shriners, in 1921 and 1923; in 1921 he welcomed his fellow Shriners in Arabic: "*wa aleikum salaam*." Jonathan Curiel, *Al'America: Travels through America's Arab and Islamic Roots* (New York: New Press, 2008), 96. This fact serves as evidence for Aliite claims that Harding was himself "Asiatic" rather than European; see the lengthy page at an anonymously run Aliite site explicitly linking MSTA, Nuwaubian Yamassee, and Washitaw images and concerns: http://www.sphinxpyramid.com/the-moorish-science-academy. This site seeks to serve as an "academy" for the education of Aliite children and adults, as well as "on online company . . . with digital products and online sales." President Truman in a Shriner fez is featured prominently in "Moorish America," a video that features a panoply of other white political leaders or anonymous citizens parading and meeting in fezzes. Posted by darazz25, April 30, 2010, https://www.youtube.com/watch?v=tOSt_SJkYTg.

34. See Nance, "Mystery"; Haddad and Smith, *Mission to America*; and Richard Brent Turner, "The Ahmadiyya Mission to Blacks in the United States in the 1920s," *Journal of Religious Thought* 44 (Winter–Spring 1988).

35. Ali, "Masterpieces of Religious Literature: Secrets of Other Creeds Revealed," in *ML*. Much of Edward Curtis's engagement with the MSTA has been invested in reclaiming that religion as "a form of Islam in the academic study of religion"; see Edward E. Curtis IV, "Debating the Origins of the Moorish Science Temple: Toward a New Cultural History," in Curtis and Sigler, eds., *New Black Gods*, 83. There are those within Aliite communities who want to be included within the diverse global ummah or Islamic community. Other Aliites, however, insist on the distinction between Islamism and Islam, and even the difference between Ali's usage of "Moslem" and the word "Muslim." More than mere "letter semantics" as B. Denham El argues, the words have distinct meanings, with "Moslem" denoting "a 'High' spiritual station and really [having] nothing to do with organized Al Islam." See Denham El, *The Divine Creed of the Moorish Scientist: An Interpretation* (CreateSpace, 2015), n.p.

36. Johnson, *African American Religions*, 299; Johnson, "The Rise of Black Ethnics: The Ethnic Turn in African American Religions, 1916–1945," *Religion and American Culture* 20, no. 2 (Summer 2010): 125–63.

37. Ali, *Holy Koran*, 47:9, 11. At other points, however, Ali reiterated the idea of race as a means of categorizing humans. "If you have race pride and love your race, join the Moorish Science Temple of America," Ali wrote in "Prophet Drew Ali Speaks to the Nations." He also spoke of "the nobler life which the future holds for the races of men," when discussing religious freedom in "Moorish Leader's Historical Message to America." Both pieces are collected in the *ML*.

38. Aliite thinkers plumb legal history to offer examples of "Moor" as distinct from "Negro," giving citations to, among other sources, a petition on behalf of the Sundry Free Moors living in South Carolina in 1790 and the Virginia Black Codes, always with an eye toward contemporary implications of the use of such legal categories. As Hakim Bey says, in his discussion of the Black Codes, "If we use those names, we likewise put ourselves in that category." "Hakim Bey The Divine Warning Entire Lecture," posted by Moors in America, April 11, 2014, https://www.youtube.com/watch?v=MSdwKVeq1kc. On South Carolina, see José V. Pimienta-Bey, *Othello's Children in the 'New World': Moorish History and Identity in the African American Experience* (Self-published, 2002), 97. To identify—or allow oneself to be identified as—"negro, colored, or black" is, as Kudjo Adwo El says, reiterating Ali, to be subject to "Civil Death," to be "dead in the eyes of the law." Adwo El, *You Are NOT Negro, Black, Coloured, Morisco Nor An African Slave!* (Califa Media, 2014), 13.

39. Lopez, *White by Law*, 7.

40. On these examples, see Joane Nagel, *American Indian Ethnic Renewal: Red Power and the Resurgence of Identity and Culture* (New York: Oxford University Press, 1997), 24.

41. Hopkins-Bey argues that "the first generation was *stripped* of their nationality and the words Negro and black were placed upon them . . . and they took on certain characteristics that were not theirs . . . They were being fraudulent. Do not act like a black person; do not act like a Negro. *Be* a Moorish American." *Know Thyself Radio*, episode "What Makes One a Moorish American?" October 18, 2010, http://www.blogtalkradio.com/themooriam/2010/10/18/what-makes-one-a-moorish-american.

42. Ali, *Holy Koran*, 47:1–9.

43. Ali, *Holy Koran*, 47:15.

44. Ali, *Holy Koran*, 47:16–17. Ali discusses "mental slavery" in "The Voice of the Prophet," and "political slavery" in "Political Slavery," both in *ML*.

45. See Spencer Dew, "Juanita Mayo Richardson Bey: Editor, Educator, and Poetic Visionary of First-Generation Moorish Science," *Journal of Africana Religions* 2, no. 2 (2014): 184–210. Temple No. 9 in Chicago was founded by M. Lovett-Bey, and Temple No. 17 in the same city was eventually run by Alsop Bey as Grand Sheikess. While no academic work has yet been done on her life and work, Mary Clift Bey was sent as a missionary from Chicago to Louisville, Kentucky, where by 1941 she was Grand Governess of a community. See A. Hopkins-Bey, *Prophet Noble Drew Ali*, 113–15. See also Debra Washington Mubashshir, "Forgotten Fruit of the City: Chicago and the Moorish Science Temple of America," *CrossCurrents* 51, no. 1 (Spring 2001): 6–20. This trajectory toward gender equality did not hold up as MSTA and Aliite history proceeded, though

there are, in this book, examples of significant female leaders and theorists, notably the Washitaw founder Verdiacee Goston, contemporary Aliite legal theorist Valahra Renita El Harre-Bey (also known as Queen V), and Moorish historian Tauheedah S. Najee-Ullah El. The prominence of female thinkers is rarest in the Nuwaubian Yamassee community, despite explicitly legal rhetoric on gender equality. "United Nuwaubian Nation of Moors Constitution," http://www.unnm.org/our-constitution. This statement is aimed directly at critics who held that the Nuwaubian Yamassee were misogynists and black supremacists. Much of this document is a kind of legal brief *against* those critics, including its affirmation of an openness to all cultures and a refusal "to hold prejudice" (18–19). The Washitaw movement, though founded by a female politician, has since become male-dominated. Members of the movement advanced claims of it being "a matriarchal empire" after their founding Empress's death, but such claims have been advanced primarily by men (with important female leaders, from Fayola Modupe to Lisa Tucker El, either withdrawing from positions of vocal leadership or being actively excluded by the community).

46. Ali, "Our Dollars and Sense," in *ML*.

47. Ali, "Political Slavery," in *ML*. See also Najee-Ullah El and Taylor El, *Moors in America*, 3.

48. Hopkins-Bey, *What Your History*, 24.

49. El Amin, *Nationality*, 116.

50. The distinction between Moor and Mu'ur is generally to flag one line of indigenous claim advanced by Aliite communities, which is that they are descendants of the original settlers of the New World who came from the lost continent of Lemuria or Mu. See "Mu: Original Garden of Eden" (according to James Churchward), in Adwo El and Salaam El, *77 Amazing Facts*, 40.

51. Asher Elbein, "Road to Tama-Re," *Oxford American Magazine*, http://www.oxford american.org/magazine/item/969-the-road-to-tama-re.

52. Julius Bailey, "Sacred Not Secret: Esoteric Knowledge in the United Nuwaubian Nation of Moors," in Stephen C. Finley, Margarita Simon Guillory, and Hugh R. Page, Jr., eds., *Esotericism in African American Religious Experience: 'There Is a Mystery'* (Leiden: Brill, 2015), 210–24, especially 211.

53. See the comparative religions as part of a "Universal Order of Love" as it is graphically mapped out in York's *Celestial Being or Terrestrial Being: Which One Are You?*, http://www.aeoebookstore.com/freebooks/Celestial%20Being%20or%20Terrestial%20Being%20-%20Which%20One%20Are%20You.pdf.

54. "Constitution of the UNNM," http://nuwaubianfacts.com/Constitution%20of%20UNNM%20ebook.pdf.

55. EWCC, October 4, 2015.

56. See, for instance, Civil Action 1:05-CV-2458-JEC, US Ex Rel v. Derrick H. Sanders, District Court for the Northern District of Georgia, Atlanta Division, where Chief Black Hawk (Derrick Sanders) had his claims of Yamassee Native American identity dismissed as "phony" on the logic that "[t]he Yamassee Native Americans are not recognized as an Indian tribe by the Bureau of Indian Affairs. The Yamassee do not have a treaty with the United States" (3,15). The Bureau of Indian Affairs receives from Aliites occasional petitions for recognition as Native American. See, for instance, the BIA document, "List

of Petitioners by State (as of November 12, 2013)," https://www.bia.gov/sites/bia.gov
/files/assets/as-ia/ofa/admindocs/ListPetByState_2013-11-12.pdf and one Aliite (legal) response critical of BIA treatment of Aliite claims, Silver Cloud Musafir (Navin-Chandra
Naidu)'s "Complaint Against R Lee Fleming in His Capacity as Director, Office of Federal Acknowledgement, United States Department of the Interior," April 21, 2015, http://
www.scripturalaw.org/Letter-of-Cmplnt-Against-Lee-Fleming.pdf.

57. Lacey Sharp, "Former Richwood Mayor Dies," KNOE.com, April 30, 2014, https://
web.archive.org/web/20140512222500/http://www.knoe.com/story/25397593/former
-richwood-mayor-dies; and "Empress Goston's Legacy Continues in 40th Anniversary," *Monroe Free Press*, June 19, 2017, http://www.monroefreepress.net/2017/06/19/em
press-gostons-legacy-continues-in-40th-anniversary/.

58. Members of the Washitaw claim Ali as "anointed Washitaw" in Shabazz Bey's language;
see *We Are the Washitaw*, 29. Dr. Ali Muhammad and Bigbay Bagby Badger insist that
Ali shares "bloodline" with the Washitaw royal family. "Noble Drew Ali: Prophet of the
People," posted by Paypal.me/Turtlegangnyc, June 27, 2104, https://www.youtube.com
/watch?v=xIewokB4JtQ; and EWCC, August 30, 2015.

59. See the cover image for the public Facebook group, "I Am Washitaw This is My Flag
Challenge," posted by William Woods, February 28, 2016, https://www.facebook.com
/photo.php?fbid=1673118702962241&set=gm.1083376228379749&type=3&theater.

60. "Brother Red Hawk—The Untold Story of the Washitaw Part 3," March 5, 2013, http://
www.youtube.com/watch?v=3Vw6K6RmVhI&list=PLYIseHPXyzyyFwolh7SxrZ5uAz
PBITxtm. This video is no longer available.

61. EWCC, October 9, 2016.

62. https://www.govtrack.us/congress/bills/84/hjres396/text.

63. Hussein Ali Agrama, "Secularism, Sovereignty, Indeterminacy: Is Egypt a Secular or a Religious State?" *Comparative Studies in Society and History* 52, no. 3 (July 2010): 495–523, 500.

64. Saba Mahmood, "Secularism, Hermeneutics, and Empire: The Politics of Islamic Reformation," *Public Culture* 8, no. 2 (2006): 323–47, especially 328.

65. Mayanthi L. Fernando, *The Republic Unsettled: Muslim French and the Contradictions
of Secularism* (Durham, NC: Duke University Press, 2014), 20.

66. Talal Asad, *Formations of the Secular: Christianity, Islam, Modernity* (Stanford: Stanford University Press, 2003), 5.

67. Sidney Mead, "The 'Nation with the Soul of a Church,'" in Russell E. Richey and Donald G. Jones, eds., *American Civil Religion* (New York: Harper & Row, 1974), 46.

68. See Vincent W. Lloyd, "Introduction: Managing Race, Managing Religion," in Jona-
thon S. Kahn and Vincent W. Lloyd, eds., *Race and Secularism in America* (New York:
Columbia University Press, 2016), 1–195.

69. Johnson, *African American Religions*, 303.

70. W. Clark Gilpin, "Secularism: Religious, Irreligious, and Areligious," *The Religion
and Culture Web Forum*, March 2007, https://divinity.uchicago.edu/sites/default/files
/imce/pdfs/webforum/032007/secularism.pdf, 7 and 8.

71. Charles Taylor, "Modes of Secularism," in Rajeev Bhargava, ed., *Secularism and Its
Critics* (Delhi: Oxford University Press, 1998), 46.

72. Denham El, *Divine Creed*, n.p.

73. Étienne Balibar, *Secularism and Cosmopolitanism: Critical Hypotheses on Religion and Politics* (New York: Columbia University Press, 2018), 134.

74. This emphasis on separation anticipates the work of Michael Walzer in "Liberalism and the Art of Separation," *Political Theory* 12, no. 3 (August 1984), 315–30.

75. Ali, *Holy Koran*, 47:16.

76. Ali, *Holy Koran*, 47:10–11.

77. Fernando, *The Republic Unsettled*, 98.

78. Ali, "Divine Warning," in *ML*; and "Moorish News Presents . . . Moorish Sovereignty vs. 'Sovereign Citizens,'" posted by Sheik Love El, October 28, 2017, https://www.you tube.com/watch?v=W7eD6ciZkA4.

79. See "The Phantom Wahhabi: Liberalism and the Muslim Fanatic in Mid-Victorian India," *Modern Asian Studies* 47, no. 1 (January 2003): 22–52, especially 48.

80. Matthews-El, *Moorish America's Archival Palladium*, 81.

CHAPTER TWO

1. https://www.state.gov/documents/organization/27807.pdf, 15.

2. Jessica Cattelino, *High Stakes: Florida Seminole Gaming and Sovereignty* (Durham, NC: Duke University Press, 2008), 189; and *Chisholm v. Georgia*, 2 U.S. 419 (1793) at 479. See also *Afroyim v. Rusk*, 387 U.S. 253 (1967); and, for a history of Supreme Court opinions on the sovereignty of the citizen, Patrick Weil, "Can a Citizen Be Sovereign?" *Humanity Journal*, January 2, 2016, http://humanityjournal.org/blog/can-a-citizen-be-sovereign/.

3. Carl Schmitt, *Political Theology: Four Chapters on the Concept of Sovereignty* (Chicago: University of Chicago Press, 2006), 5.

4. As Paul D. Halliday has shown, "pluralist forms of sovereignty" are not new and were the norm for centuries before Jean Bodin or Thomas Hobbes, let alone Carl Schmitt. See Halliday, "Law's Histories: Pluralisms, Pluralities, Diversity," in Lauren Benton and Richard J. Ross, eds., *Legal Pluralism and Empires, 1500–1850* (New York: New York University Press, 2013), 261–77, especially 268.

5. Cattelino, *High Stakes*, 190.

6. http://www.rvbeypublications.com/id27.html; and "Return of the Ancient Ones to the 21st Century—Introduction to Wash*taw History—II," http://www.blogtalkradio .com/truthpastor/2009/08/30/return-of-the-ancient-ones-to-the-21st-century--in.

7. Ali, *Holy Koran*, 3:2.

8. Thomas Blom Hansen and Finn Stepputat, "Sovereignty Revisited," *Annual Review of Anthropology* 35 (September 2006): 295–315.

9. William Connolly, "The Ethos of Sovereignty," in Austin Sarat, Lawrence Douglas, and Martha Merrill Umphrey, eds., *Law and the Sacred* (Stanford: Stanford University Press, 2007), 135–54, especially 137.

10. Kinda El, "Sovereignty," *Clock of Destiny* (2016), clockofdestiny.com/index.php /sovereignty/.

11. Kinda El, "Sovereignty."

12. Agamben, *Homo Sacer*, 83. Agamben is a theorist with whom some Aliites engage; see El Amin, *Nationality*, 65.

13. Hansen and Stepputat, "Sovereignty Revisited," 295.

14. Anne M. Kornhauser, *Debating the American State: Liberal Anxieties and the New Leviathan, 1930–1970* (Philadelphia: University of Pennsylvania Press, 2015), 99.

15. Goston, *Return*, 417.

16. By legal discourse I mean that mode of speaking through which one engages the law. Legal discourse is seen as the most efficacious means of advancing arguments, a way of stating claims that can lead to real social change. I follow Sally Engle Merry in understanding discourse as "systematic, impersonal modes of talking which govern the production of culture . . . a specialized language, a particular jargon." Merry, *Getting Justice*, 110.

17. Hopkins-Bey, *What Your History*, 24.

18. Nance, "Respectability," 635.

19. Milton Rakove, *We Don't Want Nobody Nobody Sent: An Oral History of the Daley Years* (Bloomington: Indiana University Press, 1979), 93.

20. Ali, "Political Slavery," in *ML*.

21. "Sa Neter Instigates Confrontation at the Brother Reggie vs. Bother [*sic*] Sharif Debate," posted by Moorish World, April 17, 2016, https://www.youtube.com/watch?v=r8zzCnl9MNI.

22. Mahdi L. McCoy El, "Why We Moors MUST Rock the Vote," *Moorish American News*, September 16, 2014, http://moorishamericannews.com/moors-must-rock-vote.

23. McCoy El, "Why We Moors MUST Rock the Vote."

24. Sharif A. Bey, *The Blueprint: Moorish Musings on Noble Drew Ali's Divine Plan of the Age*. Ali's Men Publishing, n.d., n.p.

25. In his investigation of this "tense and ambivalent" relation between the sovereignty of the citizen and the sovereignty of the government, Andreas Kalyvas argues that in American politics, the dominant mode of sovereignty is not "the traditional notion of sovereignty as the higher and final instance of command," as in Schmitt, but rather "the concept of sovereignty as the creative, founding act of the constituent subject," what he terms the "constituent sovereign." Andreas Kalyvas, "Popular Sovereignty, Democracy, and the Constituent Power," *Constellations* 12, no. 2 (June 2005): 223–44, 227, 226. As the concept of constituent sovereignty keeps alive the notion of an original revolutionary collective of citizens who serve as ancestral representatives of an ongoing "people," enshrined in the Constitution itself, the sovereignty of the constituency recognizes that living, shifting force, always active (and courted) within democratic politics.

26. "Open Letter to (so called) Black Caucus," June 1, 2015, http://moorishamericannationalrepublic.com/news/open-letter-to-so-called-black-caucus/.

27. Audra Simpson, *Mohawk Interruptus: Political Life Across the Borders of Settler States* (Durham, NC: Duke University Press, 2006).

28. El Amin, *Wake Up*, 14.

29. Sharif A. Bey, *The Blueprint*.

30. In such public appearances Nuwaubian Yamassee were sometimes confused with fraternal societies. See the claim of Clarke County, Georgia, sheriff Ira Edwards that when

he was photographed at an NAACP function with York, he took him to be the leader of a Masonic lodge. *Hart v Edwards and United Government of Athens-Clarke County*, 3:07-cv-64 (cdl) (M.D. Ga. Mar 11, 2009).

31. See Osinski, *Ungodly*, 195.

32. York was convicted in 2004 on four counts of child molestation and six counts of racketeering, for a prison sentence of 135 years. See Bill Torpy, "Judge Throws Book at Cultist: 135 Years in Prison Ordered," *Atlanta Journal-Constitution*, April 22, 2004.

33. Although it was not public, what Palmer describes as a "solidarity meeting" of Nu-waubian Yamassee that she attended nonetheless rehearses a kind of identification as a constituency with the cause of York. She says individual members of the community took turns at a podium, stating their name and declaring, in solidarity, "I am a criminal!" Palmer, *Nuwaubian Nation*, xxx.

34. See the photo gallery of images by Andrew Moran collected at Digital Journal, http://www.digitaljournal.com/topic/Nuwaubian; and the video of a Canadian protest, "Toronto Nuwaubian Protest Free Malachi K. York," posted by DroBro19, September 29, 2009, at https://www.youtube.com/watch?v=RwyPq2ME8HU.

35. In Putnam County, Nuwaubian public statements are more direct, such as the bill-board leased in 2006, on U.S. Route 411, featuring "a large photo of York in one of his elaborate, Masonic-style costumes. There is also a plug on the billboard for a website, www.heisinnocent.com. Browsers of that site are informed how they can contribute to York's continuing legal defense efforts." Osinski, *Ungodly*, 268.

36. "Constitution of the UNNM," http://nuwaubianfacts.com/Constitution%20of%20 UNNM%20ebook.pdf. See also Pamela E. Klassen, "Spiritual Jurisdictions: Treaty People and the Queen of Canada," in Paul Christopher Johnson, Pamela E. Klassen, and Winnifred Fallers Sullivan, *Ekklesia: Three Inquiries in Church and State* (Chicago: University of Chicago, 2018). Klassen discusses "treaty metaphysics" involved in the use of treaties—including physically carrying copies of texts as well as citation of them.

37. See, for instance, the reproduction at http://www.rvbeypublications.com/sitebuilder content/sitebuilderfiles/treatyofpeacefriendship.pdf or http://thelastechomovement .blogspot.com/2011/02/black-moors-and-usa-constitution-treaty.html. The treaty and related documents are included in Joseph Jeffries-El, *In Search of Nationality: A Position Paper* (Moorish Mosque, 2017), 8–27.

38. El-Amin, *Moorish-Muurish Treaties*, 19 and 20.

39. See R.A. Umar Shabazz Bey, *We Are the Washitaw*, 42. "The treaty we signed with them is no different than that we've signed with other nations. We have treaties with a number of nations," Goston is quoted as saying in a *Monroe News-Star* article by Mark S. Rainwater, "Washitaw Nation Forges Union with Republic," contained with the FBI file on Goston (acquired through FOIA request). The Republic of Texas advanced a legal argument for its own sovereignty based on the "Treaty of Mutual Recognition and Friendship" it cut with the Washitaw; see "Exhibit 237 in the case of People of the Republic of Texas and the Sovereign Nation of the Republic of Texas v. United Nations and United States," August 7, 1998, http://www.nationoftexas.com/case_exhibits/exhibit_237.pdf.

40. In a typical decision touching on Aliite treaty use, recourse to treaties by Aliites is understood as a "delusory contrivance" in *Bey v. United States Dep't of Homeland Sec.*

Immigration, No. 10-46 (FSH), 2010 U.S. Dist. LEXIS 40112, at *6 (D.N.J. April 23, 2010).

41. Such squatting is sometimes (at least for a period of time) effective. New Orleans residents spoke to one journalist about two other such sites—both in the Marigny neighborhood, one on Independence and one on Marais—similarly posted as "Claimed by Washitaw Mu'ur," seizures that had been going on "over . . . almost three years.": Shelley Brown, "FOX 8 Defenders: Top stories of 2016," December 28, 2016, http://www.fox8 live.com/story/34144827/fox-8-defenders-top-stories-of-2016.

42. Robert McClendon, "Black Nationalist 'Washitah Nation' Claims Bywater House, Changes Locks While Home Is for Sale," http://www.nola.com/crime/index.ssf/2016/02 /black_nationalist_washitah_nat.html, February 15, 2016; and Robert McClendon, "Boarding School Graduate's Search for Answers Leads to Washitaw 'Nation,' Jail," http://www.nola.com/politics/index.ssf/2016/03/washitaw_muur_nation_moor_squa .html, March 11, 2016; and Robert McClendon, "4 'Washitah Nation' Squatters Arrested for Trespassing at Bywater House," http://www.nola.com/politics/index.ssf/2016/03 /washitaw_muur_nation_moor_squa.html.

43. See *USA v. York, et al.*, 5:02-cr-00027-CAR-1. York claims to be a naturalized citizen of Liberia and to have been appointed Consul General by President Charles Taylor, a subject of legal appeal and media coverage in Liberia. See, for instance, David S. Menjor, "Who Is Dr. Malachi York?" *Daily Observer*, May 16, 2018, https://www.liberianobserver .com/news/who-is-dr-malachi-york/. York explains his claims to diplomatic status (by phone from prison), at https://soundcloud.com/usa-vs-york/malachi-york-speaks-on -liberia, posted by "USA v York," 2012. "He's actually held in jail illegally," a Nuwaubian Yamassee supporter argues, explaining the legal argument for diplomatic immunity: "Dr Malachi Z York's Diplomatic Immunity, Diplomatic Number 003828-04," posted by 9Mind News 101, April 27, 2018, https://www.youtube.com/watch?v=_olHNIHpiYI.

44. Quoted in Gaines, *Uplifting the Race*, xi. For the Du Bois text, see NAACP, *An Appeal to the World! A Statement on the Denial of Human Rights to Minorities in the Case of Citizens of Negro Descent in the United States of America and an Appeal to the United Nations for Redress* (New York: NAACP, 1947). See also *We Charge Genocide; The Historic Petition to the United Nations for Relief from a Crime of the United States Government against the Negro People* (New York: U.S. Civil Rights Congress, 1952).

45. See, for instance, Amunhotep El Bey, "The Washitaw Moors," posted July 17, 2011, http://thewashitawmoors.blogspot.com/2011/07/washitaw-moors.html.

46. See, for instance, Bandele El-Amin, *Moorish/Muurish Treaties: A Guide to Treaties and Declarations* (Indigenous Peoples Inc., 2010), 51–67.

47. See "Washitaw Speech to the United Nations on the Health of Indigenous People," posted by MuurRoots, April 19, 2009, https://www.youtube.com/watch?v=Ux5QNvKRgGM.

48. Winnifred Sullivan, *Prison Religion: Faith-Based Reform and the Constitution* (Princeton, NJ: Princeton University Press, 2011), 227.

49. Goston, *Return*, 417.

50. On Christian Patriots, see James Aho, *The Politics of Righteousness* (Seattle: University of Washington Press, 1990).

51. Merry, *Getting Justice*, 12.

52. Thomas Blom Hansen, *Melancholia of Freedom: Social Life in an Indian Township in South Africa* (Princeton. NJ: Princeton University Press, 2012), 9.

53. Achille Mbembe, *On the Postcolony* (Berkeley: University of California Press, 2001), 35.

54. See Merry on "legal rights . . . shad[ing] into moral rights" in legal consciousness. Merry, "Everyday Understandings of the Law in Working-Class America," *American Ethnologist* 253 (1986): 13.

55. On "citizenship" as a matter of values and identifications, see Yuval-Davis, *The Politics of Belonging*, 12.

56. See Paul Kahn, *Political Theology: Four New Chapters on the Concept of Sovereignty* (New York: Columbia University Press, 2012), 85. See also Justice Scalia's dissent in *Obergefell v. Hodges*, 576 US (2015), which argues that the Supreme Court circumvents democracy: "This practice of constitutional revision by an unelected committee of nine, always accompanied (as it is today) by extravagant praise of liberty, robs the People of the most important liberty they asserted in the Declaration of Independence and won in the Revolution of 1776: the freedom to govern themselves."

57. Stewart Macaulay, Lawrence M. Friedman, and John Stookey, "Introduction" to chap. 3, "Where Does Law Comes From? The Impact of Society on Law," in *Law and Society: Readings on the Social Study of Law* (New York: W. W. Norton, 1995), 169.

58. See Sam Haselby, *The Origins of American Religious Nationalism* (Oxford: Oxford University Press, 2015), 165, on "frontier revivalism" and sovereignty; Marianne Constable, *Just Silences: The Limits and Possibilities of Modern Law* (Princeton, NJ: Princeton University Press, 2005), 57.

59. Noble Drew Ali, *Plenipotentiaries and the Negro, Black, Coloured Addiction*, ed. Sis. Tauheedah S. Najee-Ullah El (Califa Media, 2014), 69.

60. *United States v. Curtiss-Wright Export Corp.*, 299 US 304 (1936). See also Mateo Taussig-Rubbo, "Outsourcing Sacrifice: The Labor of Private Military Contractors," *Yale Journal of Law and Humanities* 2, no. 1: 103–66, 141.

61. Taussig-Rubbo, "Outsourcing Sacrifice," 114.

62. Richard Tuck, *The Sleeping Sovereign: The Invention of Modern Democracy* (Cambridge: Cambridge University Press, 2015), 277. On the dynamic of "the people" as an idealized notion in modern politics, see Edmund Morgan, *Inventing the People: The Rise of Popular Sovereignty in England and America* (New York: W. W. Norton, 1989).

CHAPTER THREE

1. I refer to the imagined Washitaw case in quotation marks, "United States v. Henry Turner's Heirs," and the actual case, *United States v. Turner*, in italics. See 52 U.S. 11 How. 663 663 (1850), https://supreme.justia.com/cases/federal/us/52/663/case.html.

2. Ali also used the red flag with the green star, the flag Mulay Yusef substituted for the traditional red banner of Morocco. This flag was banned in Morocco until that country achieved independence in 1956, and some Aliites claim that Ali used this flag of free

Moors *before* Moroccans did. Hopkins-Bey, *Prophet Noble Drew Ali*, 79. As the banner of the ancient Moorish nation, this flag, according to some Aliites, could be "over 10,000 years old." *Califa Uhuru*, 141.

3. Fahim A. Knight-El, "Moorish American Sovereignty: Myth or Reality," April 6, 2014, http://fahimknightsworld.blogspot.com/2014/04/moorish-american-sovereignty-myth-or.html.

4. Ali, "A Divine Warning."

5. "Moorish News Presents . . . Moorish Sovereignty vs. 'Sovereign Citizens,'" posted by Sheik Love El, October 28, 2017, https://www.youtube.com/watch?v=W7eD6ciZkA4.

6. See, for instance, the image at http://www.iuom.org/images/MSTA_Authority.jpg.

7. Weisenfeld is the source for the funeral usage; *New World*, 163.

8. Ali, "A Divine Warning."

9. Ali, "A Divine Warning." In Ali's theology, redemption applied to the Moorish people, to correct their "sin" of abandoning their ancestral identity. "This is an everlasting movement founded by the Prophet through the will of Allah to redeem his people from their sin." Ali, "Warns All Moslems," in *ML*. "Salvation"—both "Earthly Salvation as American Citizens" and "divine salvation" via eschatological alignment of society with true law—applied to all nationalities. Ali's prophetic mission involved first redeeming his people and then leading them and other nationalities into salvation through the work of citizenship.

10. Weisenfeld, *New World*, 20.

11. On the importance of patronage and postal system jobs for African Americans in Chicago in the 1920s, see Christopher Robert Reed. *The Rise of Chicago's Black Metropolis, 1920–1929* (Urbana: University of Illinois Press, 2011), 61–62.

12. Nance, "Respectability," 639.

13. See the celebratory *Moorish Guide* article quoted in Hopkins-Bey, *Prophet Noble Drew Ali*, 55.

14. Press coverage—from the *Chicago Defender* as well as the Moorish press—is collected in Hopkins-Bey, *Prophet Noble Drew Ali*, 97–99.

15. Naynika Mathur, *Paper Tiger: Law, Bureaucracy and the Developmental State in Himalayan India* (Cambridge: Cambridge University Press, 2016); and Matthew S. Hull, *Government of Paper: The Materiality of Bureaucracy in Urban Pakistan* (Berkeley: University of California Press, 2012).

16. Mathur, *Paper Tiger*, 111 and 67.

17. EWCC, November 8, 2015.

18. *United States v. Turner*, U.S. Supreme Court, 52 U.S. 11 How. 663 663 (1850), https://supreme.justia.com/cases/federal/us/52/663/case.html.

19. See Dew, "Washitaw de Dugdahmoundyah."

20. Washitaw members routinely refer to this case as "the 1848 Supreme Court case" and refer to the decision's author, judge for the District Court of Louisiana Theo H. McCaleb, as a "U.S. Supreme Court Justice." Dr. Asaru Alim El Bey's United Washitaw de Dugdahmoundyah Mu'ur Nation webpage links to an online copy of the actual 1850 decision even while claiming that the decision was made in 1848: http://www.dralimelbey.com/united-washitaw-de-dugdahmoundyah-muur-nation-history.html.

21. Shabazz Bey, *We Are the Washitaw*, 41.

22. "We celebrate this diligently," Mustafa Salahuddin Bey-OukhaRa ZesheRa on the EWCC of June 23, 2013.

23. See, for instance "International Declaration of Empire Washitaw de Dugdahmoun-dyah Standing," n.d., http://www.washitaw.us/about.html.

24. Goston, *Return*, 23.

25. Goston, *Return*, 187.

26. Ali, *Holy Koran* 47:17.

27. Ali, "Speaks to the Nation," in *ML*.

28. Sharif Anael-Bey, "'Transracial' and the Disintegration of the Illusion of Race," June 30, 2015, *Moorish American News*, http://moorishamericannews.com/transracial-and-the -disintegration-of-the-illusion-of-race. See "Ali's Men on 125th Harlem . . . ," posted August 5, 2015, by Ali's Men, https://www.youtube.com/watch?v=a5hoMlNqWYw, in which A. Bey insists that "the color code race construct is a myth." Sharif Anael-Bey and Sharif A. Bey are the same thinker; I have opted here to cite his work (or public appearances) under the name used on that work or for that appearance, rather than to impose a consistency on his naming that he resists.

29. Ali, "A Divine Warning."

30. R. V. Bey, "You Are Absolutely Correct, There Are Only a Handful of People Who Under-stand National Principles . . . ," November 30, 2013, posted at http://www.rvbeypublications .com/sitebuildercontent/sitebuilderfiles/youarerightnotmanyknownnationalprinciples.pdf.

31. David Lawrence, "There Is No 'Fourteenth Amendment'!" *Moorish American National Republic* website, January 18, 2017, http://moorishamericannationalrepublic.com/news /there-is-no-fourteenth-amendment/. This particular Moorish group has as its motto the twin American and Moorish flags crossed behind the Liberty Bell and a citation of Leviticus 25:10, on the Jubilee ("and ye shall return every man unto his family") and a citation of the Thirteenth Amendment, sections 16 and 17—a reference to the likewise much-cited, twenty-section Thirteenth Amendment, the original text. These sections refer to the rights of states within the United States and to reparations for slavery. See "13th Amendment with 20 Sections," posted December 10, 2009, by Abundance Child, https://abundancechild.wordpress.com/2009/12/10/13th-amendment-with-20-sections/. See also Ka Saadi El, on the Moorish Science Temple of America (Allah's Temple) web-site, http://thenewmoors.blogspot.com/2010/08/14th-amendment-citizenship.html.

32. Sharif Anael-Bey, "The 14th Amendment and Noble Drew Ali's Civic Doctrine," posted December 28, 2013, http://moorishamericannews.com/the-14th-amendment-and -noble-drew-alis-civic-doctrine.

33. Sharif A. Bey, *The Blueprint: Moorish Musings on Noble Drew Ali's Divine Plan of the Age* (Ali's Men Publishing, n.d.), n.p.

34. Anael-Bey, "The 14th Amendment."

35. Kahn, *Cultural Study*, 54.

36. Adwo El, *You Are NOT Negro*, 9.

37. "Constitution of the UNNM," http://nuwaubianfacts.com/Constitution%20of%20 UNNM%20ebook.pdf.

38. This is an important theme, linked to exegesis of *Return of the Ancient Ones*, in the Unity Washitaw paperwork sold by Alim Bey via his website, http://www.dralimelbey

.com/the-official-united-washitaw-de-dugdahmoundyah-muur-nation-history.html, and featured prominently in other Washitaw nationality paperwork, such as the "Declaration of National Washitaw Moor/Muur Appelation" filed in Miami Dade Superior Court in 2012, http://www.getnotice.info/MAE/MAEDWN0001.pdf. While discussed less frequently among members of the Empire Washitaw, the case nonetheless comes up in questions, as in October 27, 2013, when a caller from New Jersey asks how to "get paperwork" so that he can, by declaring his Washitaw identity, be recognized as a citizen "as opposed to a 14th Amendment citizen." EWCC, October 27, 2013.

39. El Amin, *Nationality*, 17. El Amin is an MSTA thinker sometimes also associated with the Unity Washitaw. On his blending of these two Aliite traditions, see "Moorish Republic of New Kemit Lecture Series 1: Building the Foundation Pt. 1," Kemit TV, October 7, 2009, https://www.youtube.com/watch?v=-YqQovJaIo8.

40. Sharif Anael-Bey, "Dred Scott, the 14th Amendment, the Negro, and the Question of Citizenship," May 13, 2015, *Moorish American News*, http://moorishamericannews .com/dred-scott-the-14th-amendment-the-negro-and-the-question-of-citizenship.

41. Aliite thought often perpetuates racism by perpetuating race, which Johnson usefully defines as "the state practice of ruling people within a political order that perpetually places some within and others outside of the political community through which the constitution of the state is conceived," an always political process and practice. Johnson, *African American Religion*, 394.

42. "Mike Brown, Ferguson, Talib Kweli, Dred Scott, and Nationality," *Moorish Oakland Star*, August 26, 2014, https://moorishoaklandstar.wordpress.com/tag/dred-scott/. Likewise, Aliites argue that Dred Scott himself would have received a different decision had he only been "naturalized" as a Moor. See http://moorishamericannationalrepublic.com /news/dred-scott-plaintiff-in-error-v-john-f-a-sandford/, posted August 26, 2012.

43. "Your Local Government Recognize Noble Drew Ali," posted by Moreno Bey, January 7, 2017, https://www.youtube.com/watch?v=_8_6Ji6aptQ.

44. Hopkins-Bey, *What Your History*, 29. There is a similar proclamation, also from 2001 and also from the city of Philadelphia, proclaiming Prophet Noble Drew Ali Day for January 8, included in Hopkins-Bey's *Prophet Noble Drew Ali*, 117. Menora Bey, "Your Local Government Recognize [*sic*] Noble Drew Ali," January 7, 2017, https://www.you tube.com/watch?v=_8_6Ji6aptQ; Joseph Jeffries-El, *In Search of Nationality: A Position Paper* (Moorish Mosque, 2017), 33; Goston, *Return*, 445–46 and 435.

45. Letter dated June 11, 1997, author's collection.

46. Available at http://www.rvbeypublications.com/sitebuildercontent/sitebuilderfiles/Rahm EmanuelProclamation.pdf. This document, in particular—with its rather extreme phrasing—offers an example of how little attention is given (how little recognition, one might say) to the text of proclamations "officially" endorsed with the signature of an elected official.

47. John Comaroff, "Reflections on the Rise of Legal Theology: Law and Religion in the Twenty-First Century," *Social Analysis* 53, no. 1 (Spring 2009): 193–216, 196; Catherine Wessinger, *How the Millennium Comes Violently: From Jonestown to Heaven's Gate* (New York: Seven Bridges Press, 2000), 160.

48. Comaroff, "Reflections on the Rise of Legal Theology," 194–95.

49. Comaroff, "Reflections on the Rise of Legal Theology," 210.

50. Comaroff, "Reflections on the Rise of Legal Theology," 202.

51. Willian Pietz, "The Problem of the Fetish, I," *RES: Anthropology and Aesthetics* 9 (Spring 1985): 5–17, 6.

52. Johnson, *African American Religions*, 105, 103.

53. Wessinger, *How the Millennium Comes*, 160.

54. See, for instance, T. H. Luhrmann, *Persuasions of the Witch's Craft: Ritual Magic in Contemporary England* (Cambridge, MA: Harvard University Press, 1989); and, for an investigation of Aliite legal consciousness in relation to such magical thinking, Dew, "Moors Know the Law."

55. Kelly E. Hayes, *Holy Harlots: Femininity, Sexuality, and Black Magic in Brazil* (Oakland: University of California Press, 2011), 178.

56. Yvonne P. Chireau, *Black Magic: Religion and the African American Conjuring Tradition* (Berkeley: University of California Press, 2003), 57 and 3.

57. Hayes, *Holy Harlots*, 199.

58. Jerome Frank, *Courts on Trial: Myth and Reality in American Justice* (Princeton, NJ: Princeton University Press, 1949). See pages 37–79 for Frank's analysis of "legal magic."

59. Wilson, *Sacred Drift*, 40.

60. Wilson, *Sacred Drift*, 39–43; and *Chicago Defender*, October 5, 1929.

61. *Chicago Defender*, September 28, 1929.

62. Nelson Maldonado-Torres, *Against War: Views from the Underside of Modernity* (Durham, NC: Duke University Press, 2018), 149.

63. Patchen Markell, *Bound by Recognition* (Princeton, NJ: Princeton University Press, 2003), 5.

64. Markell, *Bound by Recognition*, 27.

65. Charles Taylor, "The Politics of Recognition," 32, athttp://elplandehiram.org/docu mentos/JoustingNYC/Politics_of_Recognition.pdf.

66. Glen Sean Coulthard, *Red Skin, White Masks: Rejecting the Colonial Politics of Recognition* (Minneapolis: University of Minnesota Press, 2014), 17.

67. Coulthard, *Red Skin, White Masks*, 39.

68. Coulthard, *Red Skin, White Masks*, 25.

69. Frantz Fanon, *Black Skin, White Masks* (1952), trans. Richard Philcox (New York: Grove Press, 2008), 220.

70. Coulthard, *Red Skin, White Masks*, 23.

CHAPTER FOUR

———————

1. Attributed to Dingle-El by Batinel, "Lost/Found Moorish Timelines in the Wilderness of North America Part III," https://sacreddriftmoc.wordpress.com/2013/01/22 /lostfound-moorish-timelines-in-the-wilderness-of-north-america-part-iii/.

2. Batinel, "Lost/Found Moorish Timelines."

3. All three Aliite religions feature occasional identification, and also dialogue and contest, with Hebrew Israelite groups, with a call for synthesis and harmony predominating among Aliite thinkers. "Prophet Noble Drew Ali came and tied in all the 'African,' 'Kemetic/Egyptian,' 'Hebrew' and 'Islamic' connections all in one, because it began as one. Today we are scattered and debating amongst one another" due to "lack of knowing global history, nationality, pre-slavery history and blood lineage," writes an unnamed Moor on the Moorish American National Republic website. "I see debates between Afrocenetric [sic] groups, Kemetic/Egyptian groups, Hebrew Israelite groups, Masonic groups, Black Indians/Indigenous Natives and Moors; what is the disagreement," January 29, 2016, https://moorishamericannationalrepublic.com/i-see-debates -between-afrocenetric-groups-kemeticegyptian-groups-hebrew-israelite-groups-islamic -groups-black-indiansindigenous-natives-and-moors-what-is-the-disagreement/. For background on the Hebrew Israelite movement as itself always a matter of exchange and innovation, see Jacob S. Dorman, *Chosen People: The Rise of American Black Israelite Religions* (Oxford: Oxford University Press, 2013); and Yvonne Chireau and Nathaniel Deutsch, eds., *Black Zion: African American Religious Encounters in Judaism* (Oxford: Oxford University Press, 1999).

4. Jamhal Flicks, "Standing on Your Square/The Need for a Moorish Science Temple," December 9, 2017, https://www.youtube.com/watch?v=yJAtajjHokU. See also "When Approached by a Public Servant—How to Stand Your Square and Stay in Control," posted by Baqi Khaliq Bey, July 26, 2015, https://www.youtube.com/watch?v=b8aZxBY5X1A.

5. "Moorish News Presents . . . Moorish Sovereignty vs. "Sovereign Citizens," posted by Sheik Love El, October 28, 2017, https://www.youtube.com/watch?v=W7eD6ciZkA4.

6. Matthews El, *Palladium*, 210.

7. Act 3.

8. Amen A. El, *The Passion and Resurrection of the Moorish Hiram: Or the Metaphysical Subjugation and Posthumous Emancipation of the So-Called Black Race* (AuthorHouse, 2007), 357.

9. Mungin Bey, *Discover the Key*, 9.

10. "Return of the Matriarch," http://www.rvbeypublications.com/id78.html.

11. Ali, "Saviour of Humanity," in *ML*.

12. "Sharif Bey Explains: What Is Moorish Science? (Even a Child Could Understand), posted by Moorish World TV, September 24, 2016, https://www.youtube.com/watch ?v=4IGFNHdoNs8.

13. Amen A. El, *The Passion and Resurrection of the Moorish Hiram*, 368.

14. Amen A. El, *The Passion and Resurrection of the Moorish Hiram*, 430.

15. Amen A. El, *The Passion and Resurrection of the Moorish Hiram*, 368.

16. EWCC, June 2, 2013.

17. El Amin, *Nationality*, 29.

18. T. King Connally-Bey, *Enter Nationalnomics (The King-dom of Divine Free-dom): The Moorish Code* (Trafford, 2014), 3.

19. Marianne Constable, *Just Silences: The Limits and Possibilities of Modern Law* (Princeton, NJ: Princeton University Press, 2005), 57.

20. http://clockofdestiny.com/index.php/sovereignty/.

21. *Juilliard v. Greenman*, 110 U.S. 421 (1884), is cited prominently in Kinda El's "Sovereignty" page for *Clock of Destiny*.

22. Lawrence Rosen, *The Anthropology of Justice: Law as Culture in Islamic Society* (Cambridge: Cambridge University Press, 1989), 20.

23. Hirsch and Lazarus-Black, eds., *Contested States*, 11.

24. Hirsch and Lazarus-Black, eds., *Contested States*, 13.

25. Richard K. Sherwin, *When Law Goes Pop: The Vanishing Line between Law and Popular Culture* (Chicago: University of Chicago Press, 2000), 69.

26. Hirsch and Lazarus-Black, eds., *Contested States*, 1.

27. Georges Bataille, *The Accursed Share: An Essay on General Economy* (New York: Zone Books, 1993), 200.

28. Hirsch and Lazarus-Black, eds., *Contested States*, 13.

29. Shyaam Al Muharrir, ed., *Murakush Jurisprudence: Case Law on 'The Moorish Science Temple of America, Part I* (Murakush Caliphate of America, 2012).

30. Mathur, *Paper Tiger*, 115.

31. *Tyrone Eunice Bey v. Hillside Twp. Municipal Court and New Jersey State Police*, Civil Action No. 11-7343 (RBK), Civil Action No. 11-7351 (RBK), LEXIS 28397, March 5, 2012.

32. "Moors in Court Got the Judge SHOOK!" posted by yahsoldier1 (Noble Amir KC-El), December 11, 2009, https://www.youtube.com/watch?v=RhCWbXwVn7A&t=59s.

33. Barry Sullivan, "Just Listening: The Equal Hearing Principle and the Moral Life of Judges," *Loyola University Chicago Law Journal* 48 (2016): 351–411, 366.

34. Merry, *Getting Justice*, 1.

35. Merry, *Getting Justice*, 17.

36. "Moors in Court Got the Judge SHOOK!" at 3:56.

37. Sherwin, *When Law Goes Pop*, 62.

38. Sherwin, *When Law Goes Pop*, 230–31.

39. "Moors vs. Police," posted by Yirimayah Israelite, January 8, 2016, https://www.youtube.com/watch?v=QJrlcUtsvUU.

40. "Moors in Court Pt. 1," posted by theDynastyM3, August 31, 2009, https://www.youtube.com/watch?v=CriJmEBgWQo.

41. Sherwin, *When Law Goes Pop*, ix.

42. "POLICE vs MOOR—Who do you think is right? Plz share ur Opinon," posted by Rick Scheu, August 2, 2011, https://www.youtube.com/watch?v=oe9Hot4TLKM.

43. Cover, "*Nomos*," 44 and 47.

44. T. R. S. Allan, *The Sovereignty of Law: Freedom, Constitution, and Common Law* (Oxford: Oxford University Press, 2013), 207.

45. *Sanders-Bey v. United States*, 267 F. App'x 464, 466 (7th Cir. 2008).

46. Anti-Defamation League, "The Lawless Ones: The Resurgence of the Sovereign Citizen Movement," 2nd ed. (2012), available at https://www.adl.org/sites/default/files/documents/assets/pdf/combating-hate/Lawless-Ones-2012-Edition-WEB-final.pdf.

47. Daniel Levitas offers a useful history of the development of tax protest and Posse Comitatus/Christian Patriot thought from the work of Bill Gale and others (such as Martin Larson's 1973 *Tax Revolt: U!S!A! Why and How Thousands of Patriotic Americans Refuse to Pay the Income Tax*). See his *The Terrorist Next Door: The Militia Movement*

and the Radical Right (New York: Thomas Dunne Books, 2002). Aho, *Politics of Righteousness*, offers a broader reading of religious influences, including the role of Mormon theological conceptions of America's founding and destiny in "sovereign citizen" ideology. See also Spencer Dew and Jamie Wright, "God's Law: Universal Truth according to Religious Sovereign Citizens," *Sightings*, Martin Marty Center for the Advanced Study of Religion, October 15, 2015, https://divinity.uchicago.edu/sightings /gods-law-universal-truth-according-religious-sovereign-citizens; and J. M. Berger, "Without Prejudice: What Sovereign Citizens Believe," George Washington University Program on Extremism, June 2016, https://cchs.gwu.edu/sites/g/files/zaxdzs2371/f /downloads/Occasional%20Paper_Berger.pdf. Representative contemporary texts include Robert Hart, *Citizen/Slave: Understanding the American Sovereign Spirit* (Pittsburgh: Rose Dog Books, 2005); William Dixon, *Sovereign Covenant: "Without Prejudice," UCC 1-207* (God Is Sovereign First Amendment Study Team, 2002); David E. Robinson, *Reclaim Your Sovereignty: Take Back Your Christian Name* (Maine-Patriot .com, 2009); and Peter Eric Hendrickson, *Cracking the Code: The Fascinating Truth about Taxation in America* (Self-published, 2010). On "paper terrorism," see Mark Pitcavage, "The Washitaw Nation and Moorish Sovereign Citizens: What You Need to Know," published on the Anti-Defamation League's website, July 18, 2016, https://www .adl.org/blog/the-washitaw-nation-and-moorish-sovereign-citizens-what-you-need -to-know; Leah Nelson, "'Sovereigns' in Black," SPLC Intelligence Report, August 24, 2011, https://www.splcenter.org/fighting-hate/intelligence-report/2011/%E2%80%98so vereigns%E2%80%99-black; Travis Gettys, "Sovereign Moors: An Anti-government Obsession Spreads to the Black Community," August 26, 2014, http://www.rawstory .com/2014/08/sovereign-citizens-express-fears-of-lawlessness-by-rejecting-laws/.

48. See Larry Kellery, "SPLC Video Reveals Dangers of 'Sovereign Citizens,'" *Intelligence Report*, February 27, 2011, https://www.splcenter.org/fighting-hate/intelligence-report/2015 /splc-video-reveals-dangers-sovereign-citizens. See also the "special edition" booklet that accompanied the DVD, with information on two specific MSTA thinkers: https:// www.splcenter.org/sites/default/files/d6_legacy_files/ir_sov_special_report.pdf.

49. See Shaila Dewan and John Hubbell, "Arkansas Suspects Had Rage toward Government," *New York Times*, May 23, 2010, https://www.nytimes.com/2010/05/24/us/24arkansas .html. For watchdog coverage, see J. J. McNabb, "'Sovereign Citizen' Kane," *Intelligence Report*, August 1, 2010, https://www.splcenter.org/fighting-hate/intelligence-report/2010 /sovereign-citizen-kane.

50. Kellery, "SPLC Video."

51. Maxwell Barna, "'Move Over, Jihadists—Sovereign Citizens Seen as America's Top Terrorist Threat," *Vice News*, August 25, 2014, https://news.vice.com/article/move-over -jihadists-sovereign-citizens-seen-as-americas-top-terrorist-threat.

52. On the origins of the SPLC, see Jeffrey Kaplan, *Radical Religion in America: Millenarian Movements from the Far Right to the Children of Noah* (Syracuse: Syracuse University Press, 1997), 136–37.

53. Leah Nelson, "'Sovereigns' in Black," SPLC Intelligence Report, August 24, 2011, https://www.splcenter.org/fighting-hate/intelligence-report/2011/%E2%80%98soverei gns%E2%80%99-black.

54. "Active Antigovernment Groups in the United States," https://www.splcenter.org
/active-antigovernment-groups-united-states; Don Terry, "Manhunt Continues for Drug
Kingpins Claiming to Be Moorish Sovereigns," *Hatewatch*, May 14, 2014, https://www
.splcenter.org/hatewatch/2014/05/14/manhunt-continues-drug-kingpins-claiming-be
-moorish-sovereigns.

55. "Nuwaubian Nation of Moors," https://www.splcenter.org/fighting-hate/extremist-files
/group/nuwaubian-nation-moors; Bob Moser, "United Nuwaubian Nation of Moors
Meets Its Match in Georgia," *Intelligence Report*, September 20, 2002, https://www
.splcenter.org/fighting-hate/intelligence-report/2002/united-nuwaubian-nation-moors
-meets-its-match-georgia.

56. Ryan Lenz, "Gunman Who Killed Three Police Officers in Baton Rouge Member of
Black Antigovernment 'Sovereign Citizen' Group," July 18, 2016, https://www.splcen
ter.org/hatewatch/2016/07/18/gunman-who-killed-three-police-officers-baton-rouge
-member-black-antigovernment-sovereign; "Washitaw Nation Comes under Investigation," *Intelligence Report*, June 15, 1999, https://www.splcenter.org/fighting-hate
/intelligence-report/1999/washitaw-nation-comes-under-investigation.

57. EWCC, July 24, 2016.

58. Richard Posner, writing for the Seventh Circuit U.S. Court of Appeals in the case of *John
Jones Bey v. State of Indiana*, No. 16-1589, February 3, 2017, pp. 5, 3, 2; http://media.ca7
.uscourts.gov/cgi-bin/rssExec.pl?Submit=Display&Path=Y2017/D02-03/C:16-1589:J
:Posner:aut:T:fnOp:N:1906655:S:0.

59. Kaitlyn Compari, "The Moorish Science Temple of America and the Legal System: Exploring the Need to Take Proactive Measures against Radical Members of an Incorporated Religion," *Rutgers Journal of Law and Religion* (May 2015): 508. This article declares
as illegitimate the "religiousness" of such actions, on the logic that they depart from
the teachings of "the" MSTA, "an incorporated religion" (538, 510, 507). This phrasing
(unintentionally?) echoes Aliite emphasis on the authority of bureaucratic recognition,
while laying out a terrifying mode of legal discernment in which "illegitimate" religious
communities and practices can be sorted, by the courts, from "legitimate" ones.

60. Kaplan, *Radical Religion*, 127–30.

61. See, for instance, Bob Garfield, "The Southern Poverty Law Center: Anti-Hate Activists, Slick Marketers or Both?" *On the Media*, September 8, 2017, http://www.wnyc.org
/story/southern-poverty-law-center-anti-hate-slick-marketers-both/?tab=transcript;
Ben Schreckinger, "Has a Civil Rights Stalwart Lost Its Way?" *Politico*, July–August 2017,
http://www.politico.com/magazine/story/2017/06/28/morris-dees-splc-trump-southern
-poverty-law-center-215312; Phillip Lucas, "Critics Skewer SPLC Hate Groups List,"
Montgomery Advertiser, February 21, 2016, http://www.montgomeryadvertiser.com
/story/news/2016/02/22/critics-skewer-splc-hate-group-list/80722176/; Ken Silverstein,
"The Church of Morris Dees: How the Southern Poverty Law Center Profits from Intol-
erance," *Harper's*, November 2000; and Ken Silverstein, "The Southern Poverty Business Model," *The Harper's Blog*, November 2, 2007, https://harpers.org/blog/2007/11
/the-southern-poverty-business-model/.

62. See "Moorish Sceince [*sic*] Temple of America: Home Office Home Rule 805 Temple #2," http://www.mstahohr805.co/law-abiders.

63. EWCC, July 3, 2016.

64. Varda, "Drew Ali and the Moorish Science Temple of America," 689–90.

65. Daryl Johnson, "Return of the Violent Black Nationalist," *Intelligence Report*, August 8, 2017, https://www.splcenter.org/fighting-hate/intelligence-report/2017/return -violent-black-nationalist. For some background on Setepenra's philosophy, see Spencer Dew, "'I'm the One': Masculinity in the Philosophy of the Baton Rouge Shooter," *Sightings*, July 21, 2016, https://divinity.uchicago.edu/sightings/im-one-masculinity-philosophy-baton -rouge-shooter.

66. Matthew Teague, "The Washitaw Sovereign Citizens: Where the Baton Rouge Gunman Found a Home," *Guardian*, July 25, 2016, https://www.theguardian.com/us-news/2016 /jul/25/sovereign-citizens-washitaw-baton-rouge-gunman.

67. Jaweed Kaleem, "Black Nationalist Group Washitaw Nation Distances Itself from the Baton Rouge Shooter, Who Had Pledged Allegiance to It," *Los Angeles Times*, July 21, 2016, http://www.latimes.com/nation/la-na-washitaw-nation-baton-rouge-snap-story.html.

68. "Moorish Americans Are Not 'Sovereign Citizens'!" posted by Moorish American 720, June 2, 2016, https://www.youtube.com/watch?v=27mGnxbXW3s.

69. Seyla Benhabib, *The Claims of Culture: Equality and Diversity in the Global Era* (Princeton, NJ: Princeton University Press, 2002).

70. El Amin, *Nationality*, 65.

71. UNNM Constitution, 33.

72. Hugh Urban, *The Church of Scientology: A History of a New Religion* (Princeton, NJ: Princeton University Press, 2011).

73. Sarah Barringer Gordon, *The Spirit of the Law: Religious Voices and the Constitution in Modern America* (Cambridge, MA: Belknap Press of Harvard University Press, 2010), 12.

74. Matsuda, "Looking to the Bottom."

75. Merlin Owen Newton, *Armed with the Constitution: Jehovah's Witnesses in Alabama and the U.S. Supreme Court, 1939–1946* (Tuscaloosa: University of Alabama Press, 1995), 133; Jennifer Jacob Henderson, "The Jehovah's Witnesses and Their Plan to Expand First Amendment Freedoms," *Journal of Church and State* 46, no. 4 (Autumn 2004): 811–32, 817.

76. Kristen Tobey, *Plowshares: Protest, Performance, and Religious Identity in the Nuclear Age* (University Park: Penn State University Press, 2016).

77. Alexandra Lahav, *In Praise of Litigation* (Oxford: Oxford University Press, 2017), 1–2, 125.

78. Lahav, *In Praise of Litigation*, 110.

79. Lahav, *In Praise of Litigation*, 89.

80. *Triestman v. Federal Bureau of Prisons*, 470 F. 3d 471, 474 (2d Cir. 2006); emphasis in original.

81. Richard Posner, *Reforming the Federal Judiciary: My Former Court Needs to Overhaul Its Staff Attorney Program and Begin Televising Its Oral Arguments* (CreateSpace, 2017). This book also echoes the wider *pro se* movement in its style of composition and auto-hagiography.

82. "Pro Se 101: Jurisdiction and Due Process," *New Kemet TV*, April 11, 2015, https://www .youtube.com/watch?v=mIvpT-xsu20&feature=share.

83. EWCC, September 25, 2016.

84. http://cdn2.btrstatic.com/pics/showpics/large/440453_SHVPwB7C.jpg.

85. "Moorish American Party: Save Our Streets," posted by Moorish American Party, August 2, 2010, https://www.youtube.com/watch?v=y3io8eqTZ5I.

CHAPTER FIVE

1. See, for instance, Sunny Vansertima, "All Seeing, Eye of Horus, Pineal Gland," posted April 12, 2016, http://www.nobledrewalifoundation.com/seeing-eye-eye-horus-pineal/. B. Denham El reads the eye as "alluding to the unity of ALLAH and Man," in his *The Divine Creed of the Moorish Scientist: An Interpretation* (CreateSpace, 2015), n.p. A Yamassee claims that "our signature is on the dollar bill . . . we're the seeing eye," in "Walter Davis Interviews Leaders of Yamasee [*sic*] Nation," posted by Walter Davis, August 29, 2012, https://www.youtube.com/watch?v=UukHX7gmZMQ. Washitaw members trace the image of the all-seeing eye back to ancient Mu; see http://www .my-mu.com/bon/b03-2014.html. They repeat the claim that it ends up on the dollar as a sign of indebtedness to Moors. Alim Bey, "The Official Website of the United Washitaw De Dugdahmoundyah Mu'urs Nation," http://www.dralimelbey.com/the -official-united-washitaw-de-dugdahmoundyah-muur-nation-history.html. The eye is equated with Allah in "Neophyte Questions for Free Asiatics, Chapter 18," http://www .ancientorderoffreeasiatics.com/Neophyte.html. For a reading of the eye as "global trophy displaying the subjugation and domination" of Aliites, see Elihu N. Pleasant-Bey, "The Great Seal Was Never for the Moors But about the Moors" (Seven Seals Publications, n.d.), http://universalzulukemeticmuurs.net/wp-content/uploads/2012/02/Truth -About-The-Great-Seal.pdf.

2. Simone Browne, *Dark Matters: On the Surveillance of Blackness* (Durham, NC: Duke University Press, 2015), 10.

3. Derek Hicks, *Reclaiming Spirit in the Black Faith Tradition* (New York: Palgrave Macmillan, 2012), 90.

4. See "I Have Always Heard Moors Say 'The Verbal' Statements of Prophet Noble Drew Ali, What Exactly Are Those," January 29, 2016, https://moorishamericannational republic.com/i-have-always-heard-moors-say-the-verbal-statements-of-prophet-noble -drew-ali-what-exactly-are-those/.

5. The more famous of the two is the smaller group shot in front of Unity Hall, where the MSTA rented its headquarters and ran a cafeteria. In this shot, a banner for the convention hangs above the door. This image is in the collection of the Schomburg Center for Research in Black Culture, Photographs and Prints Division, available online at https://digitalcollections.nypl.org/items/510d47de-1a2a-a3d9-e040-e00a18064a99. The second image features a larger crowd, with multiple Moorish and American flags in the back, overlaid with typed text identifying local luminaries who were speaking at the convention. This image is reproduced at http://www.thethinkersgarden.com /wp-content/uploads/2015/03/moorish-science-temple-1.jpg.

6. "Moorish Head Makes Plans for Conclave," *Chicago Defender*, July 21, 1928, A4. The camel is a central symbol in the MSTA, identified with the trait of endurance. The "Koran Questions for Moorish Americans" catechism states of the camel that, in ancient days, "The Moors rode camels and the Europeans walked and rode goats." *Califa Uhuru*, 150. Pictures of camels sometimes stand as punctuation in or alone on a page in Aliite texts. For instance, *Califa Uhuru*, 16; and Matthews-El, *Moorish America's Archival Palladium*, 230. Aliites also practice what they call "camel-backing" as a way of engaging in conversation, continuing ideas (like "piggy-backing" on someone's comments, only removing the reference to the filthy pig and replacing it with the animal most associated with Moorish history and pride).

7. The *Chicago Defender* described an earlier parade, celebrating Thompson's 1915 mayoral inauguration, by saying, "All nations were there with their multi-tongues, colors and costumes." See "Thompson Inaugurated," May 1, 1915, 1.

8. Susan G. Davis, *Parades and Power: Street Theatre in Nineteenth-Century Philadelphia* (Philadelphia: Temple University Press, 1986), 113.

9. Shane White, "'It Was a Proud Day': African Americans, Festivals, and Parades in the North, 1741–1834," *Journal of American History* 81, no. 1 (June, 1994): 13–50, especially 50.

10. Hopkins-Bey, *Prophet Noble Drew Ali*, 53.

11. *Califa Uhuru*, 200.

12. *Chicago Tribune*, September 29, 1929.

13. "Declaration involving . . . Moorish-American descent amount to nonsensical gibberish." *Fuller v. Maryland*, No. PWG-14-3405, WL 1517393 at *1 n.1, March 31, 2015. Aliite claims to identity have been dismissed as "patently frivolous" and Aliite legal arguments as of "dubious legal significance." *Aaron Riley Bey v. State of Louisiana,* No. 08-cv-0250, United States District Court for the Western District of Louisiana, Shreveport Division, LEXIS 91606, July 11, 2008.

14. Ali, "Saviour of Humanity," in *ML*.

15. Susan Nance, "Respectability and Representation: The Moorish Science Temple, Morocco, and Black Public Culture in 1920s Chicago," *American Quarterly* 54, no. 4 (December 2002): 623–59, especially 631.

16. *Chicago Defender*, June 8, 1929.

17. *Chicago Defender*, October 20, 1929.

18. "Ali's Mysticism Didn't Foretell Prison Term," *Chicago Defender*, January 11, 1930.

19. Weisenfeld, *New World*, 43.

20. The World's Columbian Exposition, which gave birth to African American Shriners, featured a Moorish palace and demonstrations of Islamic prayer, and also brought to Chicago both a camel and Houdini himself. See Christopher Robert Reed, *"All the World is Here!" The Black Presence at White City* (Bloomington: Indiana University Press, 2002). On the stage magician Black Herman, see Yvonne P. Chireau, "Black Herman's African American Magical Synthesis," *Cabinet Magazine* 26 (Summer 2007), http://cabinetmagazine.org/issues/26/chireau.php.

21. Wilson links this performance to legends of Ali's circus background. See Wilson, *Sacred Drift*, 17; and Turner, *Islam*, 92.

22. Weisenfeld, *New World*, 43.

23. Notably Grover Cleveland Redding's Abyssinian Order. See Chicago Commission on Race Relations, *The Negro in Chicago: A Study of Race Relations and a Race Riot* (Chicago: University of Chicago Press, 1922), 480; and "Frenzied Fanatics Burn Flag; Followers of Radical Cult Kill 2 Wound 2," *Chicago Whip*, June 26, 1920.

24. For comprehensive treatment of Ali's *Holy Koran* and its relation to its antecedents, see Nance, "Mystery," 127–37.

25. Ali, *Holy Koran*, 46:5.

26. Fauset, *Black Gods*, 49.

27. Wilson, *Sacred Drift*, 30.

28. Ali, *Holy Koran*, 17:14.

29. Ali, *Holy Koran*, 19:37.

30. Ali, *Holy Koran*, chap. 1 (there are no verse division in chap. 1).

31. Susan Palmer, *The Nuwaubian Nation: Black Spirituality and State Control* (Burlington, VT: Routledge, 2010), 130, 132.

32. Palmer, *Nuwaubian Nation*, 105, 146.

33. See "Why Do We Undergo So Many Changes," in *The Holy Tabernacle Ministries Guide to Better Living*, http://www.nuwaubianfacts.com/guide_to_better_living.pdf, 82.

34. Palmer, *Nuwaubian Nation*, 10.

35. Palmer, *Nuwaubian Nation*, 367.

36. Palmer, *Nuwaubian Nation*, 10.

37. Malachi York, *The Holy Tablets*, 6:1:20–28, p. 685, and 7:9:9–19, p. 731. *The Holy Tablets* is available online through a Nuwaubian Yamassee website, http://holytablets.nuwau bianfacts.com.

38. Malachi York, *Sons of Green Light* (n.d.), http://www.salaammasjid.com/pdf/Lesson 7SonOfTheGreenLight.pdf; York, *The Holy Tablets*, 6:1:20–28, p. 685.

39. York, *The Holy Tablets*, 2:1:1–2.

40. York, *The Holy Tablets*, 7:9:9–19, p. 731.

41. York, *The Making of the Disciples* (1992), quoted in Palmer, *Nuwaubian Nation*, 9–10.

42. York, *The Holy Tablets*, 2:7:21, p. 743.

43. York, *The Holy Tablets*, 19:1:1–9, p. 1587, 9:6:17–27, p. 1641. "I am from Rizq the eighth planet in the nineteenth galaxy Illyuwn, far outside of this one. I am sent here to give you the true guidance." 19:6:1–7, p. 1640. "The Anunnaki is an ancient Sumerian term which was given to the beings who came down to earth and pro-created (BARA) homo sapiens." Malachi York, "The Sacred Teachings of the Nubians" (1996), https:// www.bibliotecapleyades.net/sumer_anunnaki/anunnaki/anu_22.htm.

44. Tyson Lewis and Richard Kahn, "The Reptoid Hypothesis: Utopian and Dystopian Representational Motifs in David Icke's Alien Conspiracy Theory," *Utopian Studies* 16, no. 1 (Spring 2005): 45–74, 45.

45. York, *The Holy Tablets*, 12:381–93, p. 899. The role of illustrated portraits in *The Holy Tablets* fits with this call for racial pride, at once countering the whitewashing of famous figures (Jesus, Adam, Moses) and presenting reference points for the assorted heroes and villains of the Yorkian myth ("Anu, the Heavenly One," "Crill, Leader of the Rumardians," and "Zahrah, the demon who seduced the eloheems"), 989. See also "Anu Elyun Elyun El!"/"Are You a Celestial Being," http://mysticchat9.webs.com/areyouacelestialbeing.htm.

The Aliite author called African Creation Energy does something similar with "The Personification of Science," an "allegorical story" in which the characteristics of scientific inquiry are represented as African American superheroes. See *The Science of Sciences and the Science in Sciences: The Scientific and Mathematic Method in Ancient and Traditional African Culture and Philosophy* (Self-published, 2010), 171–76.

46. York, *Sons of Green Light*, n.p.

47. "The Ku Klux Klan (KKK)!" in Goston, *Return*, 351–56.

48. Goston, *Return*, 103.

49. Goston, *Return*, 355.

50. Goston, *Return*, 353.

51. Goston, *Return*, 354.

52. Goston, *Return*, 354.

53. See the hoodoo ritual of the black cat bone as described in Zora Neale Hurston, *Mules and Men* (New York: Harper Collins, 1935, 2009).

54. Goston, *Return*, 352.

55. This fez is featured in the memorial image in Yaffa Bey, "Washitaw Empress Verdiacee Ascended," May 11, 2014, http://www.yaffabey.com/washitaw-empress-verdiacee -ascended/.

56. Chris Roth, "'Emperor' of Black-Nationalist 'Washitaw Nation' Claims Individual Sovereignty in New Jersey Gun Case," September 10, 2014, *Springtime of Nations*, http:// springtimeofnations.blogspot.com/2014/09/emperor-of-black-nationalist-washitaw .html.

57. R. A. Umar Shabazz Bey dedicates *We Are the Washitaw* to Chief Allison "Tootie" Montana (1922–2005) of the Yellow Pocahontas Tribe. A photograph of the chief in his Indian regalia is featured on the acknowledgments page of the book (3). Dauphin Washington of the Empire Washitaw has referred to Mardi Gras Indians as "the Indian tribes of Louisiana" and welcomed them to Empire events, including his mother's funeral. EWCC, February 28, 2016.

58. George Lipsitz, "Conjuring Sacred Space in Gulf Coast Cities," *Journal of the American Academy of Religion* 86, no. 2 (June 2018): 497–525.

59. George Lipsitz, "Mardi Gras Indians: Carnival and Counter-Narrative in Black New Orleans," *Cultural Critique* 10, *Popular Narrative, Popular Images* (Autumn 1988): 99–121, 103. See also Michael P. Smith, *Spirit World: Pattern in the Expressive Folk Culture of Afro-American New Orleans* (New Orleans: Urban Folklife Society, 1984), 43, 66, on Sauk Indian Chief Blackhawk as object of worship. See also Emily Suzanne Clark, *A Luminous Brotherhood: Afro-Creole Spiritualism in Nineteenth-Century New Orleans* (Chapel Hill: University of North Carolina Press, 2016). Lipsitz notes that, for Mardi Gras Indians, "the crowds along their route [are treated as] participants, not just as spectators"; "Mardi Gras," 115. On the performative nature of Mardi Gras Indians, see Joseph Roach, "Mardi Gras Indians and Others: Genealogies of American Performance," *Theatre Journal* 44, no. 4 (December 1992): 461–83.

60. Lipsitz, "Mardi Gras," 101, 104.

61. Lipsitz, "Conjuring," 501.

62. "Moorish Head Makes Plans for Conclave," *Chicago Defender*, July 21, 1928, A4. On

"custom-made Moorish Garb" and M. Tiggs-El, first seamstress and sewing instructor for the MSTA, see Hopkins-Bey, *Prophet Noble Drew Ali*, 56.

63. Susan Palmer and David G. Robinson, "Minority Religions and the Law," an interview for the Religious Studies Project, December 14, 2015, http://www.religiousstudiespro ject.com/podcast/minority-religions-and-the-law/.

64. FBI MSTA file, part 6, p. 83, https://vault.fbi.gov/Moorish%20Science%20Temple %20of%20America/Moorish%20Science%20Temple%20of%20America%20Part %206%20of%2031/view.

65. FBI MSTA file, part 4, p. 27, https://vault.fbi.gov/Moorish%20Science%20Temple%20 of%20America/Moorish%20Science%20Temple%20of%20America%20Part%204 %20of%2031/view. One home had "a large American flag was displayed." FBI MSTA file, part 20, p. 24, https://vault.fbi.gov/Moorish%20Science%20Temple%20of%20America /Moorish%20Science%20Temple%20of%20America%20Part%2020%20of%2031 /view. FBI MSTA file, part 1, p. 35, https://vault.fbi.gov/Moorish%20Science%20Temple %20of%20America/Moorish%20Science%20Temple%20of%20America%20Part%20 1%20of%2031/view. "He stated that he is not a negro, but a descendant of the Moors. Agent [redacted] advises that Bey has all of the appearances and characteristics of a full blooded Negro."

66. FBI MSTA file, part 15, p. 85, https://vault.fbi.gov/Moorish%20Science%20Temple%20 of%20America/Moorish%20Science%20Temple%20of%20America%20Part%20 15%20of%2031/view.

67. FBI MSTA file, part 6, p. 83, https://vault.fbi.gov/Moorish%20Science%20Temple%20 of%20America/Moorish%20Science%20Temple%20of%20America%20Part%206%20 of%2031/view. Turner-El is notable, as well, for his role in a Bronx court case leading to MSTA children being exempted from attending public school on Friday, the Moorish Sabbath. He was profiled in the *New Yorker* in 1940. See Patrick D. Bowen, "Grand Sheik Frederick Turner-El: A Moorish-American Trailblazer," 2014, http://www.academia .edu/6246670/Grand_Sheik_Frederick_Turner-El_A_Moorish-American_Trailblazer.

68. The FBI, for its part, found such confident declarations to be all the more suspicious. Sylvester Johnson has detailed how FBI agents categorized MSTA members as "pathological . . . mentally imbalanced, delusional, or intellectually weak," victims of a "propaganda . . . not an actual religion," and as attempting to manipulate others with their claims, "masquerading behind a fake identity" in order to engage in "religious fraud." Johnson, *African American Religions*, 319–20.

69. See Tisa Wenger, *Religious Freedom: The Contested History of an American Ideal* (Chapel Hill: University of North Carolina Press, 2017), 64. See also Sylvester Johnson, "The FBI and the Moorish Science Temple of America, 1926–1960," in Sylvester Johnson and Steven Weitzman, eds., *The FBI and Religion: Faith and National Security before and after 9/11* (Berkeley: University of California Press, 2017), 55–66.

70. FBI MSTA File, part 3, p. 15, https://vault.fbi.gov/Moorish%20Science%20Temple%20 of%20America/Moorish%20Science%20Temple%20of%20America%20Part%20 15%20of%2031/view.

71. FBI MSTA File, part 11, p. 23, https://vault.fbi.gov/Moorish%20Science%20Temple%20 of%20America/Moorish%20Science%20Temple%20of%20America%20Part%20

23%20of%2031/view. See Weisenfeld on the "range of attitudes toward the Japanese and the military service," *New World*, 220. Fathie Ali Abdat presented the turn toward visible, vocal patriotism in the C. Kirkman Bey faction as tactical, noting "a clear paradigm shift" from previous, pro-Japanese sentiment by 1943, when that community's newsletter, *The Moorish Voice*, began highlighting "Moors currently in the US Military," requesting readers to "send in the name of all the members drafted into the military Services of the United States of America." Adbat also notes that Kirkman Bey himself "saw action with the famed 92nd Division in France during World War I" and states that Kirkman "was wounded by bomb fragments in the bloody Argonne forest battle" and had two sons in the navy. Fathie Ali Abdat, "The Sheiks of Sedition: Father Prophet Mohammed Bey, Mother Jesus Rosie Bey, and Kansas City's Moors (1933–1945)," *Journal of Religion and Violence* 3, no. 1 (2015): 7–33, especially 23.

72. *Paa Madjayu Dakun: The Protector's Records*, vol. 1, edition 4, June 7, 2009, http://an nuhassa.com/PDF%20Docs/Publication4_PaaMedjayuNewsletter.pdf.

73. See Wright and Palmer, *Storming Zion*, 142; "Nuwaubians Send Odd Common-law Bills to Local Officials," July 8, 2002, http://savannahnow.com/stories/070802/LOCnuwau bians.shtml#.V1wzc7srK7o; and "Nuwaubians Arrested in Common-Law Scam," December 31, 2003, *Southern Poverty Law Center Intelligence Report*, https://www.splcenter .org/fighting-hate/intelligence-report/2003/nuwaubians-arrested-common-law-scam.

74. See Associated Press articles "Sect Bases Prophecies on Egypt, Spaceships," *Calgary Herald*, July 28, 1999; and "Georgia Sect Alarms Neighbours and the Law," *Hamilton Spectator*, July 31, 1999. See also Larry Copeland, "Race, Religion, Rhetoric Simmer in Ga. Town," *USA Today*, September 13, 1999.

75. Elbein, "Road to Tama-Re."

76. Osinski, *Ungodly*, 17.

77. Elbein, "Road to Tama-Re."

78. "Illegal Detention: A Plot for Destruction," July 16, 2003, http://www.nuwaubianfacts .com/images9/Aplotf28.gif.

79. Malachi York, transcribed by Ah Sen Ptah Tum, March 11, 2004, in *Paa Madjayu Dakun*.

80. Osinski, *Ungodly*, 134.

81. Palmer, *Nuwaubian Nation*, 132. The local media were described as all "a part of the 'good ole boy' circle." Malachi York, transcribed by Ah Sen Ptah Tum, March 11, 2004, in *Paa Madjayu Dakun*. See also "Untold Truth—Dr. Malachi Z. York," posted by Menhu Hotep Ankh, September 26, 2014, https://www.youtube.com/watch?v=iWodbgJDdN4, 19:26.

82. Wright and Palmer, *Storming Zion*, 134.

83. Rob Peecher, "Arrest Nuwaubians' Latest Trouble: Group Has Had Confrontational, Controversial History in Putnam," *Macon Telegraph*, May 9, 2002, posted by Yamassees, http://www.nuwaubianfacts.com/2002May9-a.htm; "Yamassee Native Americans—Tribal News," http://www.nuwaubianfacts.com/images5/kathyj54.gif.

84. Malachi York, transcribed by Ah Sen Ptah Tum, March 11, 2004, in *Paa Madjayu Dakun*.

85. Khnum Ka Ankh, in *Paa Madjayu Dakun*.

86. Khnum Ka Ankh, in *Paa Madjayu Dakun*.

87. Palmer, *Nuwaubian Nation*, 81.

88. Elbein, "Road to Tama-Re."

89. Palmer, *Nuwaubian Nation*, 131.

90. Quoted in Palmer, *Nuwaubian Nation*, 80; emphasis in original.

91. *Paa Madjayu Dakun*. On these officers, see *Hart v. Edwards and Athens-Clarke County, Georgia.*, Case No. 3:07-CV-64(CDL), U.S. District Court for Middle District of Georgia, Athens Division, decided March 11, 2009, 2009 U.S. Dist. LEXIS 18836.

92. "Yamassee Native Americans—Tribal News," http://www.nuwaubianfacts.com/images 5/kathyj54.gif.

93. EWCC, March 26, 2017.

94. Matt Reynolds, "Recalling the FBI Raid of Late Washitaw Nation Leader's Home," *Franklin Sun*, May 2, 2014, http://www.hannapub.com/franklinsun/recalling-the-fbi -raid-of-late-washitaw-nation-leader-s/article_de819b14-d233-11e3-91b9-001a4 bcf6878.html. Reynolds states that "full membership" in the Washitaw cost $520 at the time of The Raid. Documents obtained from the FBI through an FOIA request offer a list of prices for documents, including birth certificates, passports, international motorist certifications, motorized conveyance registrations, right to travel documentation, and "Traffic Stop Strategy & Affidavit," as well as copies of *We Are the Washitaw* and *Return of the Ancient Ones*. These documents were printed from a Washitaw-affiliated America Online website by FBI agents on March 14, 1997.

95. EWCC, July 29, 2015, and June 2, 2013.

96. EWCC, July 9, 2017. Washington also said, in the same call, "The FBI and I made an agreement that I would issue no more [paperwork]."

97. This trajectory emphasized Washington's leadership, elevating him from the equality implied by "Brother Joe." It was also an attempt to negotiate ongoing Washitaw claims (made by overwhelmingly male voices) that the movement is "matriarchal." "Dauphin" was adopted as a title that flagged Washington's subservience to the post of "Empress," even though the current Empress, his daughter, only communicates through him (much as his mother did during her final years, when she was in a nursing home).

98. EWCC, November 11, 2015.

99. EWCC, August 25, 2013.

100. EWCC, July 7, 2013.

101. See the petition at https://www.change.org/p/u-s-house-of-representatives-honor-court -decisions-of-heirs-of-henry-turner-v-united-states-1848-cause-number-32-and -land-awarded-to-verdiacee-tiara-washitaw-tuner-goston-el-bey-by-the-state-of-loui siana-1993.

102. EWCC, March 5, 2017.

103. EWCC, August 13 and 20, 2017.

104. A repeated formulation; see, for instance, EWCC, October 27, 2013.

105. EWCC, August 30, 2015.

106. EWCC, November 19, 2015.

107. EWCC, November 15, 2015.

108. EWCC, January 4, 2014. A hadith exists in which Drew Ali also used the threat of action from "federal agents" to enforce his command. See *Califa Uhuru*, 200.

109. EWCC, April 24, 2016.

110. EWCC, October 25, 2015.

111. EWCC, June 21, 2015.

112. EWCC, August 17, 2014.

113. EWCC, July 10, 2016.

114. EWCC, June 2, 2013.

115. "Moorish Science Temple 2nd Moorish American Parade Part 1," posted by Grand Major Temple, October 16, 2017, https://www.youtube.com/watch?v=4WJj72aB4TI.

116. EWCC, July 10, 2016.

CHAPTER SIX

1.   Seven Star Hand, *Noble Drew Ali Plenipotentiaries*, 52. Sheikess Love El wears a metal framework of a pyramid over her turban as she lectures. See, for instance, "Moorish News Presents . . . Moorish Sovereignty vs. "Sovereign Citizens," posted by Sheik Love El, October 28, 2017, https://www.youtube.com/watch?v=W7eD6ciZkA4.

2.   Mustafa El-Amin quoted in Keith Moore, *Moorish Circle 7: The Rise of the Islamic Faith among Blacks in America and Its Masonic Origins* (AuthorHouse, 2005), 149–50.

3.   Henry Louis Gates, *The Signifying Monkey: A Theory of African American Literary Criticism* (1988), 25th anniversary ed. (New York: Oxford University Press, 2014). Gates describes "signfyin(g)" as a rhetorical technique in "intertextual relation" to hegemonic discourse, challenging the status quo via reinterpretation. Knowledge contests between Aliite thinkers can often resemble a game of the dozens, each thinker aiming to demonstrate more finesse at "research." Aliite usage departs from the "signifyin(g)" tradition in that, while there is a free play involved (in linkage of interpretation to pretext), "research" is understood as an archaeology, a return to *true* roots, and thus the articulation of an uncontestable counter-hegemony (51).

4.   "Noble Drew Ali," *Clock of Destiny* (2016), http://clockofdestiny.com/index.php/noble-drew-ali/. See also Herbert Berg, *Elijah Muhammad and Islam* (New York: New York University Press, 2009), 14.

5.   Posted by Adonai Dey Haile, May 1, 2015, https://drive.google.com/file/d/0B2QiGabseq 3sOExIZF8xdElQaWc/view.

6.   "Undisputable Facts" are discussed in York, *The Man from Planet Rizq*. On the notion of "proof," see, for instance, Adwo El and Salaam El, *77 Amazing Facts*.

7.   For the phrase "there is convincing evidence," used in the title of this chapter section, see Sheik Way-El, "What Exactly Is a Moor," http://moorishsciencetemple.org /what-is-moor/.

8.   "Brother Red Hawk—The Untold Story of the Washitaw Part 3," posted March 5, 2013, http://www.youtube.com/watch?v=3Vw6K6RmVhI&list=PLYIseHPXyzyyFwolh7Sxr Z5uAzPBITxtm. This video is no longer available. See also Goston, *Return*, 75, on the centrality of research.

9. EWCC, June 16, 2013.

10. R. A. Umar Shabazz Bey, *Pyramids in America: A Traveler's Guide* (Baton Rouge: Indigenous Concepts, LLC, 2010), 87.

11. *The Divine Creed of the Moorish Scientist: An Interpretation* (CreateSpace, 2015), n.p.

12. "Addressing Misunderstandings of Purpose Concerning the Prophet Noble Drew Ali," n.d., http://rvbeypublications.com/id76.html.

13. Shem El, "Call to Action for Mansur Ball Bey," n.d., http://moorishamericannews.com /call-to-action-for-mansur-ball-bey.

14. www.nuwaubian facts.com; "On Dr. Malachi Z. York," posted by Menhu Hotep Ankh, February 2, 2015, https://www.youtube.com/watch?v=a-TEaRb4b2k.

15. "Taj Tarik Bey: Moorish Heritage in the Americas," October 29, 2014, http://www.you tube.com/watch?v=KrXVPGq-CsY. This video is no longer available. A visual trope of Aliite knowledge from the earliest days of the MSTA is the stack of books, prominently displayed. In several pictures of Ali we see the prophet with a stack of texts near at hand. See "Prophet Noble Drew Ali Working in His Office," https://moorishsociety.word press.com/2012/04/18/prophet-noble-drew-ali-working-in-his-office/. In the surviving images of the Moorish School in Philadelphia in the 1940s (published at https:// sacreddriftmoc.wordpress.com/), we see a continuance of this display of books as symbols of learning and its centrality in Aliite thought. Contemporary Aliites extend this also to documents that offer evidence of acquaintance with texts and knowledge. Alim El Bey's personal website—which holds that he is a royal authority within the United Washitaw De Dugdahmoundyah Mu'ur Nation—includes images and descriptions of multiple diplomas, from high school (East Bladen High School) through his affiliations (in both MSTA and Ansaaru Allah Nubian Islamic Hebrews as well as Holy Tabernacle Ministries, two Nuwaubian Yamassee groups), his college study (Fayetteville State University, "majored in Sociology [specialized in Religion] minored in History [African Studies])," and his ministerial license through the free Universal Life Church website. www.dralimelbey.com/about-us.html.

16. Goston, *Return*, 191–208. Nuwaubian thinker Phil Valentine calls himself a "decoder." "On Dr. Malachi Z. York," posted by Menhu Hotep Ankh, February 2, 2015, https:// www.youtube.com/watch?v=a-TEaRb4b2k.

17. Shabazz Bey, *We Are the Washitaw*, 15, 39.

18. EWCC, April 6, 2017.

19. Stephen Finley, "Mathematical Theology: Numerology in the Religious Thought of Tynnette Muhammad and Louis Farrakhan," in Stephen C. Finley, Margarita Simon Guillory, and Hugh R. Page, Jr., eds., *Esotericism in African American Religious Experience: "There is a Mystery"* (Leiden: Brill, 2015), 127–37, 211.

20. Goston, *Return*, 190, 34.

21. Goston, *Return*, 35.

22. EWCC, October 25, 2015.

23. See, for instance, Najee-Ullah El and Taylor El, *Moors in America*, 9–13; "Washitaw, Yamasee [*sic*], Iroquois, Cherokee, Choctaw, Blackfoot, Pequot & Mohegan (and/or All Indigenous People of America)," http://www.stewartsynopsis.com/washitaw.htm; and Shabazz Bey, *We Are the Washitaw*, 6, 8 9.

24. Najee-Ullah El and Taylor El, *Moors in America*, 42–43.

25. Goston, *Return*, 357–76.

26. Timothy Myers-El, *The Huevolution of Sacred Muur Science Past and Present: A Theoretical Compilation* (Bloomington: Author House, 2004), 82–83.

27. See Shabazz Bey, *We Are the Washitaw*, 37; and Goston's undated appearance at the Florence Jackson Academy in Atlanta, "Return of the Ancient Ones—Pt. 1/3—Empress of the Washitaw Verdiacee Gosten El Bey," posted by Sirius Times Media, December 20, 2015, https://www.youtube.com/watch?v=eXLlyzR7ASQ.

28. Najee-Ullah El and Taylor El, *Moors in America*, 82. See also Cheryl Lofton Wooding-Bey, "Thanksgiving," http://rvbeypublications.com/sitebuildercontent/sitebuilderfiles /thanksgivingbycheryllofton.pdf, which describes Europeans roasting and carving the bodies of Moors in a cannibal feast.

29. "Nuwaubian Facts 2," posted on November 29, 2009, by Nuwaubian Fact, https://www .youtube.com/watch?v=LMsBmu5eYXA. See also the energetic Aliite lecturer linking "Europeans" with the "zoo type of the dog," in "Ta Seti An, The African Science behind the African Zoo Types of Ancient Kemet," posted by Antar Gholar, February 21, 2014, https://www.youtube.com/watch?v=D7dTXOoIkl4.

30. "Constitution of the UNNM," http://nuwaubianfacts.com/Constitution%20of%20 UNNM%20ebook.pdf.

31. Adwo El and Salaam El, *77 Amazing Facts*, 96. El-Amin echoes this in his *Wake Up I Free Ka*: "I want you to challenge what I write by researching it for yourself" (8). The title references Jamaican-born journalist J. A. Rogers's 1934 work, *100 Amazing Facts about the Negro: With Complete Proof* (St. Johns: Brawtley Press, 1995), a precursor text to many Aliite collections of evidentiary knowledge, most strikingly in its use of visual images, such as the claim of "Negroid aspect" with regard to the face of a Swiss mask of St. Maurice and inclusion of an image of an Olmec head as "indisputable proof . . . that [the Negro] did not start as a slave to white people" (1 and 4). Rogers, however, was meticulous about including citation of sources—indeed, more than half of his book (pp. 23–51) details the "proof" for the thematically arranged "amazing facts" he offers, resulting in a text that resembles conventional scholarship (and places the reader in the largely passive position of the consumer of conventional scholarship), in contrast to Aliite texts, which encourage the reader to actively pursue his or her own "research."

32. http://www.nuwaubianfacts.com/.

33. Quoted in G. S. Rami A. Salaam El, *Moorish Jewels: Emerald Edition* (2014), 3.

34. Adwo El and Salaam El, *77 Amazing Facts*, 1.

35. Mungin Bey, *Discover the Key*, 44.

36. African Creation Energy, *The Science of Sciences*, 75.

37. The Nuwaubian term for this practice is "Sound Right Reasoning," a linking of word with meanings through phonic associations, which can play out in a group as either creative collaboration or contest. For an example, see "Taj Tarek Bey on the Battlefield," posted by Blacknews 102, October 9, 2012, https://www.youtube.com/watch?v=a5yGoE78YBo. Susan Palmer noted that the Nuwaubian Yamassee, when holding forth on etymology, "tended to ignore Latin and Greek roots and violate the rules of semantics, relying exclusively on accidental phonetics." *Nuwaubian Nation*, xxv.

38. Adwo El cites "NAme, NAtional, NAture, NAtural, NAtive, Nazarene, Natal, Nazareth, Navel (Nav El), Navy, Navigate, Nautical, North America (N.A.), Naga, Napoleon (shot the nose of the Sphinx), NAïve, NArcotics (inducing sleep or stupor), Narrative (a story of description of actual or fictional events, i.e. slave narratives)." Adwo El, *You Are NOT Negro*, 5.

39. Mungin Bey, *Discover the Key.*

40. Augustus Bey, *Moslem Girls' Training Guide* (1928), rev. and ed. Tauheedah S. Najee-Ullah El (Califa Media, 2014), iii. The same instructions appear in several other Califa Media books.

41. Thus, Sharif A. Bey can switch from *Ballentine's Law Dictionary* (1948) to *Oxford New English Dictionary* (1901) in order to offer two valences on the term "human being." See *The Blueprint: Moorish Musings on Noble Drew Ali's Divine Plan of the Age* (DeWitt: Ali's Men Publishing, n.d.), n.p.

42. "Taj Tarek Bey on the Battlefield," posted by Blacknews102, October 9, 2012, https://www.youtube.com/watch?v=a5yGoE78YB0.

43. See, for instance, "The Young Nuwaubian Vs the Hebrew Isrealites [*sic*]." At https://www.youtube.com/watch?v=ENzPT-rIylM, posted Saneter Studios, August 17, 2015. While ultimately an example of "building" or collaborative conversation, the impulse to read street encounters as battles is obvious in "Bro Ankhkakek Asks Nuwaubians Some Questions On Dr York & Who Writes The Books," https://www.youtube.com/watch?v=EeI4USB1W40, posted by Asaru Nine Ether, May 10, 2015. These street battles can also involve representatives of non-black ethnic religions, as in "Nuwaubians vs. Mormons in Mississippi part 1," https://www.youtube.com/watch?v=zgbSC33tKM0, posted by Francis McMurtry, May 24, 2013.

44. Goston, *Return*, 414–15. As popular as etymology is as a means of establishing and advancing the authority of individual thinkers, Aliites often trace terms back to ancient African languages, real or imagined. Etymology serves the movement as a way to reclaim language itself. As one Washitaw thinker has argued, "You can't have a nation without a language . . . by speaking English, we do credit to the one who conquered us." EWCC, June 6, 2013. Likewise, a Nuwaubian Yamassee, citing a line from E. A. Wallis Budge's dictionary of hieroglyphics, can say "Here's a DEFINITE root for the word MOOR (MWR)" precisely because it comes from an ancient African context. See "Etymology of the Word Moor," http://nuwaubian-hotep.blogspot.com/2013/04/etymology-of-word-moor.html.

45. Goston, *Return*, 416. By signifying on names, words, and languages, Aliite thinkers can claim superiority and rights of supersession over other traditions, as when etymology is used by Washitaw thinkers to equate them with the Nation of Islam's tribe of Shabazz or even to argue that they were, as proven by the sound of syllables, the original rulers of China.

46. Palmer, *Nuwaubian Nation*, xxii.

47. "Dr. Malachi Z York—Views and Visions from TAMARE," posted by Asaru Nine Ether, February 20, 2015, https://www.youtube.com/watch?v=Lp_5IBEetV0.

48. Goston, *Return*, 5; York, *The Holy Tablets*, 19:6:300–301, p. 1654. See also Amen A. El, *The Passion and Resurrection of the Moorish Hiram*; African Creation Energy, *The Science of Sciences*; and Myers-El, *Huevolution*, 24.

49. Palmer, *Nuwaubian Nation*, xxii.

50. York, *The Holy Tablets*, 10:12:341.

51. York, *Sons of Green Light*, n.p.

52. Ali, "Masterpiece of Religious Literature: Secrets of Other Creeds Revealed," in *ML*. Ali also argued that religious teachers, historically, "have always had only a reflection of the truth and not the real thing," a distinction between such teachers and prophets like himself. "Religious Controversy," in *ML*.

53. York, *Man from Planet Rizq* (Holy Tabernacle Ministries, 1996), 120.

54. Goston, *Return*, 139.

55. Newton, *Armed with the Constitution*, 38.

56. Jenna Reinbold, "Traditional Marriage on Trial: The Supreme Court, Same-Sex Marriage, and the Fate of Secular Argumentation," *Journal of Church and State* (November 20, 2015): 4.

57. Mungin Bey, *Discover the Key*, 9; and "'Dr' Reggie Disrespects Moors & Gets Destroyed by the Truth of Moorish Science," posted by IAMHH Temple, January 17, 2016, https://www.youtube.com/watch?v=pfbA3h5AqAA.

58. "Queen Valahra Renita El Harre-Bey: Moorish Law (Full Lessons)," posted by Keishon T. Kessee El-Bey, June 6, 2013, https://www.youtube.com/watch?v=iNihE3McnRk; "Yehoshua EL Moon Phases & Moorish Science/Mathematics," posted by Joshua Pollitt, January 13, 2014, https://www.youtube.com/watch?v=WoicS8CFsNI; and "Maku Speaks . . . 'Why Are the Moabites and Canaanites'? For the Moorish Science Temple of America!!!" posted by "The Yamassee Tribe of Native Americans, the United Nuwaubian Nation of Moors Government," September 18, 2015, http://www.unnm.org/#!Maku-speaks-Who-are-the-Moabites-and-Canaanites-For-the-Moorish-Science-Temple-of-America-/cnn3/55fb76f00cf2a7bb74affd93.

59. Hopkins-Bey, *Prophet Noble Drew Ali*, 46.

60. Hopkins-Bey, *Prophet Noble Drew Ali*, 86.

61. http://www.nuwaubianfacts.com/.

62. Amunhotep El Bey, "The Washitaw Moors," July 17, 2011, http://thewashitawmoors.blogspot.com/.

63. EWCC, December 7, 2014, April 17, 2016, and October 9, 2016.

64. EWCC, June 2, 2013, December 13, 2015.

65. Johnson, *African American Religion*, 292.

66. EWCC, September 20, 2015.

67. Wenger, *Religious Freedom*, 12; Isaac Weiner, "The Corporately Produced Conscience: Emergency Contraception and the Politics of Workplace Accommodations," *Journal of the American Academy of Religion* 85, no. 1 (2017): 31–63. See also Wenger, *We Have a Religion: The 1920s Pueblo Indian Dance Controversy and American Religious Freedom* (Chapel Hill: University of North Carolina Press, 2009).

68. EWCC, October 9, 2016, for instance.

69. Shem El, "Moors and Religious Freedoms," July 24, 2014, http://moorishamericannews.com/moors-religious-freedoms.

70. Sharif Ali, "About the Fez: History and Significance of the Moorish Fez Hat," http://www.fezcaps.com/p/about-fez.html; see also Myers-El, *Huevolution*, 2; Matthews-El, *Moorish America's Archival Palladium*, 128.

71. Mungin Bey, *Discover the Key*, 11.

72. Hopkins-Bey, *What Your History*, 13.

73. Malachi York, *The Holy Tablets* 19:6:159. York is also referencing—and equating his own book with—the "Problem Book" chapter of W. D. Fard's *The Supreme Wisdom*, a central scriptural text for the Nation of Islam and the Five Percent Nation of Gods and Earths movements, a book that "teaches . . . a thorough knowledge of our miserable state of condition in a mathematical way." http://supremewisdom.webs.com/theprob lembook.htm. This reference also indicates that, just as Aliite communities share—and seize—each other's terms, teachings, and texts, the Aliite movements likewise exist within and among a broader spectrum of African American religious thought. As many Moors claim that Noble Drew Ali taught Master Fard (the founder of the Nation of Islam movement), many Washitaw claim that the NOI's Louis Farrakhan met and took advice from Empress Goston. The Nuwaubian Yamassee movement generally takes a harsher approach, appropriating NOI terms (like the title "Problem Book") while dismissing NOI teachings and leaders in favor of the "factology" of Master Teacher York. See, for instance, York's lecture "Dr. Malachi Z. York Explains Hidden Foundations of the Nation of Islam," where he contrasts his own self-sacrificing service to the truth with NOI leaders' self-serving hypocrisy and history, in which they "play games, gather lots of people and look good, put on costumes and look good," rather than really working to save "black" people. Posted by January12th1970, March 23, 2010, https://www.youtube.com/watch?v=DOJVYGlOpdo.

CHAPTER SEVEN

1. George Steiner, *After Babel: Aspects of Language and Translation* (Oxford: Oxford University Press, 1975), 222.

2. Cover, "*Nomos*," 9.

3. William H. Pease and Jane H. Pease, *Black Utopia: Negro Communal Experiments in America* (Madison: State Historical Society of Wisconsin, 1963); and Robin D. G. Kelley, *Freedom Dreams: The Black Radical Imagination* (Boston: Beacon Press, 2002).

4. See Tracey E. Hucks, *Yoruba Traditions and African American Religious Nationalism* (Albuquerque: University of New Mexico Press, 2012), 341.

5. Sylvester Johnson writes: "Nelson-Bey also reassured local authorities by taking in an individual placed on probation by the local court system. By the account of circuit court judge Frank Binford, Nelson-Bey not only kept the judge informed of the individual's behavior but eventually reported that the man was violating probation, turning him over to court authorities who returned him to jail." Johnson, "The FBI and the Moorish Science Temple of America," 61.

6. Claude Greene Bey, *Moorish Guide*, January 15, 1929. See also items from November 30, 1928, and February 1, 1929, collected in Hopkins-Bey, *Prophet Noble Drew Ali*, 87–88.

7. On other Moorish settlements, see Turner, *Islam*, 105–16; and Weisenfeld, *New World*, 223.

8. "The Moorish Science Temple of America's *Moorish Voice*, Being a Monthly Magazine Circulated Amongst Temples and Moors, Issues from 1943," kobek.com/Moorish%20Voice/.

9. *Moorish Voice*, May 1943, 19, 7.

10. *Moorish Voice*, August 1942, 11; and May 1943, 19.

11. *Moorish Voice*, August 1942, 3.

12. *Moorish Voice*, August 1942, 20; *Moorish Voice* from 1943, cited in Weisenfeld, *New World*, 223.

13. Ruth Howell Bey, published in *Moorish Voice*, May 1943.

14. Douglass, "What to the Slave Is the Fourth of July?"

15. *Moorish Voice*, August 1942, 20; and May 1943, 11.

16. *Moorish Voice*, August 1942, 13.

17. *Moorish Voice*, August 1942, 19.

18. *Moorish Voice*, August 1942, 24, 25.

19. *Moorish Voice*, April 1940, 8. This story is recounted in the "Humor Column," near another anecdote: "What do you think of a Brother who actually comes in the Temple and sits down before he realizes that he hasn't put on his Fez?"

20. *Moorish Voice*, August 1942, 24.

21. *Moorish Voice*, May 1943, 2.

22. *Moorish Voice*, November 1942, 40.

23. Adam Heimlick, "Black Egypt: A Visit to Tama-Re," November 14, 2000, http://www .nypress.com/black-egypt-a-visit-to-tama-re/.

24. Elbein, "Road to Tama-Re."

25. Palmer, *Nuwaubian Nation*, xxxiv.

26. Geoff Manaugh, "Tama-Re, or the Egypt of the West," January 27, 2010, *BLDGBLOG*, http://www.bldgblog.com/2010/01/tama-re-or-the-egypt-of-the-west/.

27. Palmer, *Nuwaubian Nation*, 83.

28. "Nuwaubian Nightmare," *Washington Times*, June 2, 2002, http://www.washington times.com/news/2002/jun/2/20020602-030741-8461r/.

29. Wright and Palmer, *Storming Zion*, 129.

30. A page of "beautiful pictures," http://www.nuwaubianfacts.com/tamare.htm; and "Old Photos of Tama Re," posted December 18, 2010, http://nuwaubian.blogspot.com /2010/12/old-photos-of-tama-re.html.

31. "Nuwaubian UNNM Tama-Re: Land of the Sun, June 26th, 1997, Saviours Week Dr MalachiZYork," posted by DrMalachiZYork, March 14, 2010. https://www.youtube.com /watch?v=3CqdneRhWm4. "Brings tears to my eyes," writes Khadija Norwood, in the comments . "tamare," posted by younglo98765, March 20, 2013, https://www.youtube .com/watch?v=nI-GOWHW8eg.

32. "hubi hubi," posted by thegreat770, June 17, 2010, https://www.youtube.com/watch?v =nnqt10JTugc.

33. "Gov. Raid on Nuwaupian Nation," posted by illeife, February 2, 2011, https://www .youtube.com/watch?v=zL-sKtPDtTI.

34. "Tama-Re: Egipt of the West," posted by Tama-Re: Egipt of the West, August 10, 2011, https://www.youtube.com/watch?v=HaUNv_YBeYY. The newspaper is seen at 2:08. "Egipt" is frequently used in Nuwaubian Yamassee discourse to contrast their (true)

claims about ancient Africa with the lies associated with academic Egyptology, as well as to distinguish their national (cultural) engagement with the Egyptian from the contemporary nation-state of Egypt.

35. Elbein, "The Road to Tama-Re."

36. "Tama-Re: Egipt of the West."

37. "Tamare This Is Why They Attacked Dr Malachi Z York," posted by MultiverseCinema, April 14, 2009, https://www.youtube.com/watch?v=OZkyzwS8DL0.

38. "Nuwaubian Love— Savior's Day 2003," posted by Al Carter, May 5, 2012, https://www.youtube.com/watch?v=coNiVes_FME.

39. "Nuwaubian Children: Where Is the Abuse?" http://nuwaubianfacts.com/.

40. "Beautiful Video of Tama-Reans," posted by AllEyesOnEgyptTV, August 23, 2009, https://www.youtube.com/watch?v=rzkIaG6z4GU.

41. "Nuwaubians have show [sic] NEW LAND, Capital sits in Temple, GA," posted by United Nuwaubian Nation of Moors, July 14, 2016, https://www.youtube.com/watch?v=zTVESM80f5s.

42. EWCC, September 25, 2016.

43. EWCC, November 13, 2016.

44. EWCC, June 2, 2013; emphasis added.

45. EWCC, September 20, 2015.

46. EWCC, May 26, 2013.

47. EWCC, June 2, 2013.

48. EWCC, October 27, 2013.

49. EWCC, June 2, 2013, and October 27, 2013.

50. Matthews-El, *Moorish America's Archival Palladium*, 43; and Shabazz Bey, *We Are the Washitaw*, 5.

51. EWCC, January 1, 2017.

52. EWCC, August 20, 2017.

53. Goston, *Return*, 419–20.

54. Goston, *Return*, viii.

55. Goston, *Return*, viii.

56. EWCC, September 3, 2017.

57. EWCC, March 26, 2017. See also Brother Salomon's testimony of being "greeted by the wind" at Poverty Point. "Return of the Ancient Ones to the 21st Century—Introduction to Wash*taw History—IV," *Truth Radio*, September 27, 2019, http://www.blogtalkradio.com/truthpastor/2009/09/27/return-of-the-ancient-ones-to-the-21st-century--in.

58. EWCC, October 22, 2017.

59. EWCC, July 9, 2017.

60. *The Goddess Lives in Upstate New York: Breaking Convention and Making Home at a North American Hindu Temple* (Oxford: Oxford University Press, 2005), 61–62.

61. EWCC, July 9, 2017.

62. Derek Hicks, *Reclaiming Spirit in the Black Faith Tradition* (New York: Palgrave Macmillan, 2012), 90, 107; Ashon Crawley, *Blackpentecostal Breath: The Aesthetics of Possibility* (New York: Fordham University Press, 2017), 32.

63. Quoted in Hicks, *Reclaiming Spirit*, 168.

CONCLUSION

1. "7 Moors Proclaimed Their Nationality, *Angel in Training TV*, November 22, 2014, https://www.youtube.com/watch?v=S1naOSaxwbk.

2. "Moorish Leader's Historical Message to America," in *ML*.

3. Karl N. Llewellyn and E. Adamson Hoebel, *The Cheyenne Way: Conflict and Case Law in Primitive Jurisprudence* (Norman: University of Oklahoma Press, 1941), 20.

4. In Charleston, the "very language of 'replacement' suggested that the hoped for polity of white nationalists was one in which citizens were born, not made." Michael G. Hanchard, *The Spectre of Race: How Discrimination Haunts Western Democracy* (Princeton, NJ: Princeton University Press, 2018), 211.

5. Gregory Korte and Alan Gomez, "Trump Ramps Up Rhetoric on Undocumented Immigrants: 'These Aren't People. These Are Animals,'" *USA Today*, May 16, 2018, https://www.usatoday.com/story/news/politics/2018/05/16/trump-immigrants-animals-mexico-democrats-sanctuary-cities/617252002/.

6. Matthews-El, *Moorish America's Archival Palladium*, 179.

7. Matthews-El, *Moorish America's Archival Palladium*, 213.

INDEX